Praise for *The Consu*

"A must-read for all change agents trying to help their teachers move from the lecturing mode to being facilitators of learning, using digital content and curriculum. *The Consumerization of Learning* captures all essential points in making these challenging transitions possible and effective as they significantly influence student achievement."

—Dr. Jasna Aliefendic
Coordinator of Technology Integration & Staff Development, Garland ISD

"LeiLani has been asking essential questions as she investigates the educational system across the United States. In approaching trends and gaps from a business lens, she is able to highlight areas that may seem obvious after she points them out but may have gone largely unnoticed or unconsidered from an education focused lens. In the three years of knowing LeiLani, I've gained new insight and perspective shifts, learned about broader trends, gaps and predictions for future movement in digital content and strategy, and been able to fit together puzzle pieces I didn't know I was missing before. She has a forward thinking vision for the future of education, paradigm shifts, organizational shifts, with students at the center."

– Dr. Michelle Zimmerman
2016 NCCE Outstanding Technology Educator of the Year,
Educator/Researcher, Renton Preparatory Academy

"LeiLani brings together educational leaders from across the country in unique forums to challenge them to think differently about technology in education. She has an amazing vision for what technology in education will look like in the very near future. Her new book is a testament to the new reality of the digital transformation taking place. She explains how technology in education is being implemented and suggests systems of change to adopt digital learning and knowledge. These systems of change represent a very authentic and real-world approach to *'upset'* the present culture of education and transform into a truly digital one that will result in better learning outcomes."

– Keith A. Bockwoldt
CETL, NSBA "20 to Watch", Director of Technology Services,
Township High School District 214

"LeiLani is a true visionary with a passion for the power and future of digital curriculum. She truly has a heart for teachers and students. *The Consumerization of Learning* brings meaning & context to the chaos of the millions of digital resources available to educators, and provides invaluable tools and frameworks to aid in the understanding, evaluation, and selection of digital curriculum. LeiLani has done and continues to do the work that we wish we had the time and resources to do. She is an education pioneer, research partner, valued colleague, friend."

– Karla Burkholder, Ed.D.
Director of Instructional Technology, Schertz-Cibolo-Universal City ISD, TX

"I keep asking for more, more, more! What LeiLani is saying in this book is unique – it is years ahead of where educators are now. Education is buried in testing, Common Core, charter schools, personalization, etc. – the minutiae of today. But, LeiLani's book is a breath of fresh air – it is a thought-provoking, visionary book that every educator – teacher, administrator and parent must read. Change, as LeiLani describes it, is absolutely happening. Educators can join in... or be left behind."

– Dr. Elliot Soloway
Arthur F. Thurnau Professor, Dept. of CSE,
College of Engineering, School of Information,
School of Education, University of Michigan at Ann Arbor

"The research that LeiLani has conducted and artfully summarized in *The Consumerization of Learning* is presented in a way that positions education leaders to adopt common language and understandings of the rapidly changing landscape of K-12 education. As we collectively work to redefine what we believe about learning, how people learn, and what role technology plays in modern learning environments, leaders recognize that technology is an essential piece of the education puzzle, but that it is not the driver. *The Consumerization of Learning* offers unique perspectives that spark important conversations about the transformations taking place around us."

– Beth Pocius
Manager, Blended and Digital Curriculum Implementation and Support,
Seminole County Public Schools, FL

"The creators of Amazon know the future of retail is direct to consumer. The founders of Uber know the future of transportation is on-demand. The visionary at Tesla understands that the future of energy creation and storage is distributed. LeiLani Cauthen knows the future of Education shares all three of these characteristics. In *The Consumerization of Learning* she shares her expansive knowledge of what it all means."

–Erik Heinrich
Former IT Director, San Francisco Unified School District

"Listening to LeiLani Cauthen talk about the consumerization of learning has helped me reconsider the negative bias against the concept of consumerism as a term to define human activity. In 2013, Leilani started having conversations about leveraging technology to design personalized learning environments and close performance gaps with district leaders across the USA. With laser-sharp vision, she focused on one condition that would determine whether educators can step up to the challenges of 21st century learning so our students can grow up to be contributing and competitive participants in the global economy: Education leaders must have enough technical knowledge to make the right choices, such as what to purchase, create, or curate; how these pieces will plug, play, and provide relevant data to inform learning, and how these elements may or may not support the design of relevant and authentic learning experiences. Read *The Consumerization of Learning* before you rush to purchase the next shiny learning product!"

– L. Beatriz Arnillas
Director IT, Education Technology, Houston Independent School District

The Consumerization of Learning

The Consumerization of Learning

How educators can co-opt
consumer-grade digital courseware to
transform learning in the Age of Experience

by LeiLani Cauthen
CEO, the Learning Counsel & Founder, Knowstory

Outskirts Press, Inc.
Denver, Colorado

The Consumerization of Learning
How educators can co-opt consumer-grade digital courseware to transform learning in the Age of Experience

v3.0

Outskirts Press, Inc.
http://www.outskirtspress.com

ISBN: 978-1-4787-8232-2

Cover Design: the Learning Counsel

PRINTED IN THE UNITED STATES OF AMERICA

Contents

BOOK 3 – FICTIONAL FUTURE

Prefa

Facing Down the Learning Content Disruptio

by David Kafitz Ed.D.

The education sector is facing some serious disruption in learning content, implementation, and methods, as it goes from paper to digital in all things. The disruption has elements of consumer technologies impinging into what used to be the normal course of business in schools.

We are truly in the eye of the storm. Unfortunately, many schools and districts are implementing 1:1 initiatives with no, or at least an underdeveloped, strategy to truly make the shift. This is a billion dollar market and every district has huge responsibilities and massive pressures from parents and communities at large to deliver the best possible education. Equity in education is a very important consideration and the expectation by most parents and students today is digital. If a school isn't using devices and delivering digital curriculum for individualized learning, it's generally considered that the leaders are holding children back.

With computing devices on campuses and in schools all over the world, the teacher/professor has fought to maintain his position at the head of the class. And their superiors in the front office have supported them with the familiar mantra of "the teacher knows best." No one wants to disrupt the power structure of teacher centricity. Unwittingly, these administrators and teachers, however well intentioned in their purpose, have been blocking the progress that transitioning to learning digitally promises.

Digital content and curriculum has been built to serve the student. Some of it is highly interactive, many with gaming features built in to "gate" forward a student once an objective is achieved, packaged with glossy user interfaces and slick management features and more. It can put the student on a personally charted knowledge path. There is also a promising pedagogical shift with some digital curriculum that allows for the teacher to no longer be standing in front of the class as the *source* of knowledge. He or she is mobile, working with each student or groups of students, facilitating. Helping teachers make this happen is a major challenge for administrators.

"Consider how you, as an adult, like to learn something: you try it, you fail, you look to someone with experience as a guide so you can find your path and keep working at it. Teachers will need to be more like personal trainers, like coaches."

-Kurt Madden
Chief Technology Officer
Fresno Unified School District

As Kurt Madden, the CTO of Fresno Unified, put it, "Consider how you, as an adult, like to learn something: you try it, you fail, you look to someone with experience as a guide so you can find your path and keep working at it. Teachers will need to be more like personal trainers, like coaches." The great redemption of this is that the teacher is now remarkably more efficient in delivering personalized learning to each student. Personalization, customization, and giving individualized service – these are the hallmarks of the new economy we already expect, except in education.

Of course this culture shift has been fraught with problems and false starts. There is great digital curriculum content, and curriculum that is less than great. Just like there were great textbooks and not so good ones. Much of the "middle-of-the-road" curriculum that can be found will be something like an eBook with pictures to click on for extended captions. This type of digital curriculum still allows for a more teacher-centric model while adding interest for the student. It's a "safe" step, one that gains the most teacher support initially.

Any resistance to the fully automated digital object world, where software is automatically teaching with teachers intervening where necessary, will grow less and less as more teachers experience a classroom of enthusiastic students, have less lesson planning to do, and also see a 15-25% increase in achievement in formative and summative assessments. In fact, Julie Garcia, a teacher in a San Diego middle school, recently completed a two-year study comparing traditional classroom schooling on math versus use of digital math curriculum for at-risk elementary students who had significant learning deficits. The study showed remarkable results:

> *"As educators, we are always asking ourselves, are the resources we make available to our students moving the needle? What is the right mix of direct instruction, one-on-one time, and engaging software? I ask myself these questions every day. We are charged with giving our students the best possible opportunities and experiences for success throughout their schooling years and beyond.*
>
> *During my nine years of teaching middle school math, trends have surfaced and sparked an interest in me to dig deeper into the use and efficacy of digital resources as intervention in my math classes. What started as part of my program to gain administrator certification has led to a two-year research study that sought to prove the efficacy of my work in the classroom and the*

digital resources we use. In order to obtain objective results, I designed and implemented a way to collect, analyze, and interpret data that compared students who used a digital intervention with those who did not.

When performing research, I gave my class of 8th grade algebra readiness students at Black Mountain Middle School in San Diego the opportunity for improvement. Many of these students scored between two and three grade levels below grade-level average on their NWEA MAPs test, creating the need for additional intervention and support to prepare them for success in high school math. Pairing a digital supplement with direct teacher instruction effectively increased test scores, raised achievement levels, and improved cognitive ability."

It's not an easy thing for leaders to tell teachers, "We're going digital now. Throw out your textbooks. Oh, and all basic sense of order you've had for the last twenty-five years." But suffice it to say, gone are the days when a teacher can say, "Pull out your textbooks and turn to page…" and not have at least one child *who has never even seen a book before.* With lecture capture in higher-ed, even repeat-performance lectures are no longer needed and institutions can literally just "replay" earlier lectures and "rack-mount"-up another course using previously captured digital lectures and materials.

Disruption is at hand for the way leaders lead and how teachers organize lessons. Many are lost in how to cope with it all. Many are making their own content while juggling a dramatically altered schedule where they are supposed to individualize for every student. With so much random motion brought suddenly and shockingly in by the addition of thousands of digital devices, a new leadership mindset is needed. No good leader leaves all their troops without their basic support. Nor does a good leader allow their institution to literally have every teacher running in different directions. In an age when accountability and pressure to perform are at an all-time high for schools, organizational solutions are urgent.

Many places *have* started to take on the question of how to deal with mass curriculum change on a district-wide or state level. Device tactics have unleashed a mad scramble for learning content systems, repositories, workshops, and events. Many institutions need a strategy, not from the view of the devices only, but from the very architecture of learning delivery.

This book is about turning attention on the *actual* digital transition needed and the leadership needed by top administrators, not just teachers. Teachers will always be important, and we will need more of them, but in a new way.

An exciting teaching and learning journey lies before us. Let's go.

Backstory

Chapter 1
Introduction

Consumerization is the act of making something desirable and consumable by the individual.

> *Think of consumerization of learning as the personalization of it on computing screens using the capabilities of the software that make it intuitive and highly adaptive just for that learner. It teaches using highly developed programming. If schools fully discover and adapt around its ingenuity, it has the power to give teachers back time spent custom building every digital resource themselves, time that can now be turned with attention on students, to create more hands-on learning activities, and to guide students in the fullness of a digital learning experience.*
>
> *Consumerized learning is also an alternate delivery mechanism that has the potential to disintermediate on cost, immediacy, and effectiveness. It's time for schools to co-opt this trend.*
>
> *To win with it.*

This book is divided into 4 major sections. The first section deals with the backstory of the Learning Counsel, a mission-driven organization founded in late 2013 to help schools with context and research in their shift to digital curriculum.

Book One is a look at the problems and education's current environment. These serve to give context to the shift and drive home why consumerization is happening and what it means.

Book Two is about the solutions to advance the interests of both institutions and individuals seeking to learn or to teach others to learn. It's about bringing order into the digital transition.

Book Three is fiction. It is a made-up story of the future and included simply to illustrate how things could go *potentially.* Early readers have found it the most enjoyable part. I think that fact is both promising and challenging.

I've tried to include as many examples as possible of real-life schools, facts and figures from various studies, and references. At one point, it got to be way too much and a lot was cut, or else this book would have been way too long.

The most interesting thing realized, as I wrote and looked at which schools were being covered and where, is that it has been the smaller places who have acted like incubation points. Oh, not smaller as in *size* all the time, but in social stature and expectation. For example, I would have expected the city of San Francisco, with its proximity to Silicon Valley, and its citywide Wi-Fi coverage, to be at the forefront in all aspects of digital transition in education. Not so, at least when I first got on the road in 2014 – not by a long stretch. Nor many of the Silicon Valley schools, even the wealthiest. The same goes with other tech havens.

I have a theory that many places which have established an elite reputation for excellence stop struggling as much about their structure even while they continue to excel in discrete function. Teachers may be celebrities, but the place and ways haven't changed except by tiny portions. The school structure has solidified along old lines of success and interests, and it grows weightier by the year. This is why the places that are so impressive in digital transition are off in lesser-known places, fighting small skirmishes for excellence and throwing in everything – including their very structure – in order to last at all. They are the desperate edge. For them, the mere function of learning is *so* at risk, their quiver of workable old-school ways so empty of results, that they don't even think of themselves as brave when they rush headlong into dramatic tech transition. They drop all pretenses and reorganize for a correct fit.

The problem with any educational institution's status-quo complacency is that we are not in a fight any more about function. It's entirely a fight for *structure*.

My intention is to help schools, individual teachers, parents, and students win their rightful place in the new economy with a careful reimagining of their position.

Chapter 2
An Epic Road Trip

Fear and Disbelief

I have been working non-stop on a nationwide tour of eighty-seven cities, speaking about what is happening. Since January 2014, I have helped the education sector with strategy and tactics designed to help them survive the consumerization of learning unruffled, though changed.

Today, teachers and schools everywhere are in uncharted waters of digital learning objects constructed much like the most engaging games, ones that use increasingly sophisticated machine learning within their inner workings, sporting algorithms that are exceedingly precise at customizing the views to the learner.

I first gave a talk about "Surviving the Consumerization of Learning" to three hundred K-12 school administrators and educators at Monmouth University in New Jersey on May 20, 2016. I presented the idea that schools would eventually level up to join the rest of corporate America in the Experience Economy.

About a dozen people came up to me after I spoke and were very grateful for the insights, but a couple of them said some things that struck me as very odd. They voiced their concern that the idea of consumerization of learning "needed to be stopped," or "That's *horrible* what you talked about. What are we going to do?"

At first I thought to myself, "Whoa, that person somehow got what I said all twisted up and backwards." But that wasn't it, really, because I had

Key Points

- Learning consumerization is a force that institutions need to reckon with, but most don't believe it.
- The tech transition in the education sector has largely been mismanaged through lack of really visionary leadership from inside the tech reality.
- What consumerized learning *could* be when it is fully matured is a direct route to quality knowledge, on demand.
- It's not true that it will be without all human interaction or lessen the fact that human teachers are an important part of a lot of learning.

staff come up to me and say that they'd heard the same sort of things from various other educators who had been in attendance. "Curiouser and curiouser," I thought, with a finger on my chin.

Then I realized I'd just presented an idea that schools are being potentially competitively overwhelmed by something outside of themselves, namely the consumers of learning and commercial markets who are bypassing schools with various digital learning objects, like apps, what is known as "courseware" or digital lesson software, eBooks, various learning games, and online courses of study, such as those found at Khan Academy, Udemy, Fuel Education, and thousands of others.

I came to understand this actually *is* a sort of horror to schools, and many conversations since that point have proved more and more that just mentioning this possibility is akin to asking for a fight.

"**Consumerization** is the specific impact that consumer-originated technologies can have on enterprises. It reflects how enterprises will be affected by, and can take advantage of, new technologies and models that originate and develop in the consumer space, rather than in the enterprise IT sector. Consumerization is not a strategy or something to be 'adopted.' Consumerization can be embraced and it must be dealt with, **but it cannot be stopped**."

-Gartner IT Glossary http://www.gartner.com/it-glossary/consumerization/

While I was speaking, I had said to all those present that the reason schools don't properly confront and shift to adopt the consumerization trend for learning is because they didn't experience any part of it when they were in school. It's an interesting exercise that leaders and administrators must be able to do – step into the shoes of their users, the digital natives. Personally, I think schools are not doing it at levels of appropriate response one would expect because they have been distracted, and perhaps purposefully. They are consumed with testing and standards, devices and networks, constant negative bashing from the outside – all things that distract and suppress attention on the real change of learning consumerization. It is just so surprising that few people *see* it when it is so plainly evident.

The world has changed. Outside the school, media is no longer a one-way "tell" directed at you without any way for you to talk back as in the days of only television and radio; today, media is online and interactive. It "responds." The travel industry used to be made up of thousands of agencies with physical offices in cities worldwide, as were insurance agencies. Retail is being transformed significantly, with more and more closures, and millions of square feet of store space is going unleased as shopping online explodes.

> "If we don't work hard to improve every day, transform what we do for young people, the competition will eat us up. One can go out there and find their K-12 experience online, and cheaply. As communities, as leaders, as school boards who are grappling with that, we must make some decisions and make some shifts quickly."
>
> *Dr. Luvelle Brown*
> *Superintendent*
> *Ithaca City School District*
> *7 June 2016*

What I find so interesting in my observations about the consumerization of learning is that it is an *inevitability*, not mere musings. Inevitable because consumer demand, industry marketing, and uninhibited access through the Internet are creating an unstoppable force. The fact is that as I write this, consumerized learning is a reality that is already here. I am imploring schools and teachers to see this train coming, to do what is in their power to shift.

The worry by some about any software learning being a dehumanizing force, lessening human interaction, is evidence that they don't know what it *is* and can't imagine how tech could *help* teachers and schools, because all they have ever seen is a tech incursion bringing mass confusion. In this they are entirely right. We should be ashamed of how the tech transition in the education sector has largely been mismanaged through lack of really visionary leadership from inside the tech reality. Product pushing, the non-profit arms of major corporations funding the marketing saturation of tech through seemingly innocent give-aways and thought leadership fests, and just the whole explosion of potentialities, has needed a firm hand to guide schools through.

What consumerized learning *could* be when it is fully matured is a direct route to quality knowledge – on demand. It's not true that it will be without all human interaction or lessen the fact that human teachers are an important part of a lot of learning. What can happen is that teachers are on-demand, as many software systems offer currently with "pop-up" interactive video chat in shopping systems, and that teacher specialists offer office hours for specific mentoring. The perpetually popular live physical classroom is also probable in that schools will be offering a surge of more social hands-on and project-based activities to further enliven learning around the now largely digital object world. It is how they will stay relevant. Sophisticated systems with complete customizations for each learner will already offer intersection points for teacher decisions and assistance.

With this change comes huge opportunity for individuals in the teaching profession.

I have been driven by the fact that it is not enough to sit on the sidelines and comment like a bleacher journalist; what's important to do for schools today is to show them what is happening and why, so they can see what would be obvious in survival tactics inside that future.

That is what this book is about – schools and teachers having enough understanding of all the dynamics in the market to survive the future.

So far, my continuum of change scratched out in 2013 (with schools starting first at writing strategies, going through several other stages, and much later arriving in the new Age of Experience, where most of corporate America and commerce is today) is proving true as to the stages in between.

Let's start first with the continuum of change we have been talking about in every city and through which we are helping school district leaders move stage by stage each year. After that, let's look at the problems and solutions.

We might as well consider the truth of where good software development *could* take us when educators are not buffeted by the high winds of constant change and waves of niftiness coming out of the tech sector. When policy makers and leaders get down to business to take advantage of tech, to command it and not let it command them, then I can rest.

Until then, my favorite part of the entire massive journey, which definitely *wasn't* sleeping overnight in Dallas Love Field due to tornadoes, was this:

I have no words to describe my soaring pride in each individual I have met and my amazement at the epic struggle of the American people to not just be better than other nations or the next state in how we help our kids learn and excel in life. No, the strivings are more touching than that by far. It is to just be *perfect*, without regard to any other nation, any other school, or any other teacher, really – it's to give perfect learning for that neighborhood, at this time, and in this circumstance, or that one single student, right here, right now. Perfect.

No other word describes the totality of what is sought. It is a miracle you don't find in other industries.

It is so wrenching to be one who sees it in every town, that look on some executive's face as he or she asks me, "But what app can help *this* (fill in the blank)?" Or, "How can I get my teachers to (fill in the blank)?" Or, "We don't know how to pay for it." In their eyes I see the reflections of millions of children's faces. Millions.

It breaks my heart.

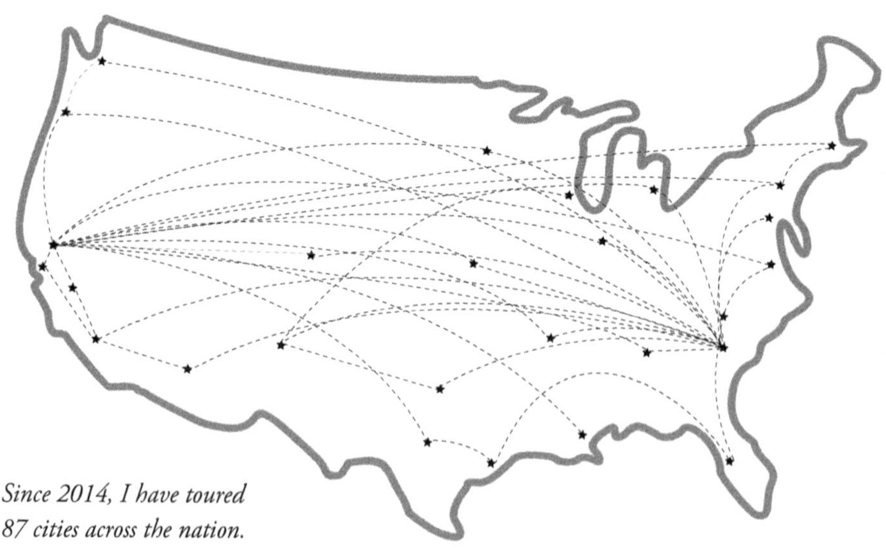

Since 2014, I have toured 87 cities across the nation.

Chapter 3

Reaching the End Point

Is there an end point of the digital transformation for institutional education? There is an end point, but getting there will require what may seem like never-ending and exhausting change in both public and private schools across the U.S. What I have learned is that it is really a journey of five to ten years. It's achievable.

In most of the cities I visited, I shared a vision for where the bulk of the market is going and how fast, based on our research and our direct observation. From the very beginning, this vision included a change continuum that ends in what is known as the "Age of Experience." It's an economic term and represents our present age as beyond merely a focus on information and technology. It is conceptually a time when our **"online and offline identities are converging...accelerating the development of experience-driven products."**[1] Most teachers and school administrators agree to the logic of it, their journey of change ending at this point, because it resonates well with their internal terminology, such as "blended learning." Education executives are relieved to hear about an end point in view, because they don't want to keep shifting the pieces and parts of their operations around indefinitely, guessing as to workability of their plans. Continuous disruption has a feeling of having some deep wrong that can't be named. Change is needed, but disruption is something more.

Key Points

- Education is headed toward every student receiving truly personalized learning after transitioning through a tech maturity curve to the "Age of Experience."
- Schools and districts will know they have reached the Age of Experience when they find themselves considering the depth of individualizations they can do.

"Economy of Experiences sheds light on the fundamental process of change whereby society is currently searching for new forms of value creation. The 'Experience Economy' is the first symptom of this process. The Economy of Experiences is more than 'feed me' or 'entertain me.' Businesses and organizations have a larger, more significant role to play in supporting individuals in their search to find their own way and a significant role for themselves.

"It starts by placing individuals at the center of their social context as well as events that are important to them in the world in which they live. In order to facilitate these, we present new business models in which co-creation plays an important role. Concrete design principles are given that can be used as a basis for creating meaningful experiences."[2]

Most leaders understand that continuous disruption leads to destruction of the organization. When you engage in too much change getting into the thin threads that hold together a working organization of people and things, you can wreck productivity and morale. The whole enterprise can wither and die. This happens to companies all the time when some new competitive force hits their market or industry, but to most people in education, it is an alien thought.

Educators can weather this storm with a proper view to the architecture of their digital assets and a real strategy straddling the digital and physical worlds.

Educators cannot conceive of a world where their industry isn't able to stay the way it's always been. They feel that if it changes, they will lose all sense of order. Federal compliance requirements, new testing, new standards, a growing population of students, economic pressure, and an urgency to integrate technology make for one wild ride for any leader. This is especially for leaders who are not trained or apprenticed in any kind of business or programmatic execution and have mostly risen in the ranks from their training as a teacher.

The proffered idea of an "Education Market Activity Continuum," a cycle of change from one starting point through to an end point in this instance, is starting with a mass move by schools into strategy and then is seen as maturing all the way up to a focus on experience. It began as an average, where the market was in 2013-2014, where schools mostly stumbled about

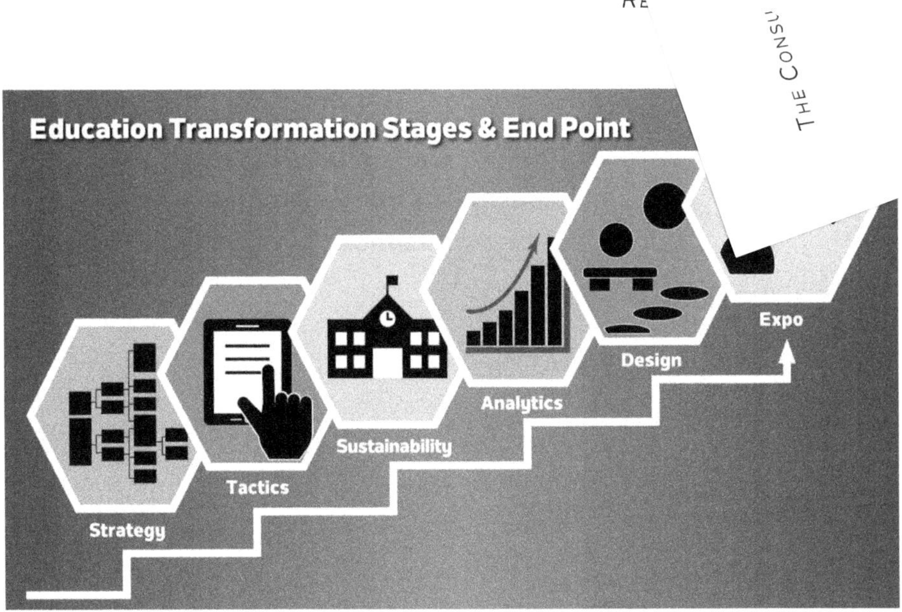

as they either considered or implemented computing devices. Since schools have implemented computing devices as a tactic without a real understanding of their use or contextualized how the environment would change in many instances, not having a real strategy was the first pitfall.[3] In 2014 and 2015, schools had been experiencing this pitfall, and we got on the road to help them by the thousands come to grips with what it would be like to have an actual strategy. These strategies included various programs that could collect inventory of what they already owned digitally, took into consideration policies and practices, engaged in a programmatic approach to professional development, and more. These were not individual things no one had ever thought of before, but new considerations with regards to the executions of the whole of those programs in concert. This was the mark of actual success.

The continuum stages define the digital transformation in education, going from strategy consideration and implementation, all the way through to a refinement that will arrive at the same place as other industries who have moved through the technology revolution – the Age of Experience.

In 2016, The Learning Counsel leveled up to discussions about tactics, true to the market's current dynamics. Most schools and districts in 2016 were in "buy mode" for digital curriculum, but not always with the necessary tactical maps behind them. Buying was willy-nilly in many districts without a plan to administer cost negotiations with the thousands of publishers or a proper vetting of the purchased or custom home-built digital learning objects.

In 2017 and beyond, The Learning Counsel is continuing to both support the natural change and drive forward the Education Market Activity Continuum with a series of Special Reports and live events.

These Continuum stages define the digital transformation in education, going from strategy consideration and implementation, all the way through to a refinement that will arrive at the same place as other industries moving through the technology revolution – the Age of Experience. Let me define each of these stages and describe what is involved in each.

Strategy Years

For schools, the strategy years are characterized by a real concern about devices and networks. They are the year or years where a district starts off with devices and ends with a plan to implement digital learning or vice-versa. It is characterized by a lot of discussions about equity and home access, and the right *kind* of device per grade. Also, a lot of effort goes into substituting old ways with a digitized way, but not necessarily a *digital* way. This stage does not necessarily recognize the highest capabilities of digital technologies and merely substitutes old ways for a new mode with the lowest orchestration of software – merely documents and links to outside resources. Schools haven't even entered real strategy if they haven't gathered as a body to create an orderly process that consents to some commonalities in the transition. A real digital transition strategy, the way we are now defining it, is an organizational motion, not individual random motions by teachers or tech directors with random answers to dozens of unaligned questions about how to be, how to teach, or how to meet standards.

In the Strategy Years, a school needs its advance guard of enthusiasts and leaders. There is a lot of depth to the strategy conversation. Many schools and districts have done well at this, but they are in the minority considering the whole nation.

Tactics Years

After setting goals and programming out a strategy, schools find they are in a couple of heated years of tactics arguments. These arguments will be over the broad, general plan of access and fairness for all teachers and grades, because many schools find they can't use the same device for all ages. Others find they can't do live online testing without breaking the network, or don't even have the hope of equal access any day of the normal school week due to the high numbers of odd devices hitting their networks that they never planned on. This phase includes discussions on the utility of the pieces of things, like what file standards should be used, and what types of curriculum software features work the best.

In this phase, the tendency of administrators is to let these conversations take place amongst the rank-and-file teachers, with only an admonishment to coordinate with the instructional and technology staffs. This is a tactic in itself, barely recognized for what it is; that is, a lack of closely supervised leadership. Leaders with this approach either do not see the relevancy or they cannot grasp the significance. They often say, "We let the teachers make all the choices," as to what and how they will use various technologies including the software elements.

The lack of tactics leadership leads to such wonders as vast and unsustainable quantities of digital files, tens of thousands of which are barely tracked and typically hard to find. Most are irrelevant or quickly out of date. Also, many critical resources are left on the individual's own desktop, frequently not even backed up. Or the teacher allows the students to log into outside services that are collecting huge amounts of student data. These services are hidden from view but are used to commercially advertise or otherwise corner a student's interests. This means that the student is potentially locked into a categorization right during their highest mental development years as a "frequently sick" or "game-oriented" individual. Lack of tactics leadership involves more than just the risk; it also leads to the continued overwhelming of teachers who are trying to cope and get the job done.

Tactics conversations will probably rage forever, but there will be a couple of years of heavy discussion about all the digital learning objects, who should have what objects, who should make the objects (public or private), the missing objects that need to be built, and the things that fall away as useless. A true tactics conversation involves discussions about a fully digital coverage model, how the school can transition from paper and printing to the highest degree possible, and proving exactly how their informational and teaching models lower cost and gain model efficiency.

Sustainability Years

When I say "sustainability," I'm not talking about being green by being ecologically aware and doing your bit with recycling. The idea I'm presenting is the ability of your district to sustain a new working model for teaching and learning. In other words, is the school or district able to deliver, in a stable, long-term manner, complete packages of learning for their students digitally and graduate them, not necessarily based on grades, but by readiness and skills to enter the world of 2020 and beyond?

Evidence of a school that is ready to enter the "sustainability conversation" starts by discussing restraints and then bursts through them. The first time I heard sustainability mentioned unsolicited by a school was September 13, 2016 in Tampa, Florida, when Dr. Tina Barrios, Assistant Superintendent of Information Systems and Technology of Polk County School District, said regarding tech innovation in schools, "I think that where we are at now is: how are we going to sustain it?"

The sustainability conversation is going to go deep in the next few years. Schools will run into all kinds of archaic legislation, competition from consumerization, faulty funding lines, and old policies that will have to be overturned to have a bit more breathing room for their transformation. Some of this has already gone on, but with this continuum, we're talking about the motion of the bulk of the market. In any case, there will be a couple of years for most schools and districts where top policies will be altered and conversation will center on sustainability.

Education administrators will know they are coming *through* the sustainability arguments when they have reoriented themselves to think *as a software company* would think. This means that they have started to enter the same frame of reference as all other industries have done. They will be solidly confronting the reality of the digital age, that to communicate with populations of students and teachers and control them well through the end goals, you must be on the same "channel" with them.

That channel is, of course, online for the great majority of communications. It is robustly well beyond the local individual face-to-face interactions and on a global scale, bringing fantastic efficiencies in knowledge access that allow for local purveyors-of-knowledge to change what they do to be more service-oriented and a less autocratic source of learning. It will be necessary for teachers to actively seek this mutation, because the next few stages definitely require them to formulate a keen sense of differentiation in order to use technology's many iterations of analytics, to redesign their daily routines with in-person and online guidance, and to come to grips with the demands of this age—the Age of Experience.

Analytics Years

The analytics years start with a realization that there are dashboard qualities to much of the software, and that the tons of tests and data signify more than is being utilized for the betterment of education. It also includes conversations about the aspects of "malalytics"or "harmalytics," those things being collected and displayed and consuming massive amounts of administration that are just unnecessary or so uncomfortable they are harmful.

Most of the Education Industry is already consumed with testing and assessment. There is an abiding fear of ever-more analytics. The ability of testing instruments to affect immediate and non-trivial adaptations of learning to the individual student, true individualizations, has yet to be fully realized. In addition, these adaptations have yet to be quantifiable on a national scale so that big testing can be done away with. The trick is in the timing. Most testing to date is summative, or comes at the end of a course of study, which tends to be rather high stakes in that the test is taken and then goes to points unknown to be graded before coming back an indefinite period later to roost in the permanent student record. Most of the time it is as much as six months later.

These tests, in most instances, are barely useful for teaching and learning. It is almost useless even for evaluating the accountability of teachers. The big data that comes out of this work is endlessly massaged and manipulated, sometimes on a politically motivated aim to show strength where there is none, or conversely, put into ruin another. These big data analytics are not necessarily transparent even if they are public. The mysteries of the actual questions used in the tests, the methods of testing, the timing of the test, and countless other variables, including the weather and how well the child was fed that day, can all be part of the confusion that leaves educators feeling downtrodden even when the results are good.

When the real aim is real learning, big high-stakes tests have been gaining ground in one distinct and negative way – they are seen as an us-versus-them disciplinary and control effort by those they are imposed upon. Students and teachers alike feel that analytics about themselves through a universal test distinctly separated in time from the original learning is dehumanizing. It forces more memorization and concentrations on what exactly will be in the test rather than learning. Such tests should be called what they really are – surveys to rate a nation's students and teachers comparatively in a value bell curve of best to worst.

Formative assessments, those done inside the daily routine of learning (i.e., close to the learning in time) are immensely useful to the student as feedback loops. New highly developed and designed courseware, which provides various avenues for the student to go down with repetitive variants to questions until the student gains one hundred percent mastery, have the promise of even removing the need for formative assessments.

The ability to collect formative data on a level that might even include how long little Suzy's eyes remained locked on one aspect of a problem, how many times she had to go back to one part because of how a question was worded, how frequently she had to click on words to get definitions of them, how slow or fast she was, how much time it took to formulate a sentence for an essay, and how much the device spell-corrected – all of those are analytics points, the likes of which will be coming to teachers in future courseware.

In the analytics years, schools will be looking at the meaning and utility of all these inventions of technology, and they will be looking beyond that at the collation of these data points into something more, possibly a more efficient learning path. Definitely at the higher-valued digital aspects of learning experience that cause nuances of data collection we have not yet dreamed about. All of this type of data is already being collected online by big industry for tracking consumer behavior and used in ways and with algorithms that would astound the average person. We all think that somewhere, someone can know *all* about you merely by how you shop and surf online.

When the Education Industry reaches the moment when many schools and many private industry partners have accrued awesome amounts of data, it can begin to be used in alarming and edifying ways. Some of the alarming things are already happening. There will be a rise in concern that so many organizations and teachers are not trained in Internet defense, and they are most certainly unfamiliar with algorithms and analytics usages. This will become a fascinating discussion point. Possibly surprising and saddening things will have happened as a national body by the time we get into the Analytics Years with accrued big data. It is highly likely that things will force more new legislation by this time. Schools and districts will know they have arrived in the Analytics Years because they will be talking a lot about data collected, about what's useful and what's not, and administrators and teachers will have their digital dashboards to help them align their efforts towards a full service-orientation for each individual student. Analytics will be used on a vastly more significant scale, but not to discipline teaches and students. Data used by the individual, for the individual, and for the relationship of teaching and learning will be part of the discussion.

Design

Coming through the Analytics Years will have caused many in leadership to question things that have never been really in question before. These will include even down to the very root basics of *what* is taught, the actual core subjects. It will get into the very foundations of the organizational structures beyond the questions of online and face-to-face and well into networked mixes of school branding over "white-labeled" learning modules. Administrations will have knit together, for example, a group of best-in-class instructors who are ported in over live internet feeds to teach various lessons at precise moments, courseware and games will be slotted in for certain lessons, and live technology-oriented projects will replace the old science and social studies classes with Crime-Scene-Investigator-like labs, or even playwriting to script an ancient classical Roman scene that is video edited by the students after performing.

Because of all the new learning modalities, administrators will find themselves remodeling and retrofitting their brick-and-mortar structures to fit. Now that learning is 15-40 percent (40 percent is considered optimum) purely screen interface, with students "in the screen" reading or moving through courseware and educational games, the physical environments will need shifting and the remaining 60 percent of time will need to focus the energies and socializing in new ways. For example, quiet reading areas with bean-bag chairs or giant cushions that allow students to lounge comfortably will be part of the environment, alongside group meeting areas with mobile furniture, and lab rooms and cubbies for quiet personal work similar to industry. Group spaces, even "social emotional" spaces, that provide for social sharing in the old "whole group" way, will be necessary, even whilst students and teachers may use social media as a back-channel for chat not seen by all simultaneously.

Schools will move towards a well-designed institution and instructional model such that their streamlined and innovative approach can be articulated easily and marketed for student recruitment purposes. How well a whole school or program is "designed" will be contextualized as if by professional marketers and software developers for best appeal in a highly competitive landscape – just like colleges and pretty much all service companies have had to do. Private industry is already viewing the "Design Economy" in the rear-view mirror. For over twenty years there has been exponential growth of new non-linear manufacturing models and boutique services firms. The Dyson vacuum cleaner is a good example of the new design era. It was an old product and an old industry, revolutionized by a new concept. Accompanied by a super-marketing effort with an engineer leading the effort, Dyson is one of many companies whose corporate DNA fits well with society's clear expectations of good design, good mission, good communication, and "enough." Excess is shunned by the present age, so in the Design Years, if administrators open the door to input from their teacher and student populations, one of the first things they will learn is that a large portion of what they always thought was bountiful learning is considered excessive and superfluous and should be replaced by more adapted and individualized learning journeys to ready the student for life.

The Design era, a.k.a. the Tech or Digital or Information Age, is the same as the four earlier stages outlined in this chapter. Good design is generally predicated on good strategy, thorough tactics, an eye to form and cost sustainability, analytics of outputs, and a service orientation. Most manufacturers and software developers have a "version two" and so forth after their initial "minimally viable product" version one. This later version has higher design, a better interface. Good design is a seamless underlayment to real and easy expansion. By itself, good design is like having a good character, warm smile, hearty laugh, and strong handshake. When you have those things, you have a somewhat magical magnetism. You "grow" without heavy and exhausting effort.

Education will be joining the Age of Design, because education, like all of the continuum of years spoken about in this chapter, will inevitably level up to where the rest of industry has already gone. In the Design Years, a tangible shift in how institutions communicate and articulate themselves as parts of a community, real or virtual, will become apparent. This could also be called the Golden Age of School Administration such that a new higher level of executive skill will enter in. It could be known as the "coding" of education if the viewpoint of institution-as-intelligent-software-interface gets popular like it currently is in industry.

Schools will know they are in the Design Years when they are most focused on their survival in their markets, like when they are gaining more competition from local private schools and unschooling or consumerization. When demands for more and more charters and other separate avenues are ever higher despite the technology they have brought in so far, then schools are at a crisis point of their design. Tweaking and augmentation, using analytics, and a few new hires and some firings of personnel are not cutting it; they need a clean slate. In addition, they will have reached the Design Years when their leadership and a few forward thinkers in that school or district realize that the sum of all their disjointed, mostly teacher-level efforts, with a few pronunciations by leadership against the demand of its population, is still inadequate.

This is where an awareness will alight such that, compared to other super-tech imbued industries, our institution does not have a disciplined and refined cohesive highly technologically enhanced administration that delivers on its promise. It is not constructed to win; it must be deconstructed and then rebuilt into a winning platform exactly like industry must do when it is marginalized or run out of business by competition. It must find its "hook" in the present economy and social structure, which will undoubtedly be founded on tech with all other elements playing second fiddle to that central channel.

The Point about Time

Before moving on to discuss the last "Experience" stage, let's make a point about *why* this is all happening. In every city for the past twenty or so, I have mentioned that there are four pillars of the universe we all know and love. Those are: space, matter, energy and time. Those are the "things" of our universe upon which all else is built. As mankind, we have built an ecosystem of each one of these, in turn standing on the shoulders of the one before. We first focused on survival by busily conquering spaces. We had to hold a lot of space to find enough game or fish, and later farm, so defending and holding onto our little corners of the world was very important. Kings and Queens and all sorts of regimes and governments have warred for nation-states. Later on, in the focus on space, people have taken on mortgages and decorated. Our learning in the early part of the original Earth space-race was parents-as-teachers and monasteries for higher learning.

Mankind then moved on to the Industrial Age and conquering matter, building bridges, inventing air flight, and in general making a lot of stuff.

The next evolution was into energy and all things having to do with it, including all trade and making computers and the Information Age. This Age, also known as the Knowledge Age, was the vast accumulation of things-to-know while also distributing those widely. Since money is what people are paid for their labor as an exchange mechanism, it is a form of energy. Like manipulating electrical grids, that Age has included financial market manipulations and more. Governments have focused in this Age on oil and any means of producing energy directly, but, as an Age, mankind's dedicated focus on energy as an issue is almost over.

The last pillar of the universe, and the one that is now drawing the most attention from advanced societies, is *time*. What the present generations are most focused on is how they can have a *good life*. They consider that knowledge is "done." It's on the internet, isn't it? Born-digital learners often think that someone, somewhere already knows something about anything, and that that knowledge can be found. They are therefore prone to focus on *experience*, including learning-as-experience. The Millenial generation is even into the "Tiny House Movement," abstaining from mortgages and going mobile with their *living*. They are less interested in things, in buying and acquiring since things are so easily obtainable, and more in their own ride through the years emotionally and exploring the external world. This is, from an economic point of view, a vast and interesting new frontier to be conquered. Conquering *time* as a consumable, as something aided by the delivery of services of all kinds, has many potentialities for new industry. For *learning*, it could mean developing delivery mechanization to compress some parts of knowledge acquisition into exceedingly short acquisition timeframes by learners and for other parts of knowledge, expanding them out into challenging and intellectually thrillingly theatrical journeys.

Experience

After the Design Age comes the Age of Experience. Schools will level-up from design to education-as-experience with online and physical interactions so artfully crafted together and personalized that the life-journey of the student will be mapped and adjusted with consummate ease. Some might just call this "personalized learning," an idea that has been around awhile. Actually, very often schools get the definition of "personalized learning" a bit backwards – personalization in the software field is really something *you do yourself*. Individualization or differentiation is what a school or teacher would do *for* the student. What can be done with the full capabilities of software design realized, including virtual reality and intelligent learning engines that adapt lines of inquiry for an individual student, are promising an unlimited potential for experiential learning.

In reality, the world could be going someplace with institutional education of truly majestic impact through a far higher capacity to individualize and transport learning from mediocre into new highs of students achieving real intellectual creativity and employability. "Geniuses" will abound, because the system is built to help them excel on their greatest potential path. The ramifications economically are beyond description.

Stepping into the Future

Not familiar with the idea of the Age of Experience? With the rise of Amazon, Google, Apple, Facebook, and Microsoft battling for collections of devotees, big business has entered a level of branding and product that is self-evidently called "Experience." Disney is the high watermark brand of this concept. If you've been to Disneyland, you've had an experience. If you've joined Amazon Prime, you know that they will send you emails at midnight to see if you will rate one of the movies you just streamed off their site. Facebook sends those nifty anniversary videos to keep engagement at a high whine, capturing attention in order to capture everything else you do. Starbucks is a prime "experience brand" with all the theatre of making a cup of coffee individualized.

Large brands, as cultural phenomena, provide valid clues for where education will need to arrive as an end point, and not because it is an ideal, but because it will be an expectation driven by other consumer experience. This is no different than the computer-tablet revolution, which happened first to shift consumer culture. As industry filed in behind it to offer more technical benefits, it delivered even greater *social* functionality, which in turn shifted culture again to expectations of things like same-day grocery order delivery and more, which in turn shifted industry, and so on.

Education will need to be providing personal value, as judged by the individual person. The only way to do this is to make it a self-determined and experiential thing, being self-determined through the vast possibilities that exist, while also taking care of students to reach minimal goals of reading, writing, mathematics, science, and social studies. Attaining this experiential level will be above typical design into best-of-breed brand. This is the difference between a local community college's cache and the Ivy League schools' already. Attaining this through technology interface woven in with human interaction is a high art, so the Age of Experience is above design and into a more artistic rendering of the attainment of knowledge as a service. It is aesthetic, even fun.

Schools and districts will know they have reached the Age of Experience when they find themselves considering the *depth of individualizations* they can do. Right now, individualization, a.k.a. "personalization" by most teachers, is the art of mildly adapting the same whole group lesson so that the slower student gets remediation to catch up, or that the student with hearing difficulty is given a special headset to listen in on some video, or that fast-Johnny gets to go play more math games online, or other educational leisure activity, because he has already finished everything. In schools where this definition of differentiating instruction is in play, you will see progress boards, typically with little gold or colored stars showing the progress of each individual student against a known set of lesson plans. Teachers busily unleash the faster kids, while helping the slower – rewarding with time the lowest common denominator, which actually penalizes the faster students more. Parents see these boards and silently gloat about their child being the one with the most stars, or are saddened by the child with so few. It is for this reason that the Age of Experience will be forced upon the Education arena. Consumers know that full adaptation is available from mentors and the sea of knowledge available on the Internet and will seek those things out rather than allow the inequity of not-truly-adapted environments. Costs to do so are coming down and incentives to achieve are going up. When schools are having real conversations that almost obliterate the "whole group" learning modality conceptually in all directions, then real individualization can start occurring and real experiences shift.

Another direction schools will go in the Experience Age is towards giving real hands-on and theatre-style or field-trip type moments to balance the screen-time learning. This is the number one thing that can be done to provide relevancy and criticality to physical school – but it will come at a high cost structure. The promise of things, like social virtual reality, may mitigate some of this, but it is still screen time. The art of real-life activity, things that draw out collaboration and communication between students locally and with like-minded others globally, will be the customization that schools promote as their marketable brand, because any high motion and interaction experience is so appealing to all students. As education comes through the technology transition, there predictably will be a renaissance in sports, music, art, labs, and more – all tied to tech and analytics.

With device wearables, virtual and augmented reality, and the internet of things, this end-point to the transition seems to come full-circle to where we *were* before we started the tech transformation: still with functioning schools but transformed beyond recognition in many cases. This predicted end point is more like a network with a bright center chandelier-like hub that is perhaps a physical place but is most definitely a virtual one, around which students coalesce, but surrounded by thousands, if not millions, of contributive bulbs, points of individual light that individual students float out to visit in random patterns before reporting back to the central hub and later graduating up to another hub. This allows every individual to have an individual experience, impossible to do at scale until a high-level of technology is absorbed into every fiber of the Education enterprise. The end of this book looks at this hypothetical future.

The structure of education upon arrival by any institution to this loosely-defined end point is in question, but for certain the function will have been modified.

Since form typically follows function, we have some interesting years ahead for all teachers and administrators to adapt through before arriving in the Age of Experience.

[1] Mike Wadhera, The Information Age is over; Welcome to the Experience Age, *Tech Crunch*, https://techcrunch.com/2016/05/09/the-information-age-is-over-welcome-to-the-experience-age/ Posted May 9, 2016.

[2] Albert Boswijk, Ed Peelan, and Steven Olthof, Economy of Experiences, http://www.experience-economy.com/page/view/37/our-book, 2012.

[3] *Los Angeles Times,* "LA School District Demands iPad Refund from Apple," http://www.latimes.com/local/lanow/la-me-ln-ipad-curriculum-refund-20150415-story.html, April 2015.

Book 1

The Problem & Current Environment

Chapter 4
Conquering Time

In the future, super-actualized software systems will provide teachers with all the information they need to supervise their students individually with crafted learning programs.

As mentioned earlier in the discussion of the Experience Economy, mankind is bent on conquering the next major aspect of the universe: *time.*

Now we're in the Experience Economy, and top companies are getting greater shares of interest and displacing old-line companies not built for this new value system. Nearly all of the companies in the Fortune 500 have some time savings in their offerings or experiential aspects or both.

It's fairly self-evident that to live at all is to strive for experiences, but in past eras, having a great experience was a luxury, a sort of vacation from normalcy, not a continuous feature. Living was regulated by more basic strivings. Basics are well managed today in the advanced nations. Things not so basic are even well managed. Now we are striving to manage the things that are harder to manage. And managing people, particularly children, in the direction we will them to go without over-managing them into suppressed intellect or passion for life is hard.

Technology has given us more than we have recognized before – a shift in the basis of our whole economy, and a problem, if we are not educating in the direction of relevancy for the individual in that economy.

Key Points

- Accomplishing greater efficiency of time in learning, of *authentic* and not superficial experience, is the new level for schools to reach.
- *Knowledge itself is an experiential journey.* Learning is no longer just a preparatory step towards something; it *is* the something.
- Educators have been distracted from demanding highly engaging courseware into an "everything should be free" argument.

A focus on quality time, real experiences that we hope are better than others are having, is the new value paradigm. It is what we will compete for and sacrifice other things to get and what has been building our largest commercial interests, such as social media sites that give us the experience of greater circles of friends and online retail that saves us having to physically drive anywhere.

Now that the human collective has veered into this new value paradigm, the focus is on experience, rather than ownership of space, consumption of material things, or seeking only wealth. The repercussions are vast for all institutions and heavily implicate teaching and learning.

I think this means a vastly expanded conceptualization of education because *learning and knowledge itself is an experiential journey.* Learning is no longer just a preparatory step towards something; it *is* the something. It is the new commodity, the desirable, because it is both a thing of experience and a point of leverage of one's time in this Age. Smarter is considered to also be faster, which obtains more leisure, which is more experience. That equation is irresistible. Commercial and institutional ingenuity in the digital packaging of knowledge could be limitlessly remunerative.

The trouble is the present American education system is based on a system of extremely time intensive memorization and forgetting, not feats of creativity and intelligence. It is not experiential, really. It is oriented at more generalist raw survival, "readin', writin', 'rithmetic,"and histories and basic science, without a great deal of personal exploration to arrive at a specialty oriented to skill or efficiency. The present system spews out a mass of generalists who are constructed for the Industrial

Age to live narrowly cast in menial labor-intensive tasks, and finally arrive, after years of toil, in a final few years of exhausted retirement.

This generation wants to live and not have to work as incredibly arduously as prior generations – and probably they don't have to. Already companies are experimenting with "5-hour work days" having recognized that technological work, now a significant part of the economy, is more mentally challenging than physical and that people are really "on" for really only about that much time out of an 8-hour day anyway.[1]

What educational institutions need to produce now are students who have interest in the experiential economy, who are super-attuned to time management skills and creative contribution.[2]

The Shift

With the advent of a great deal of technology, education could now enable a journey of effort accompanied by real enjoyable rewards all along the way – a life of experiences and real contributions, probably in a specialty. You could argue that people now want this not just because our forebearers may have had little enjoyment, but because right here and now so much of existence prior to adulthood has been forced to be devoid of anything dynamic. One school district made national news recently and caused a fight with their students' parents when they canceled playground time in an effort to keep primary grade-schoolers focused on onerous standards work. Another let individual teachers fight with parents about what food was acceptable for them to send in their children's lunches. Chocolate chips were not "healthy choices" inside granola bars.[3]

Education has given us a lot of non-experience. It has been way more effort and a lot less fun – perhaps even less than was enjoyed in our great-great grandparents age of the one-room schoolhouse. At least the fun then was fun on the playground, where you could climb trees, catch lizards, and skin your knee or elbows in a wrestling match or kickball game. You could potentially experience genuine interaction, and because of that, genuine joy. And every kid got a personalized education because there were a handful of kids. Things were real.

What the current youth generation seems to want the most is *authentic experience.* They will use social media endlessly to discuss anything, but the depth of what they can extrapolate imaginatively is at issue. They are experientially poor, having less and less "real" interaction. For example, they will take a picture of their well-dressed frozen yogurt and Tweet the flavor they selected, but they won't hypothesize why yogurt doesn't freeze in the smoothie machine, and perhaps ask questions like, "Is this stuff called **'propylene glycol'** in the ingredients good for me to eat or just good to help yogurt machines not freeze? And why is it labeled 'food grade' when the same-named stuff can be seen on airport tarmacs being used to de-ice airplanes? Perhaps this stuff is not good for a human body? And perhaps we should investigate why it's okay to put it in our food." That sort of authentic inquisitiveness has been being lost to generations who have been targets of information ingestion rather than creators and makers.

> "Society is currently searching for new forms of value creation. The 'Experience Economy' is the first symptom of this process. The Economy of Experiences is more than 'feed me' or 'entertain me'. Businesses and organizations have a larger, more significant role to play in supporting individuals in their search to find their own way and a significant role for themselves."
>
> *Economy of Experiences* [4]

The current crop of economically disadvantaged youth need the education barrier removed for real so they are not *superficially* experiencing learning. Without authentic, aware experience, millions of youth will be marginalized, and they know it – victims of place and time, just when the Age of Experience is starting.

Youth who have been weaned on the highly interactive video games of today are already questioning why their homework is so devoid of animation, depictions, and intelligent tangents they could explore off to the side like game-world levels and alternate modes. Because of exposure to such rich media, they see limitations on the delivery mechanisms of their learning, which are mostly flat text or simple video – and video that mostly captures a talking head lecturing. They tune out even while teachers think it's so cool that the whole class is using an app *together*, as if this is novel.

A digital re-direction to experiential education can untether any and all students from "place" and allow them to take charge of their own destinies, and additionally take the added time out of learning relevant skills. The problem with the economy where education is concerned perhaps isn't a problem at all – it's just that nearly every industry is moving into the Experience Economy while the education sector has largely been left behind. It has instead been filled with new requirements for endless testing and accommodations while not being reinvented to discard some of the earlier, now non-relevant things.

Educators have also been distracted from demanding highly engaging courseware into an "everything should be free" argument that is giving schools millions of Open Education Resources (OER) that are primarily non-animated, non-designed learning objects that do little to deliver experience because they are mostly merely documents, videos, and links. The *digital* experience is not what it could be.

Airbnb and Uber are both prime examples of a digital sharp-turn from the prior social and business norms because of the expectations for experience. It is easier to use Uber than it is a regular cab in many instances. It is more authentic and memorable to temporarily rent a house via Airbnb than a hotel. It's more local-flavored, typically, and gives access to public spaces in a different, more direct way than hotels, whose public spaces are created to be internal, such as lobbies or bars, with higher formality and less hominess. Riding in Uber means you already have your credit card loaded into the app, and you don't have to dig in to your bags to find your money or slow down at the end of the trip for the transaction. You just order it on your app, jump in, and jump out. The simplicity of this is far from what students experience in interacting with institutions.

Seeking simplicity and authenticity without pretentiousness is a hallmark of the new age. Schools who specialize in authoritarian and pretentious "we're-the-only-source" and "without-us-you-don't-get-a-degree-or-diploma-or-grade," are already secretly shunned because they are interfering with the idea of just getting on with a rich experience of life. Toll-takers like the requirements, the forced human interaction mimicking office visits and waiting in lines of old for any business, and testing transactions may seem essential, but when technology makes them invisible and seamless, learners will have a choice and a return of their desired time. They will judge an institution by how comfortable and well-managed they feel in the overall experience of learning.

Accomplishing greater efficiency of time in learning, of *authentic* and not superficial experience, is the new level for schools to reach. To do it, they need to be maestros of digital, not dabblers.

[1] https://en.wikipedia.org/wiki/The_4-Hour_Workweek

[2] UK Commission for Employment and Skills, "The Future of Work, Jobs & Skills in 2030." Feb 2014, https://www.gov.uk/government/publications/jobs-and-skills-in-2030

[3] Lauren Levy, The Reason School Lunches Were Confiscated From Children Has Parents Infuriated, October 3, 2016, http://www.popsugar.com/moms/Teachers-Taking-Away-School-Lunches-Arent-Healthy-42499265

[4]Albert Boswijk, Ed Peelan, and Steven Olthof, *Economy of Experiences*, http://www.experience-economy.com/page/view/37/our-book (2012)

Chapter 5
Gaining Momentum

There are more than 7,000 publishers in the field who are creating tens of millions of digital resources. You would have to be living in a cave to not see the writing on the wall. This is a sea of change for education.

The consumerization of the millions of learning objects out there on the internet may be a symptom of the technology incursion, but there is evidence that it is additionally a shift in people's expectations of *how* we teach and learn. Look at how much technology has changed other industries and aspects of life.

The education market is currently crossing into the digital reality that other markets, like manufacturing, insurance, and retail have already crossed. Typically, there are millions of small efforts by individuals to get sufficient momentum going in order to carry an initiative or company, or in this case, a whole market like education, out of the wading pool of novelty start-ups into the big leagues. With the dramatic influx of tablet computers in the last several years, loads of educators nationwide started this journey, carrying all of the sector with them into a digital transition.

What is interesting is that once a market reaches a certain amount of momentum, typically at around a 15% adoption, widespread change can be seen to start to happen. It starts to be noticeable, with more "buzz." It's a sort of magic point.

The 1991 book *Crossing the Chasm*[1] by Geoffrey A. Moore argued that there is a gap that exists

Key Points

- We are on the precipice of massive change in education, and consumerized learning as an agent of that may put it into overdrive to become a "theatre of experience."
- As long as education continues to not be adequately self-actualizing in the context of the greater technology reality outside of it, more and more rules and reporting and testing requirements are being pushed in to make it a wholesale mess, further and further away from any ideal.
- Learning consumerization has more than a small chance of structural significance in the future of learning distribution.

between the early adopters of any technology and the mass market because typically the masses are more conservative. He explained that many technologies initially get pulled into the market by enthusiasts, but later fail to get wider adoption because of this inherent market inertia. Institutions and markets tend to hold their own form resolutely, decrying change in service to what they know or have known of structure. It has worked. The education sector is famous for having lots of enthusiastic "one-offs," or teachers who stand out from the rest in their tech and app use. School administrators often wonder how in the world they can get "everybody else," meaning all the rest of the teachers in their school, to be the same.

Getting uniform adoption and competency by users is the bane of all technology adoption, in every sector. There is evidently not just a chasm to cross for markets, but for individuals. Some cross it more easily than others. Some run to it, while others hold the form of their own structure, especially if it has worked in the past.

The "chasm" is typified by a sort of bell-curve showing that after technology enters the scene, about 2% are the early "Innovators." Culturally, we have been known to call these the "lunatic fringe" when talking politics or social anomalies. In education, they are a more interesting rare type – one who finds, figures out, and alters their teaching to give their students something entirely different than had been being done before. They are minor miracle workers and buckers of the norm.

The next group is the "Early Adopters" and constitutes another 13% plus the original 2% for a total of 15%. In education, these are the teachers who are willful about their teaching, who may not be the first to try new tech but are always on the prowl for things that work to better learning. As soon as someone else legitimizes it, they are behind it, and soon. What's interesting is that in the U.S. today, we *have exceeded the 15% norm* for alternative educational paradigms already.

The chasm is between this 15% and the "Early Majority" or next 34% leading up to the top of the bell curve. In education, this is the hard part. The part where we can get every other teacher left to be *fully digital* and also have new levels of administrative change to facilitate a change across the board. It requires determination by leaders to lead through change, to gain, themselves, the mindset of the "Innovators" at the beginning of the curve where running entirely on technology has never been done before. It's a changed viewpoint.

There is a high potential that we are in the stage now of "crossing the chasm" as a society

CROSSING INTO K12 EDUCATION ALTERNATIVES

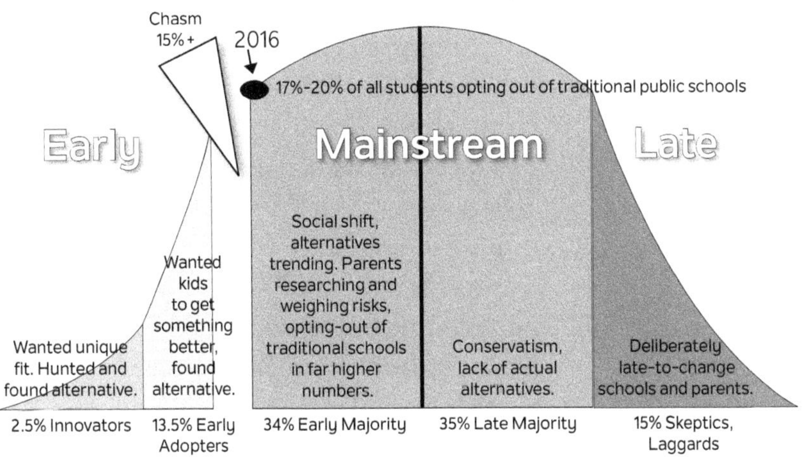
Chasm
15%+
2016
17%-20% of all students opting out of traditional public schools
Early
Mainstream
Late
Wanted unique fit. Hunted and found alternative.
Wanted kids to get something better, found alternative.
Social shift, alternatives trending. Parents researching and weighing risks, opting-out of traditional schools in far higher numbers.
Conservatism, lack of actual alternatives.
Deliberately late-to-change schools and parents.
2.5% Innovators
13.5% Early Adopters
34% Early Majority
35% Late Majority
15% Skeptics, Laggards

with education into a new digital reality. This is because once past the early adopters and transiting the chasm, when the "Early Majority" starts to transition to the new technology or adopts that social change, then there is a certain momentum that creates inevitability for every part of the market. There is a potential that learning consumerization is the bridge across the chasm for learning to a place where the majority is in alternatives to traditional institutional public schooling.

Right now in the U.S., we are already at the critical tipping point of children in the U.S. K-12 Education sector now in various flavors of alternatives to traditional public education. The alternatives to the historically typical school in the public system has reached 17%, according to the 2012 data sets of National Center for Education Statistics (NCES)[2] depicting which types of schooling environments have what numbers of the total student body in K12. Granted a large part of this is still public, just moved over into charter schools or "School Choice."

What's remarkable is that when this data is updated through 2016, it will probably show a much higher percentage have moved to alternatives since the charter schools and unschooling movement are stating record growth numbers. Based on that data, the digital shift is at least at 20%, and indications are that it will continue to be pushed politically.

From 2000 to 2012, the percentage of all public schools that were public charter schools increased from 1.7 to 6.2 percent, and the total number of public charter schools increased from 1,500 to 6,100.

Bellweather Education Partners, stating from research data by National Alliance for Public Charter Schools (NAPCS), noted in 2015 that growth has been keeping pace with previous years for charter schools, at 6% year-over-year growth. This means that 6% of students nationally, or 2.9 million students, are now in the alternative of charter schools now that 43 States have provisions for charter schools.

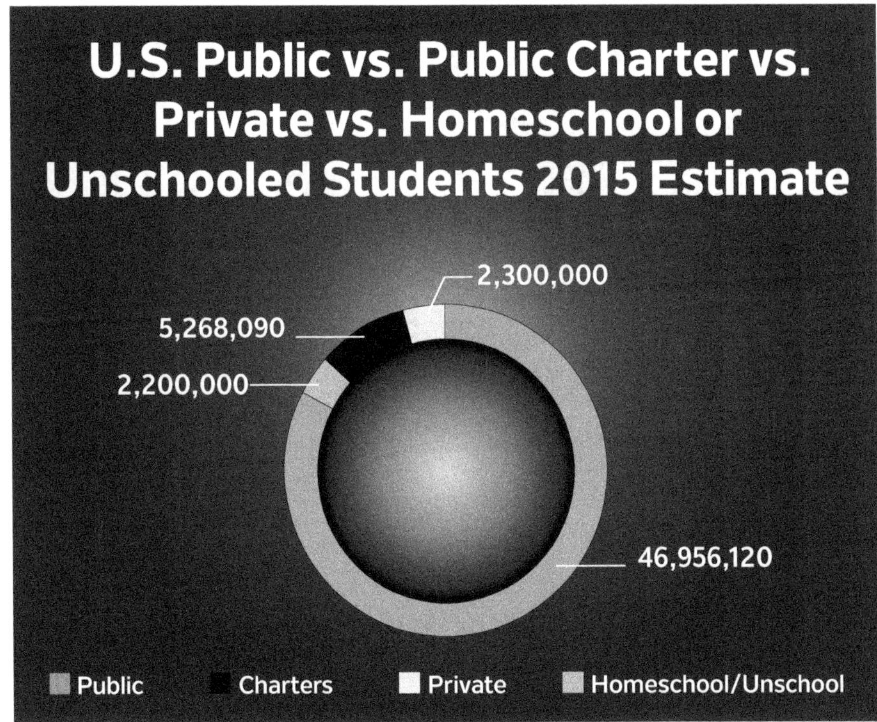

The statistic of 17%-20% is an important one in the context of more Americans seeing that we are truly in a moment of great change, an inflection point where acceptance reaches a critical mass and then starts rolling downhill to greater and greater difference from what we used to think of as our educational system. It's important to understand the *how* and *why* of something like alternative paradigms of education, just like a product or merely an idea "crosses the chasm" to where the majority start adopting it.

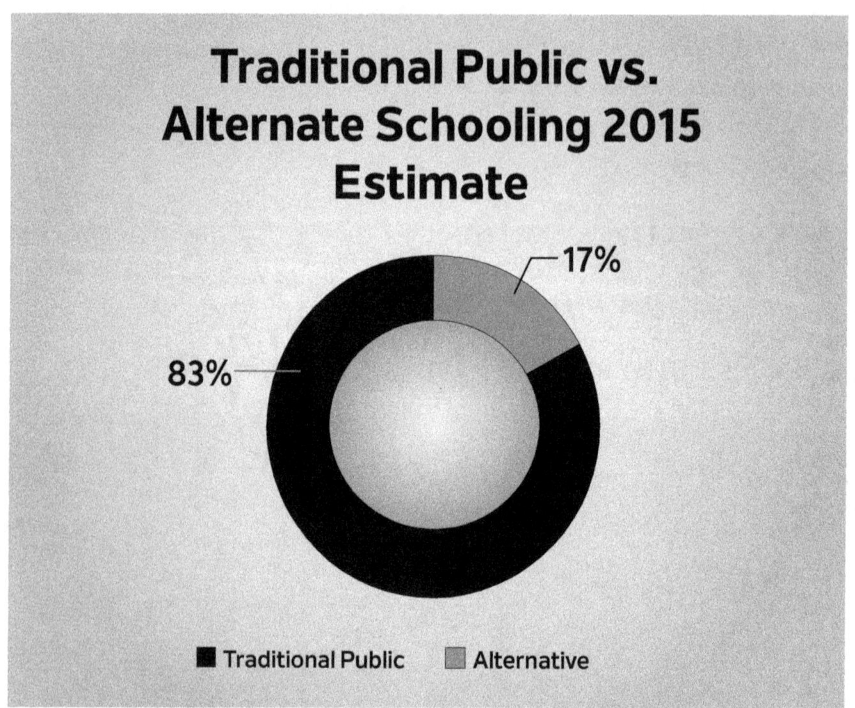

Whenever the overwhelming majority agrees that change is needed, a revolution is inevitable. It can be slow or fast, but it is inevitable. Life will find a way. Like water through your cupped hands, it will flow through to where gravity is pulling it. History has taught us that in every area, from religious to racial rights, inevitably there is a transformation politically, socially, and economically when enough people agree and a new "pull" causes it. Surprisingly, we are actually at that statistical tipping point today in the field of education. As long as education continues to not be adequately self-actualizing in the context of the greater technology reality outside of it, more and more rules and reporting and testing requirements are being pushed in to make it a wholesale mess and further and further away from any ideal.

It could it be that the revolution is none of the forms we see right now but may soon appear more like the Starbucks or iTunes revolutions – where education becomes more an online theatre of experience that is "chunked" down into individualized playlists of knowledge and seamlessly becomes imbued into the fabric of teacher-learner relationships. That could be one way. Or perhaps a sort of reworking of the educational institution could occur with new models much like Netflix and cable did away with Blockbuster and smartphones did away with going to the bank to deposit a check.

There is a high likelihood that if the transition is done right, schools can use the staff resources they presently have, including all the teachers and administrators.

The inflection point, that crossing-of-the-chasm to a new structure, one pivoting around consumerization, seems to be sweeping along without any evidence of slowing down. The multiplicity of efforts aligned with it are too numerous and with too much agreement for change. Direct, consumerized learning, with an invisible "institution" or some sort of reorganized learning officialdom that floats behind the front of online interaction much as our regulators do in many other industries, *could* be where we are headed.

One thing to note about this is that a whole lot of capital is going in to support more valuable and highly designed learning software. A report by IBIS Capital[4] looked at the national eLearning

> The global education expenditure market is projected to grow at 7.4% until 2017 (across all types of spend). E-Learning expenditure is projected to grow at 23% annually to $256 Billion by 2017, with a K-12 CAGR of 34%, higher ed Compound Annual Growth Rate (CAGR) of 28%, and corporate market CAGR of 13%.

scene, citing other primary research and their own analysis to state:

- Investment in consumer-facing e-Learning companies has increased threefold year-on-year.
- Social learning has attracted significant interest from the investment community with an annual growth rate in new investment over the last 3 years of 224%.
- The U.S. is the most active global fundraising market for e-Learning, accounting for 59.7% of total deals, with high-growth markets India and China trailing with 11.3% and 8.4% respectively.
- As consumer-faced e-Learning companies are on the rise, the distribution sector has been attracting an increasing volume of capital.
- The two largest fundraisings in 2013 were Lynda.com (Accel, MeriTech, Spectrum investing $103M) and Open English (Insight, Red point, TCV investing $65M).

These are indicators that the technically sophisticated among us have allied with the monied interests to take advantage of the potentials of digital learning, particularly items with consumer-like distributions.

I think this means learning consumerization has more than a small chance of structural significance in the future of learning distribution. The change will not be like a tsunami, despite these numbers indicating a fairly fast-moving crossing for this last great market, education.

Schools still have time. Building high-value digital curriculum software is not as simple as an animated game. Rigorous materials packaged together into flawless experiential learning take a lot of money and time. We will see a gradual evolution that will come to be seen as more like the fast-moving and wide gulfstream – teeming with life and possibility.

[1] Geoffrey A. Moore, *Crossing the Chasm*, 1991.

[2] National Center of Education Statistics, *Digest of Education Statistics*, http://nces.ed.gov/programs/digest/d13/tables/dt13_216.40.asp

[3] Alex Iskold, *Rethinking 'Crossing The Chasm*, August 6, 2007 http://readwrite.com/2007/08/06/rethinking_crossing_the_chasm/

[4] IBIS Capital, *A European Perspective on E-learning*, https://issuu.com/ibiscapital/docs/a_european_perspective_on_e-learnin

Reference Material:
National Center for Education Statistics, *Fast Facts*, https://nces.ed.gov/fastfacts/display.asp?id=30

Sara Mead, Ashley LiBetti Mitchel, and Andrew J. Rotherham, Bellweather Education Partners, *The State of the Charter School Movement*, September 2015, http://bellwethereducation.org/sites/default/files/Charter%20Research%200908%20FINAL.pdf

Chapter 6
The Blur

In the last few cities of our ongoing Digital Curriculum Discussions, there have been more varied forms of schools from private and public sectors than ever before. And they collaborate. It is heartwarming and demonstrates that the "competition" is really not what is often touted. All teachers and administrators join forces to corral and control technology.

It is easy to see in this camaraderie that the future of education is already here: a blur of options. This blur is really not hugely ideologically different than a vast array of consumer options like those for housing and home goods. You can "hotel" or Airbnb in a brief relationship with a place already fully furnished, you can rent a furnished apartment or house for long periods and decorate it yourself, you can rent an unfurnished place and then pick out all your options, you can purchase a place, you can build a place, and you can invest only and not live there at all. The blur in the housing industry is not going to go away. It has, in fact, with Airbnb, just grown another dimension to itself.

Where there used to be a two-valued system with public versus private education options, there is now a wide range of options and interdependencies. It is actually forming into somewhat of a scale that can go infinitely in both directions – from as old-school as a one-room 1800s schoolhouse with chalkboards, to the 1950s ideals with football teams, wooden flip-top desks, long hallways, PA systems, and paper report cards, and on up

Key Points

- Educational institutions can expect more varied forms, and physical presence to learn will be optional.
- Inherent value has to be either a human ability or hands-on projects that can't be surrendered to highly designed software and technology that can individualize in a mobile and highly available way.
- Institutions will need to focus on the skillful weaving of the face-to-face with the technical distributions of knowledge so that each individual is getting a totally engaging encounter and the product of real knowledge.
- People will handle the blur the way consumers handle it now in commodities and services of all kinds. They choose.

to a fully personalized and online education for "unschoolers" and home-schoolers with skyped-in pro teachers, and now even an option that literally echoes the one-room schoolhouse only highly tech-equipped.

Further illustration of this new "scale" and co-existing newly option-oriented market include:

- Charter schools are actually public outgrowths but sometimes run by enterprising private groups.

- Private academies serve to augment with study skills public sector school students in the evenings and weekends.

- Homeschoolers enroll students in state-run or district-run fully online schools with virtual "pop-up" teachers and live as-needed human interface for questions.

- Public schools providing access to online free courses by resource sites, such as Khan Academy, Udemy, and others.

- Unschoolers who take state tests to gain a diploma.

- Commercially available apps and subscription websites providing high value resources that by their nature can walk a student through all needed lessons in a gaming orientation so engaging that the student barely knows they are learning. Reports to parents can be ported over to schools for easy placement in the correct grade or study group.

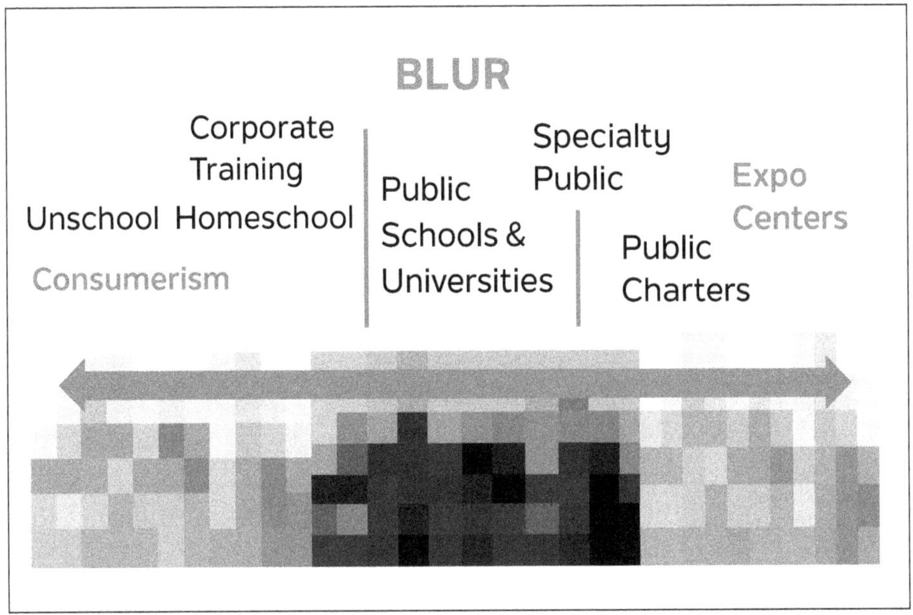

Mature markets always have a multiplicity of "fits" rather than a one-dimensional answer.

The "blur" is the new game-field of education. It has left the predictable structure and function of institutions as we have known them. Left the sort of planned village of Hershey's age that resulted in employees trying to kill him much the same as the fights anyone today can see between teachers and students on YouTube that, while not quite so violent, are growing in number. The blur proves that like the Berlin Wall in Germany reuniting a people, the proverbial wall of isolationism for educational structure has fallen, and a more free-form game of learning is returning.

As a teacher or learner, your future is a life of maneuvering between the blur of options. The real leaders will actively work at prediction of new, forthcoming options, through natural ideas spawned *because of* the blur and increasing technological capabilities.

Inside the blur, the persistence of a certain type of teacher-sourced and channeled learning as place-specific, with one-to-many-classes and age-batches and grading and so much more that is considered fact, is all being challenged. Challenges will not abate, and the smart individual or institution will adapt to master the best service model(s) for their desired constituencies.

What to focus on is the inherent value proposition of your specific teaching and your specific school, without it necessarily being something that is delivered face-to-face. That inherent value has to be something that is either a human ability or hands-on project – not one that can be surrendered to highly designed software and technology that can individualize in a mobile and highly available way. Institutions will need to focus on the skillful weaving of the face-to-face with the technical distributions of knowledge, so that each individual is getting a totally engaging encounter and the product of real knowledge.

Presence, Optional

A requirement for physical attendance with a high rate of motion going to and fro has made for an exhausting century, and we are tired. We're burning up oil and the air, and we miss having families.

With the advent of mobile communications technology, email, and more, we are once again in regular communication with family and experiencing close connection even when we live half a world away. For the last twenty years, people have been finding that distance is a conquerable phenomenon with technology, that physical presence is more optional. It's not hard to keep up a relationship, to share and laugh and learn and strive, using video chat. Remote workers and distance learning have ballooned nationally precisely because people want quality of life.

The rise in homeschooling and unschooling and the potential of consumerized learning is more than just people pulling their kids out of the old construct because of familial, moral, religious, or achievement purposes. They are doing it from dissatisfaction and because it's not necessary to have an institutional location for learning. An NCES survey showed that, "In the 2011–12 school year, 91 percent of homeschooled students had parents who said that a concern about the environment of other schools was an important reason for homeschooling their child, which was a higher percentage than other reasons listed."

The construct of schools in our culture has also assumed that socialization is necessary, but historically, prior to schools creating a focus on socialization in an effort to create social homogeneity and control larger populations of students, no such ideas were part of culture for hundreds of years. Today, socialization is totally trumped when parents realize that they and their children have lost a certain quality and quantity of life. That, with individualized instruction, their child gets the best deal available of all alternatives, including private schools. And they get to *see* the child more, perhaps even go through life experiencing being a family for more than a few minutes a day.

"Although many parents might not want to admit it, sending their children to an institutional school is a compromise. It's a compromise between one-on-one private (tutoring) and institutionalized schooling. All the research demonstrates that public or private school is a second best alternative to private one-on-one instruction. Homeschoolers regularly score 20 to 30 percentile points above public school students on standardized tests and typically out-perform private school students by 10 percentile points." [1]

J. Michael Smith
The Washington Times

The blur of options brings more dimensions to the choice issue in education – more questions, more possibilities for both sides. Potentially, the consumerization of learning holds something for both institutions and learners.

People will handle the blur the way consumers handle it now in commodities and services of all kinds. They choose, sometimes wisely and sometimes not so wisely. Sometimes they end up in the local store because it's local, and other times they do nearly all their shopping online.

[1] J. Michael Smith, " Homeschooling Strengthens Families and Communities," *The Washington Times*, April 19, 2004. https://www.hslda.org/docs/news/washingtontimes/200404190.asp

Reference Material:

http://www.bostonmagazine.com/news/article/2015/08/25/homeschooling-in-boston/2/

"The sobering evidence of social science," *The Washington Post*, George F. Will, July 6th, 2016, https://www.washingtonpost.com/opinions/the-sobering-evidence-of-social-science/2016/07/06/4a3831f8-42dd-11e6-bc99-7d269f8719b1_story.html

Chapter 7

The Jerk

There is an invisible "war for balance" happening nationally in education, one that is causing the entire field to feel somewhat jerked forward toward unknown destinations, out of any comfort zone.

This war for balance is between the inside world of education and the outside world of every other part of the economy moving faster in technology adoption. The visible friction between the way schools run and their immediate community is another level of the war. Schools and district level administrations battling their boards and finding funding sources for a shift to technology is another level of the war. Another level is with teachers trying to deploy, or fight, using technology in the classroom. The final level is a war for every single human – a war each of us have between being human and being entirely absorbed in technology. In the end, the war is an attempt by humans to balance *against* the great force of technology, to use enough to be competitive and in-fashion, but to not let it take over everything and displace us.

While traveling city-by-city, the Learning Counsel team has learned one thing really important about this ongoing war in education: that there is a frightfully uneven playing field for how sophisticated schools are with the digital transition. And that unevenness is pitching a competitive frenzy into the market. The high watermark for big players seems to be Houston Independent School District. Small private schools like Alt

Key Points

- The educational sector is experiencing "the Jerk," where we are living four years to every one we lived before (4:1), which is all part of the accelerating "War for Balance."
- It's difficult to compete as a human in a completely embedded technological world, using it, but providing a value above it to be employed and sustained.
- For schools, what is really important about "the Jerk" is that the number of new things they will have to deal with technologically will accelerate, and late entrants will risk their survival, because in a competitive landscape where positioning is everything, all the good slots will already be taken.

School, operating in major market cities like San Francisco and New York, are also a model. There are vast differences between these and the whole rest of the market.

In our third year of road-trip events, we have observed that the rate of change internal to the national education market is so far behind the change dynamics of other industries that it is literally being pulled out of its inertia by those outside forces now accelerating it faster and faster. It's like a tailwind from the other markets.

Therefore, the whole education market is experiencing what can euphemistically be called "the Jerk." Schools can no longer stand off in isolation with barely embedding technology. "The Jerk" is a physics term, not just a derogatory name to call someone. In physics, it refers to the "time rate of change of acceleration." Simply, how fast things are going. You can buy a piece of digital curriculum about "the Jerk" at the American Journal of Physics online for $30 or rent it for $4 – the type of discrete knowledge object-purchasing teachers manage to hunt down and purchase all the time. The term "the Jerk" is applicable to the rate of change of all things experienced in modern society. We are feeling that we are being jerked forward by the increasing acceleration of the rate of technology change.

Futurist Ray Kurzweil said in 2001, "We won't experience 100 years of progress in the 21st Century – it will be more like 20,000 years of progress (at today's rate)."[1]

At the Learning Counsel, we estimate that the rate of technological change in the education sector is now roughly four times as fast as it was only a few years ago. We believe it was roughly twice its normal pace in 2013 and has accelerated to an estimated 4:1 now in 2016. This is what we mean as "the Jerk."

At the same time, as the rate of acceleration of change is speeding up, many schools are simply unable to move to a more technologically advanced capability. They are too stymied by finances and low interest or fear to even start, much less keep up with how they need to "be" and "do" as a technologically savvy core of change agents. The technology and rate of change is beyond most educators' ability to understand, much less act on. They're educators, not software engineers or techie startup entrepreneurs.

Most educators have little understanding of software, how much information is gathered, and how algorithms work; they haven't been analyzing how much user interface and user experience, combined with human-like service interactions and interrogatives with machine-learning, animations, and gaming, have the power to completely customize learning. To many educators, computers mean the ability to digitize text with highlighting and definition pop-ups and links to videos or pre-recorded lectures. A teacher was not supposed to need to know how we bring all of human knowledge on-demand and convey it through a human-like personality that could emerge to "teach," with fantastic variety, anyone, anything, at any time.

> "The hardest part is really a culture shift… I think our window of opportunity is only a few years."
>
> *Kurt Madden,*
> *Chief Technology Officer*
> *Fresno Unified School District, CA*
> *2014*

It could be easy for many of us to go into an apathetic state when confronted with things so significantly complex that one's wits cannot develop a simple breakdown, only a feeling of being overwhelmed. Such overwhelm is a stagnant state; it immobilizes. It is very easy to view the world not through a lens of what is possible, but only via the structure we are currently living in. In other words, it is easy to begin to fear technology.

What is not spoken of in mainstream media is the inequity of the Jerk – how humanity as a body cannot keep pace with its own creation. The meaning of this inequity is an imbalanced state, a fraying of the culture, politics, and economy as we know it. It will not slow down.

The thing that has to be done by educators and schools is *start.* Schools are exceptional at sharing and at writing school plans.

Start with a strategy that aims at the Age of Experience. It's a good place where everyone can win.

The Jerk in Perspective

Let's put the Jerk as a concept in perspective alongside education and consider this 4:1 rate of change we've extrapolated from observing schools and look at how it applies to industry and culture.

A tiny subset of humans are producing the bulk of the new technological advances and capitalizing on them. This has been euphemistically termed the "netocracy," referring to this dominant set of corporate and government leaders defined by their powers over information, technology, and money. The utilization of technology commercially to rule has the appearance of somewhat victimizing the masses through demand generation for that technical innovation or product that sells a promise that in practice, at scale, actually is not the consumers' great savior. It's certainly *marketed* that way, as in "I have the best phone, so I am, therefore, more productive or happier," etc. This is because everyone eventually has them, which means the innovation now has actually wrought these two things:

1. An arms race of productivity using the new product, that by observation actually has actual human limitations, even whilst everyone is seemingly working ever so much harder via the augmentation of technology; and,

2. A curtailment of other more genuinely efficacious transactions, such as long-form live communication like we used to share at meals but now the family spends half the time in apps or texting. This is one of the most directly observable phenomena that proves technology is a force that changes our behavior.

What's interesting about this is that we are reaching a saturation point of tech that we can absorb.

"Despite the increase in choices, the number of apps used is staying the same. A recent Nielsen analysis found that on average, U.S. smartphone users accessed 26.7 apps per month in the fourth quarter of 2014 – a number that has remained relatively flat over the last two years. And consider this: Over 70% of the total usage is coming from the top 200 apps. However, while there appears to be a consumer threshold to the total number of apps people are willing and/or able to actively use during the month, the time they spend engaging on those apps has increased. In fact, the monthly time spent per person has increased from 23 hours and 2 minutes in fourth-quarter 2012, to 37 hours and 28 minutes in fourth-quarter 2014 – a 63% rise in two years."[2]

In terms of our ability to *use* all our "big data," derived from all our technical interactions, we are also apparently, on average, over our heads to grasp the significance. "Or consider the economic collapse of 2008. The problem of unchecked derivatives and subprime mortgages weren't problems of not enough information, but too much information. Companies disclosed mountains of data on their derivative positions, but nobody could properly evaluate the positions and inherent risks. The data was there, but we ignored it, because it wasn't possible for us to process. We all assumed someone else was doing the analysis. Technology changed faster than government regulation," said Taylor Davidson, CEO of Foresight, a company which helps startups and investors model financial projections. From his August 2011 article, he continues, "The real challenges technology companies face today are human, not technical, and that's a normal part of the cycle, not a failure of venture capital or innovation."[3]

Tech has the capacity for taking a high amount of attention, potentially causing a disregard of other basic needs, such as food and shelter, or at least making those things appear less significant than previous generations held them to be. China already has boot camps for youth "Web Junkies" who use the internet for gaming and become addicted.[4]

With the tech imperative now, education administrators, who are not top technocrats and owners of the technology, must increasingly adopt more tech while not being able to easily afford, or keep up with, each new advance. This lag on the human absorption rate of technology versus invention of new tech is such a concern that the World Bank funded a study and paper on the issue.

They even differentiated between absorption and innovation.

According to the paper, "Absorption is a costly learning activity that an organization can employ to integrate and commercialize knowledge and technology that is new to the firm, but not new to the world. For simplicity, development of new-to-the-world knowledge can be considered innovation. In other words, innovation shifts a notional technological frontier outward, while absorption moves the firm closer to the frontier."[5] Currently, the education scene is still struggling with absorption, and so is potentially inhibitive of the new tech frontier.

We are definitely in an age where it is becoming impossible for people, and even whole sectors like education, to keep up with all the tech due to the ever-faster Jerk until possibly the only thing to keep up with it is the tech itself as it gains ever-more intelligence and then artificial sentience.

Most people, and educators are no exception, are not on the offensive with technology; we are not even on the defense. We are mostly placid consumers of technology. The majority of current society has not looked far ahead – we are just trying to be effective users of the tech being sold to us.

Importantly, educators think that they must cause students to be even better consumers of technology, potentially technicians. What educators have not necessarily thought through is how to create antagonists of technology, critical questioners of tech, fostering greater *human* science to compete with the tech advance.

Struggling with the Jerk

The greatest achievements, the most sought after knowledge and new commercial developments of the next Age, will not come from purely science and technology and engineering and mathematics, but will be advancements in human understanding and ability, for one inescapable reason: we cannot reach a total overwhelm of technology without a survivalist sense kicking in as a species. We will want to protect ourselves and find a way to absorb and augment our human systems and organizational structures. We have already glimpsed this innate species-wide mechanism in two significant ways, unprecedented in history:

1. After the initial atomic and nuclear blasts killing so many in World War II, mankind woke up and declared, in near unity, that we do not want this kind of power, that this technology is a no-one-wins dead end.

2. A planet-wide realization about global warming and the significant activism to combat it regardless of the effectiveness so far.

Both of these are unprecedented in human history, which is strewn with wars for dominion that had never before held any restraint to its increasing barbarisms. The anti-nuclear-bombing and global warming movements are humanity-wide now as agreements. Even China is changing. "China aims to lay off 5-6 million state workers over the next two to three years as part of efforts to curb industrial overcapacity and pollution, two reliable sources said Beijing's boldest retrenchment program in almost two decades. China's leadership, obsessed with maintaining stability and making sure redundancies do not lead to unrest, will spend nearly 150 billion yuan ($23 billion) to cover layoffs in just the coal and steel sectors in the next 2-3 years," Reuters reported on March 10, 2016[6].

The question is, do a few new social directions really mean anything tangible about humanity and the struggle with "the Jerk"? Is there a possibility that perhaps we are capable of group consensus globally? Could we reach a new human consciousness level that, were everyone attuned to it, makes for a human equivalent of what is known as the tech "Singularity"? There is a small spark of possibility here.

> *"The Singularity is an era in which our intelligence will become increasingly nonbiological and trillions of times more powerful than it is today – the dawning of a new civilization that will enable us to transcend our biological limitations and amplify our creativity."*
>
> – Ray Kurzweil

Scores have criticized Kurzweil's prediction that the technological "Singularity" will occur in 2045. His statement rests on the very shaky assumption that Moore's Law will continue to hold true. Moore's Law, the doubling of computer processing speed every 18 months, has actually been slowing down and certainly it is not infinite unless you redefine speed as a new speed-across-accessible-knowledge. That is more the software and data side, which is really the "Big Data" issue.

In any case, speed of technology advancement will hold true at least for the time being. It will begin, in the next few years, to gain momentum and inevitably create a backlash against such ruthless change. Many will interpret this as a rejection of technology. In fact, it will be a friction between *speeds*, and speeds alone. We do not think or change as fast as technology is being thrown at us. Just consider that we don't socialize well beyond a circle of approximately 150 others (Dunbar's Number[7]). The human mind as individual mechanism in each of us does not currently directly network with other minds seamlessly like technology, at least not yet. It is an area I'm sure will be explored in the 21st century.

Right now there is a worldwide transition underway because of technology, but precious few know where the transition is really going. They *think* they know, but they are thinking along with the technology dictates of industry and not from an ideological viewpoint of where it will *inevitably* go *because of* technology at the humanity level. This is important, because it points educators in the direction of lessons for students that may just save them.

That new curriculum direction just may be the most exciting one of the 21st century: how to compete as a human in a completely embedded technological world, using it, but providing a value *above it* to be employed and sustained. And, one last cherry on top, employed in such a way that far more free time enters the picture.

We can know we are in a time of great change because literally everything about the industry of education and the effort of learning is in question. This is "the Jerk," knocking us into some alternate reality and causing us to wonder where we are.

For schools, what is really important about "the Jerk" is that the number of new things they will have to deal with technologically will accelerate, and late entrants will risk their survival, because in a competitive landscape where positioning is everything, all the good slots will already be taken.

"The Jerk" is also the new war for balance between us and machines. We are having to think about what we are and how we live alongside machine intelligence.

The good news is that enough good people see what's happening and are taking action to get a hold of, corral it, and push education change into a new, awesome future.

[1] Ray Kurzweil, "The Law of Accelerating Returns", *Kurzweil Accelerating Intelligence Essays*, 2001, http://www.kurzweilai.net/the-law-of-accelerating-returns

[2] Neilsen, "So Many Apps, So Much More Time For Entertainment", Newswire, June 2015, http://www.nielsen.com/us/en/insights/news/2015/so-many-apps-so-much-more-time-for-entertainment.html

[3] Taylor Davidson, CEO, Foresight, http://www.taylordavidson.com/2011/human-technical

[4] Shosh Shlam and Hilla Medalia, "China's Web Junkies", *New York Times, Opinion Pages*, http://www.nytimes.com/2014/01/20/opinion/chinas-web-junkies.html

[5] Itzhak Goldberg, Lee Branstetter, John Gabriel Goddard, Smita Kuriakose, "Globalization and Technology Absorption in Europe and Central Asia The Role of Trade, FDI, and Cross-border Knowledge Flows," The *International Bank for Reconstruction and Development/The World Bank*, 2008, http://www.urenio.org/wp-content/uploads/2009/11/globalization_tech_absorption_FullReport.pdf

[6] Benjamin Kang Lim, Matthew Miller, David Stanway, "China to lay off five to six million workers, earmarks at least $23 billion," *Reuters*, Mar 2016, http://www.reuters.com/article/us-china-economy-layoffs-exclusive-idUSKCN0W33DS

[7] Wikipedia, Dunbars Number, https://en.wikipedia.org/wiki/Dunbar%27s_number

[8] Heather Wolpert-Gawron, middle school teacher, 2010, "What is the Purpose of Public Education?", Blog - *Huffington Post*

Chapter 8

Culture Clash

There are many factors in our culture supporting a deeper digital transition. Some of these factors are unavoidable and have already been discussed. Others are real clash points, overlooked by educators as they strive to manage the shift to digital education. We'll examine some of these potential pitfalls in the following paragraphs. Some of what I'll point out here is generational, where older people have been brought up with a different way of learning than is potential now. The digitally integrated generation of Millennials is typically expecting that their children have increasingly sophisticated digital experiences.

Key Points

- Old cultural norms are clashing. Information hoarding is out, social media-as-substitution is in, a multi-generational reality is upon us, and we have a new paradigm for learning.
- The Standards are a cultural response to a need for order and pave the way for consumerized learning. They could perhaps be called the "Genome of Learning."
- Learning with the new "DNA" of Standards leveraged in digital curriculum has the promise to become a self-directed continuous journey filled with potential enthusiasms, camaraderie, and competitiveness, all while being usefully measured. Education's long clash with accountability has a much brighter future.

Hoarding Is Out, Sharing Is In

Old-schoolers have used the control of data for power in the past, and some of that does still go on, but new-schoolers share everything. In the past, almost exclusively, managers got to be managers because they *knew* more, having accrued more practical knowledge and having greater skill, and not just because they were in place longer. As the information age came about, managers often achieved their place or held their place because they were at the center of a web of information and used it to their advantage. Each of their direct reports gave them information that was not necessarily shared with others. Whole industries have relied on information being fairly non-liquid and the secrecy or hoarding of it to be *power.* To know something someone else didn't *was* power.

Today, except for certain financial and national security interests, it is socially *unacceptable* to leave everyone in the dark. To lead effectively is to be a consummate sharer-of-plans, to give everyone a "vision statement" and constantly update it, and keep everyone in the loop. Today's staff in almost any organization will quit if they don't know what's going on because they like the feeling of being part of something larger, not just a cog in the great machine. At least on the surface, this factor of sharing information makes the management "acceptable." As one example of this culturally, after the two World Wars, Germany's *Reichstag Dome* in Berlin was built generally in form a lot like all American State Capitol building domes, but made of *glass* to signify a new transparency to government. This is what people want – a free and open view.

People, and especially teachers, can no longer gain credibility merely by *knowing more.* That is old school. Data is findable everywhere in the open ocean of the Internet. Therefore, the usual credibility traded on for higher salaries and greater position by teachers, the "cred" of knowing more, is a nearly dead currency. It is even considered with disdain by many youth. It can barely be traded on socially, and long-term workers in every other field learned that the hard way during the recession, when masses of people were laid off only to be replaced by much younger workers or no workers at all.

The "cred" today is the exact opposite of previous generations. Instead of hoarding, they want to be the first to share and share it with as many people as they can.

How you share it matters too. Is there entertainment value? What platform was used? The implications for this across our culture are immense. It is a veritable reversal in our politics and culture, because the new generations are sharing way more than information – they are sharing emotion. What's interesting is that new generations appear to be applying emotion into a larger domain, the Internet. Emotion is used to be understood only internally to ourselves or shared intimately with spouses or family or best friends.

While there are still issues of isolated individuals, the preponderance have moved into an always-on and always-connected humankind membership. It is a first in history, and it is a gross understatement to say that a regimented uniformity to education can survive in this culture of sharing. I would go so far as to say that it wouldn't survive, because society's exposure to far more ideas and each other is reaching an entirely different realm.

This is also part of the answer to how a teacher uses what they know. It is still valuable, but it's in how you share it technologically and provide room for emotion.

Social Media as Counterweight

"If anything, social media is a counterweight to the ongoing devaluation of human lives. Social media's rapid rise is a loud, desperate, emerging attempt by people everywhere to connect with 'each other' in the face of all the obstacles that modernity imposes on our lives: suburbanization that isolates us from each other, long working-hours and commutes that are required to make ends meet, the global migration that scatters families across the globe, the military-industrial-consumption machine that drives so many key decisions, and, last but not least, the television – the ultimate alienation machine – which remains the dominant form of media. (For most people, the choice is not leisurely walks on Cape Cod versus social media. It's television versus social media.)" [2]

Zeynep Tufekci, *The Atlantic*

The Social Media Substitution

In the past, family units were depicted as having communal time of discussion. Many times this was shown as a gathering around the dinner table, a tableau that seems increasingly rare.

The new reality is meals on the run, in front of the television, the computer screen, or worse, in our cars. In restaurants, you can observe whole families temporarily absorbed into their smartphones rather than talking to each other every instant. In many instances they are individually enjoying a wider social discourse while also being with their families. They are not so "individual" as before. The facts of the meteoric rise in online community, particularly among the young, are also proof enough that the Westernized development of individualism had potentially hindered a basic instinct that is now pushing its way to the front. It could be argued that the weakening of the family unit through an idealized enforced separation into individual husband-wife-children units of family physically "cubicle-ized" into individual dwellings instead of tribes or villages has begotten an urgency amongst people for substitution.

This is not a position as to the long-term survival value of that substitution. I am simply noting the fact that youth are filling the void of family and inclusion with something, anything, to be their "group." They've of course been doing this forever and it's strengthened with the advent of the Internet. The positive thing about new online communities is that they could create a sort of culture of positivity that may be lacking in homes.

It is true that in many areas the sense of community created by a school environment has successfully bonded children with teacher outsiders. This has given children a new place for belonging outside the family. Sometimes this relationship outside the family could be considered important. In times past it was considered that modern education had a function, if left unsaid, to bond the individual as a citizen to a larger collective – to create an allegiance beyond family. Schools have helped build this broader belongingness with such things as the rites of attendance (schools, sports teams, clubs, and military) and reciting the Pledge of Allegiance, which echo religious rites.

This is very un-modern in the context of the Internet – it is an old social pattern that is still running in institutions that engineer and contrive all sorts of family dynamic substitutions. The fact that students are reputedly leaving Facebook in droves precisely *because* teachers and adults are getting onto it shows that any emotional support substitution desired is not the one that can be delivered by institutions through teachers.

The school-as-social-engineer has been disproven as an equity enabler since the 1960s[3], when major studies revealed that it is really the outside cultural setting that matters the most in educational achievement and student drive. Social media now has the capacity to form an individual custom-created support for students, a substitution that is already working on a massive scale.

Consumerized learning on top of that allows a self-navigation that may or may not break with the culture surrounding that student. We can hope that it would do so, because it may be just the thing to help break cycles of ignorance and poverty. Being non-systematized may actually provide a reduced friction with local culture for some students. When

Peers & Parents, Not Schools, Influence Achievement

"[With] data from more than 3,000 schools and 600,000 primary and secondary school students... His [James Samuel Coleman – 'Coleman Report' *Equality of Educational Opportunity*, 1966] report vindicated the axiom that social science cannot tell us what to do, it can tell us the results of what we are doing. He found that the best predictor of a school's outcomes was the quality of the children's families. And students' achievements are influenced by the social capital (habits, mores, educational ambitions) their classmates bring to school:

"One implication stands out above all: That schools bring little influence to bear on a child's achievement that is independent of his background and general social context; and that this very lack of an independent effect means that the inequalities imposed on children by their home, neighborhood, and peer environment are carried along to become the inequalities with which they confront adult life at the end of school."[3]

George F. Smith, *The Washington Post*

coming from greatly disadvantaged areas, a student with self-selected social media supports and custom consumerized learning paths that are not over-exposed to a wider class (which could possibly ridicule) and awareness of being behind, may actually find greater achievement than anything that could otherwise be done by normal institutions. This is both because the student is not overly exposed to negative influences and because the student is self-navigating, and therefore, learning to rule out negativity and seek heightened achievement as an individual.

The reality is that the purposes of creating a collective do not necessitate *some* of the functions schools have taken unto themselves. Not anymore. The Internet and technology make it entirely possible for students to lean on digital substitutes that could, in fact, be more effective.

Make Way for a Multi-Generational Society

We aren't necessarily causing people of different generations to *learn together*, but that is in fact the way it was done for all of history until the last hundred or so years. Now, however, we have come far enough along in history to have a sense of what is more natural for humanity, just as a new trend of multi-generational living is on the upsurge nationally.

The word *school* derives from "Middle English *scole*, from Old English *scōl*, from Latin *schola*, from Greek *scholē*, meaning leisure, discussion, lecture, school; perhaps akin to Greek *echein* to hold."[4]

School is something that seems to follow from our universal tendency to gather together. It has always been natural for us to form groups like the small associations called families, tribes, and villages. Historically, individuals of multiple ages learned to live and work together. Typically, the older individuals were teaching and leading the young. Right now we artificially "socialize" kids by age, completely missing a great quantity of learning that could be happening as students observe behaviors towards different stimuli by other students and adults who are of different ages.

Take, for example, the reactions seen of kids when a fire truck drives by a school yard. The older child looks bored at a fire truck going down the road, the middle school student jumps and shouts "Fire, fire, fire!" and the kindergartener shrinks back towards the safety of an adult at the loud siren noise.

There are many things learned by each of the children about each other by the mere mixing of ages. Respect, security, and different levels of care come about through this interaction and are doubtlessly irreplaceable. This type of socialization is common in small private schools but utterly missing in most public schools. Older children, unused to being around pre-school and grade-school-aged children, may be less caring or competent as parents. They have been batch-manufactured with others of like ages and become somewhat alien to multi-generational cooperation.

Search "multi-generational" learning online and another aspect comes into view: lacking an understanding of how the different generations learn is having profound effects on corporations who run into difficulties with training and developing cross-generational collaborations.

Yet today, the U.S. is in a dramatic boom of multi-generational domestic arrangements, with the economic down-turn forcing multiple-families and multiple generations to live together, the aging boomer population coming back to live with their children, and many Millennials not leaving home for lack of work or too much student debt. This new reality is on the heels of several generations where such mixing wasn't happening nearly as much. The new reality of living multi-generationally is not being mirrored in the educational environments uniformly, but talk of bringing it back has begun.

Since society is experiencing multi-generational living, a school can better match consumer reality by itself becoming "consumerized" in the respect of being openly adapted to all ages – helping to match multi-generational realities.

Mapping the Genome of Learning

If you were a programmer, you would want to break down learning into its "requirements" for programming out a sequence of code to deliver to the screen user their learning as individualized to their user preference as possible.

Individualized learning can happen with software programming when there is a map of requirements and the student is evaluated by age, ability, or professional observation for where they fit in that map. These factors of what to teach and to whom allow a program to zero in with precision. That determination has been the skill of teaching, except with an aim towards the required proficiency level. It's this final point – what constitutes proficiency – that is the stickler.

Professional educators have long been in a world without an autonomous standard of achievement. College transcripts from one to another are often fraught with imbalance, lost credit hours, and worse, no recognition of some courses. Students leaving high school end up in remedial courses, at their cost, and some never get over that hump to start getting credits towards degrees.

In addition to the desire by learners to have an outcome, a banner of achievement like a degree or diploma, taxpayers and governments want accountability. The accountability and outcomes conundrum is a heated one in the education sector for sure, but it is also highly unlikely it will ever go away. A demanding business community has heavily influenced the focus on outcomes, and the clash with this by educational institutions generally serves to make schools look irresponsible.

The far more heated debate over the relatively new Common Core Standards as models and definitions of what proficiency looks like, those newest racks to which schools are pinned, are part of the stew of change by which both student and teachers are being measured. They may not be inherently bad as an idea, merely a new, more atomized version of requirements that on a macro level are similar to textbook adoptions that had previously been the province of School Boards. There were still standards, just localized and highly opinionated ones. Ultimately, the content may be substantially similar, but the change in methodology to these hundreds of briefly-worded Standards, things more akin to machine language like zeros and ones, has been fought with a vengeance.The simplicity, the black-and-white of these things, feels like learning is being put into a developer's code assembly. The richness of human experience, the story, seems to be lost in the rendering of the Standards. Moreover, it seems like the ultimate invalidation of our thousands of years of accumulated knowledge. The enormous body of knowledge and potential is brought down to a numbers scale so we can "evaluate" each human.

We are meant to use these bits, the Standards, to dress and accessorize the full learning extravaganza around. What will be measured are still the Standards. Teachers and schools are told they have full choice around the attainment of those by students. Really? Teachers everywhere protest the Standards from a gut feeling that they and the learning have just been demoted into being more machine than human somehow – a string of code, a DNA.

It is possible, though, to take the view that *through* the new DNA-like Standards and software, teaching has been repositioned into better control *through* machines. Did the language of the teaching operation need this to adapt and allow for the transformation of education?

The Standards are a cultural response to a need for order and pave the way for consumerized learning. They could perhaps be called the "Genome of Learning."

Culturally, we have always had a predilection to measurement and crave grades and diplomas and signs of achievement. We need to have some means of knowing that something did occur. Standards put the "what" into what will be tested. With new software technology, new means of analytics can include more non-evaluative means of demonstration, such as time observed, quantity of practice, and other methods of confirming a student has done the thing for which they are now considered complete. Things like samples of writing can be machine analyzed for spelling and grammatical error without reference to the piece as "good" or not. For example, a simple paragraph describing what the student saw on a field trip, allowing for some who are learning to write to be autodidactic, while at other times the software will need real human teachers to determine how "good" and perhaps on-point the writing was. Machines could give a "pass" on simple essays without teacher review, for example, allowing faster feedback and a gain in student self-confidence while also giving a grade or mark. And, of course, there is the popular philosophy of "failing forward" with game based learning. There are also industry memory-enhancing games, essentially tests, commercially available from Luminosity, Neuronation, and others.

Building on smaller signs of achievement that are machine-intelligence enabled can allow for much greater individual personalization between students and teachers. A teacher may see only a "final" piece and can discuss its relevancy and "voice" rather than grammar and spelling errors. Constructs of sentences and the flow of thoughts one from another can be thoroughly evaluated, which is a way of using computing to draw the teacher and learner into a higher-level conversation about the work. As software technology advances, the specificity of data pre-collected on individuals *as they learn* in formative assessments will give us a gentler means of testing and perhaps, like games, a welcome experience.

Learning with the new "DNA" of Standards leveraged in digital curriculum has the promise to become a self-directed continuous journey filled with potential enthusiasms, camaraderie, and competitiveness, all while being usefully measured. Education's long clash with accountability has a much brighter future.

[1] Jason Bittel, "Therapy by Internet May Be More Effective Than You'd Think," Slate, Aug. 1, 2013, http://www.slate.com blogs/future_tense/2013/08/01therapy_by_internet_may_be_more_effective_than_you_d_think.html

[2] Zeynep Tufekci, "Social Media's Small, Positive Role in Human Relationships," *The Atlantic*, Apr 25, 2012, www.theatlantic.com/technology/archive/2012/04 social-medias-small-positive-role-in-human-relationships/256346/

[3] George F. Will, "The Sobering Evidence of Social Science," *The Washington Post*, July 6th, 2016, https://www.washingtonpost.com/opinions/the-sobering-evidence-of-social-science/2016/07/06/4a3831f8-42dd-11e6-bc99-7d269f8719b1_story.html

[4] Merriam-Websters. http://www.merriam-webster.com/dictionary/school

Reference Material:

"Do you know your neighbors?" *PEW Research Center*, June 18, 2010, http://www.pewresearch.org/daily-number/do-you-know-your-neighbors/

National Center for Education Statistics, *Fast Facts*, https://nces.ed.gov/fastfacts/display.asp?id=91

J. Michael Smith, HSLDA President, "Homeschooling Strengthens Families and Communities," April 19, 2004, https://www.hslda.org/docs/news/washingtontimes/200404190.asp

Chapter 9
Cascading Failure

One evening at a recent education conference, there was a showing of the documentary *Most Likely to Succeed*, in which an interviewer asked a mother why she had put her school-age child into an alternative education school. She responded with, "Something is going on."[1] She, like millions of other people, has a vague awareness that something is wrong, something ominous, about our educational system. This mother being interviewed in the documentary, pointed out that college-graduate students are arriving back home to live with their parents, and this is a truth of the present age.

> **Key Points**
>
> • Educational institutions are experiencing cascading failure and contributing to it in the greater economy; the technology villain may just also be the savior.
>
> • The villain? *The sum of the (tech) effect*, and more interestingly, *which technology is missing and unapplied.*

Education has let down millions of people and it can no longer be candy-coated respectably. But surely all those educators and all that policy and kind intent are not awry. It worked *before* respectably well, so what's the real "why" of it all?

There is a lot of finger pointing as to fault. The constantly changing major federal programs have an appearance of messing everything up, the teacher unions are blocking change, the parents are checking out and not helping their kids, and on and on. None of this is necessarily the *primary* truth. In fact, with the amazing ingenuity of the American people, it is simple to argue that the big "Why" *has* to be none of these things or we would have solved it by now.

The big "Why" is the unlooked-for issue, the one no one dare blame so we don't even look – but ha! – it's technology infiltration, of course. The

Internet really *does* change everything. Yet that's just the surface layer.

Now technology itself is just that, an ingenuity of some kind or other. It's persuasive. It's ubiquitous. We love it because it makes us better, cooler, and shows off our smartness. Education technology as its own category of technology is amazing and goes all the way up the scale into shock and awe if you have the time to stop and review it all. That is just about all the Learning Counsel does, so in this, we speak from authority. It's not the individual bits and pieces of the greater tech scene; no, those are great. Rather it's the *sum of the effect*, and more interestingly, *which technology is missing and unapplied.*

Now, there are lots of indicators that the education system is in some ruin. Studies show high numbers of students can't read well, when in truth that has probably always been so, but it is only recently easy to aggregate large numbers of studies all together at once and see them in statistically significant ways and find lots of anecdotes. High school graduates are also under-prepared for college, again something that has probably always been so but is more pronounced, because higher education institutions have had to shift faster to stay ahead and are therefore also going dramatically out of sync with K12, which has been slower to change.

Politically, what policies coming from what level are attempting to fix these? Was an action taken on a broad or local enough scale or both to truly ameliorate the wrong? Not yet. But there has been a lot of blame, shame, and regret, and inappropriately so.

The wealthy of America, and now a large part of the middle class, have already left the traditional public education system for various alternative flavors of education, including the fairly new "unschooling" movement. What's left in public education are a whole lot of low-income students, typically considered a more difficult set to handle, because they unfortunately come loaded with more emotional problems and barriers, like actual hunger, and special needs students requiring more expensive assistance by specialists.

> "In a report released (by the) Southern Education Foundation, researchers found that 51 percent of children in public schools qualified for free lunches in 2013, which means that most of them come from low-income families. By comparison, 38 percent of public school students were eligible for free or reduced-price lunches in 2000." [2]
>
> Motoko Rich, *New York Times*

It seems patently unfair to thereafter hold public education to blame for what can most appropriately be labeled a cascading failure of our socio-economic system.

Something *is* going on, and many have been arduously pursuing its definition. What hasn't been done is to draw together all of the competing elements *outside* of education to look at where education must *inevitably* go to "fix" it. After all, cascading failures usually begin when one part of the system fails, which causes all the nearby nodes to then take up the slack for the failed component.

> "A **cascading failure** is a failure in a system of interconnected parts in which the failure of a part can trigger the failure of successive parts. Such a failure may happen in many types of systems, including power transmission, computer networking, finance, human bodily systems, and bridges.
>
> Cascading failures usually begin when one part of the system fails. When this happens, nearby nodes must then take up the slack for the failed component. This in turn overloads these nodes, causing them to fail as well, prompting additional nodes to fail one after another in a vicious circle."[3]

We can think of education as a key single point of failure of the human system where it is supposed to have provided a means to keep up with change, to prepare people now and in the next generation to compete adequately.[4]

If the starting "why" is technology and ubiquitous information accessible anytime and anywhere, and those things together are at a faster rate of change than human systems like education can keep up with, well, you will get a series of failures that "cascade" or fall one after another. Cascading failure, essentially a term most often associated with electrical systems, when applied in this case, is signifying that the pressure on the education node in the network is greater than that node is built to withstand.

Fail-over from the system's shorting-out is falling to alternatives – private schools, unschooling, charters, and now, pure open-market consumerization of learning. The surge shorting out the education system is technology, not only inside education, but its rate of impact on all other aspects of human life, including its insistency that humans are ready to be employed to further serve it (technology-as-industry). This is a vicious tripling of education's requirement to meet society's needs to use technology and serve technology, while itself being imbued with technology.

Technology allows teachers and institutions to achieve fantastic levels of individualized instruction with truly independent paths for each student – simply because technology in its present and burgeoning state actually *can* do things beyond human scales. One machine can keep track of and calculate statistics of millions of students at once. One program can inexhaustibly redirect lessons with slight alterations to lines of questioning and examples and exercises with infinite patience until a student gets the right answer.

Our highest-level political officers and our system have not created a new human corollary to meet the explosion of technology. Friction of inconceivable proportions has resulted. It is the challenge of our Age, and we are not meeting it head on.

An analogy of this observation would go like this: Schools are like the U.S. Postal Service. At one point, probably in the 1950s, schools hit an extremely high note of utility, churning out useful products at great scale and efficiency: students nearly perfectly suited to that Age for employment, the waning Industrial Age. Similarly, the USPS was a central pillar of social communication since 1775 and the first appointment of Benjamin Franklin as Postmaster General. It grew to such mammoth proportions that today it could be the second-largest employer in the United States – after Wal-Mart – with about 600,000 workers. If the USPS were a private company, it would rank about 28th on the Fortune 500 list. However, according to a 2016 *Government Accounting Office* report, "Since mail volumes peaked in 2006, USPS's financial condition has deteriorated as technology and the Internet have changed how businesses and consumers use the mail, resulting in eight consecutive years of net losses and debt totaling the statutory debt ceiling of $15 billion."[5]

USPS's financial condition has been designated as "high risk" by the U.S. GAO (Government Accountability Office). The USPS cannot fund its current level of services, operations, and obligations from its revenues and urgently needs to restructure to reflect changes in mail volume, revenue, and use of the services.

Like private schools, homeschooling, unschooling alternatives, and additionally, the new complexity with charter schools, the postal market fractured in the 1980s with the phenomenal growth of FedEx and UPS through innovations in speed, overnight delivery, and context like trusted international delivery. Both companies usurped a huge portion of the industry of mail service. FedEx and UPS did this with superior technologies of both logistics and digital tech.

USPS is still there but marginalized by more extremes each year, and calls for privatization have begun. The USPS is part of our constitution, just as public education is considered a common right and is extensively covered in law. According to the GAO, "Large unfunded liabilities for postal retiree health and pension benefits – which were $78.9 billion at the end of fiscal year 2015 – may ultimately place taxpayers, USPS employees, retirees and their beneficiaries, and USPS itself at risk."

The USPS was one of the first nodes to fail in what is essentially a worldwide cascading failure, rippling out from the technology onslaught.

Lightning works similarly, essentially doing a voltaic arc between two fields, fast-moving clouds at friction against a slower-moving earth, each with different potentialities, seeking to strike the one with the lower potential, earth. So it seems with the enthusiastically-led technology attack, we are mesmerized by its seductive force and drawn in, reasoning to ourselves that we are better because of it even as we are knocked down by it. All of the force of technology innovations is directed against a humanity that is not, on an international scale, educated or organized enough to manage it well.

We are way past turning around in any case. First the U.S military, largely because of technology, closed bases and stripped itself of excess real estate and cost; now the USPS is blinking red on the national dashboard, and education is right there with it.

Other nodes in the great human network have been as affected, and all have cultural and common practice aspects concerning how they are shaping the education saga.

Education, so far, has taken minor steps at reformation, usually with an advocacy for a changed-in-context routine overlaid on the present system, not wholesale re-imagination.

This tinkering, a play with definitions and methods of teaching and learning, is proving inadequate to the task, because it simply does not acknowledge what is happening on the greater world stages of economics, culture, politics, and technology.

It is a positive thing that the tinkering continues, that the strivings of millions still aim to create goodness out of the circumstances of our complex environment for students. Still, we have an ever-widening gap between the haves and have-nots in terms of learning in public education. The disenfranchised are not just those have-nots but actually even the haves, because the system is headed for a collapse of epic proportions where everyone loses. If it languishes overlong as the postal service has done, it will increase the number of other nodes failing across the human network. Education is the keeper of our collective future.

The recent recession was a cascading failure that was carried out at a scale and speed across a wide amount of humanity through technology that even the insiders could not have quite grasped would happen. Critics and predictors of doom were off by a wide value about the actual cataclysm financially for people otherwise trusting of systems that had previously engendered vast respect. There is no doubt that if an immediate replacement to our banking institutions had been at hand it would have been whole-heartedly embraced, and henceforth any alternative to a "status quo" would certainly gain converts quickly. Instead, "too big to fail" declarations propped up a system nearly bankrupt of morality and accountability in its leaders.

America has lived and adapted through earlier cascading failures, the most applicable one being the political shifts since 1776 with the Declaration of Independence. We invented a new type of democracy and a form of government and were thereafter swept into a series of changes felt worldwide. These changes, such as the ending of slavery, had a dramatic increase in literacy rates.

The rampant bullying by the English King at the time led to the original Tea Party in Boston and sparked the single point of failure that divorced America from external rule and coincidentally set the stage for freedom for all. In that instance, the larger political system entering a moment of cascading failure also entered a new technology of political structure, and the resulting outcomes were truly rewarding.

That technology, democracy, forced further failures of the old guard systems as far away as France, which had its own revolution shortly thereafter and conditions that echoed into the 21st century with the civil rights movement and so much more, shouldering the way into greater freedom, greater life for countless millions, and pressing back, evermore, on the idea of solely self-interested rule politically or institutionally. Today, we have a full belief in equality and democracy and that everyone can and should read. Yet despite provisions for a free education for everyone today, only about two-thirds of students in fourth grade meet reading proficiency standards,[6] per the National Assessment of Educational Progress and the National Center for Education Statistics. And those numbers are much lower for students who come from low-income households.

Those are just the reading figures. It would be easy to assume that such low numbers necessarily indicate that all of teaching and learning is therefore doing ever more poorly in the higher learnings built upon the foundation of reading. Yet the higher learnings of old are no longer necessarily the meaningful learnings of today. We think we know, but we cannot actually know, because we are not winning against the successive transmissions of change overwhelming us.

There is, right now, a great distance between the promise of equality and actual equality, between our ideals and our practice, and perhaps that is a human condition and not a systemic issue. Reading proficiency was getting better for a while with our great new education experiment (system) of the 20th century, reaching a high tide in the 1970s where literally everyone was gaining before reaching some sort of apex and starting to stagnate and now dwindle.

What's important is that we have all lived within a fairly new system, one built on industrial principals for a certain Age, with a focus on learning homogeneity and conformity that *won big gains for most of us*. We cannot believe that in our single lifetime, a quantum change would have occurred. We want for our kids what we had, only better. We have not torn down the old building we built, perhaps too enamored with our past success, like a former medal-winning athlete or prizefighter. We can't talk about today, because we are stuck in yesterday.

To really come to grips with what we must do as individual learners, as teachers, as school and district and government leaders, we need to fully analyze the real villain of this cascading failure and come to grips with what would solve it, for real.

Because the technology villain may just also be the savior.

[1] Documentary; "Most Likely To Succeed," MTLSFILM.org, http://www.mltsfilm.org/

[2] Motoko Rich, "Percentage of Poor Students in Public Schools Rises," *NY Times*, January 2007, http://www.nytimes.com/2015/01/17/us/school-poverty-study-southern-education-foundation.html

[3] "Cascading Failure", *wikipedia*, https://en.wikipedia.org/wiki/Cascading_failure

[4] Anya Kamenetz, "System Failure; The Collapse of Public Education," *The Village Voice*, April 2013, http://www.villagevoice.com/news/system-failure-the-collapse-of-public-education-6437951

[5] "U.S. Postal Service's Financial Viability," *Government Accounting Office*, 2016, http://www.gao.gov/key_issues/us_postal_service_financial_viability/issue_summary

[6] Reid Wilson, "Low Income Students Falling Behind on Reading Proficiency," Jan 2014, https://www.washingtonpost.com/blogs/govbeat/wp/2014/01/30/low-income-students-falling-behind-on-reading-proficiency/

Chapter 10
Enter Chaos

Following on the idea of cascading failure, it's natural to wonder in what direction the American education system will go now, what will be changed that is equivalent to those changes seen to have completely altered other industries.

Chaos theory is originally a study in the field of mathematics and looks at how a set of conditions that seem random are actually determining a later outcome. Some have called the theory "the butterfly effect" for a story about how the beating wings of a butterfly might create air movement that ultimately has a weather system effect. It presupposes even small motions can make big differences.

The idea of a loose determinism of extremely discrete elements and disassociated people which move seemingly randomly and disjointedly to create a wide diversity of outcomes, all while there are still traces of an underlying base order, is chaos theory in a nutshell. It can also be applied to social systems. Theories of why social and even policy systems should live "on the edge of chaos" to achieve in-the-moment relevancy and handle immediate environmental change are part of the philosophic discussion of such authors as Niklas Luhmann, James Gleick, and Edward N. Lorenz.

Chaos is both an end point and a beginning. It is an observable phenomenon that companies and institutions typically start out small, emerging as an idea out of the chaos of life. If they survive a long time, they go through a sort of golden era where they are very successful. They keep growing

Key Points

- Chaos is the natural, next reality for the rigid educational system enabled by technology, and the new structure is likely a consensus network "un-structure" facilitated by adapted consumerized learning.
- The new reality will not necessarily be hierarchical and as bureaucratic as it has been, but will be using consensus networks and business intelligence systems as a more useful way to distribute education – fully leveraging and using technology, not just teaching with it. In addition, there will be various outposts for projects, arts, sports, and experiential learning.
- Soft skills and emotional supports are part of the needful thing in the face of chaos in digital transition.

and get weightier and more structured. If there are no checks and balances as there should be in governance, or competition in the private sector, the inclination to use their dominance for even better positioning financially or otherwise is great. Eventually this starts a sort of decay. Bureaucratic infighting and inertia is typically the result. The recent Great Recession is strong evidence of the step beyond that for a whole industry (banking), of corruption and greed. Similarly, worldwide governmental abuses of power are also well known across history.

What's interesting about this phenomenon of aged organizations is that they eventually are caught out. Something comes along to change and devolve that operation, just because it ceases to "fit." The institution or company goes through fast revolution or slow, sometimes agonizingly slow, devolution and shrinking of its power over time. Eventually, it falls again to chaos. It's a sort of scale of low-to-high, then lasting a while at that apex, and from that high-to-low, like life itself from birth through to death. It's a circle.

Educators in our highest offices of administration are mostly in their 50s and 60s. Their parents enjoyed the highest moments of our educational system in the 1950s into the 60s. They themselves were being educated just at the moment when things started to wane in the 70s and 80s and the American drug scene exploded onto campuses. Those administrators have been working at building greatness again ever since, and many times have achieved some things that are great. Still, those are islands in a roiling sea of change.

Chaos is not inherently bad as a new arrival point. Chaos now for organizations, with computer and software technology on the scene, is a different chaos than a hundred years ago. A virtual structure can arise from the ashes.

The point is that chaos is the probable natural next system of the present Age for the education sector. Parents nationally are having conversations continually about alternatives; the mood of dissent is here.

A new education administrative "un-structure" that is still a sort of structure, just not necessarily hierarchical and as bureaucratic as it has been, using a networked community administration and business intelligence systems as a more useful way to distribute education, seems like the natural next stage. It will be fully leveraging and using technology, not just teaching with it. Chaos and the "un-structure" is thusly enabled, given a "base" by technology that earlier ages did not have. Having a base is a requirement by theorists of chaos theory.

We already see that our politics and the economy experiences trend waves and absorb the shocks of minor policy shifts, while managing overwhelmingly large populations of people and things in a dizzying array of alternatives. The idea is that if there is a means to have enough chaos, then major shifts can be managed *by the chaos* into a new level of equilibrium.

If a system is too rigid, well, it just breaks or slowly deteriorates.

If it is a large enough system allowed to sicken due to a lack of flexibility and infect the society and adjoining systems leaning on it, the negative effect can be catastrophic.

Chaos assumes that natural forces *cause the needed structure* for the function at hand. For example, a large city may organize to have a mass transportation system due to congested roads and the need for rapid movement of people from one place to the next. In another example, if a small town's population grows from fifty to 4,000 it will form eventually a few utilities like a grocery store, lumber and construction goods, a bar, a church or two, and perhaps electrical distribution and water purification. It will hit a certain equilibrium until a new sort of chaos comes in. If a new business that requires 5,000 more workers than are presently available comes to that town, it will draw people to move to the town, and there will be a disequilibrium in housing and all other utilities until more are built. There will be a temporary chaos in housing, food, and other services until it is adequately managed. That same town may, at a much later date, get a new service that carries groceries directly to every house and farm from online ordering. This may cause one grocery store to scale back to just minimal goods and the other to become a high-end restaurant that also sells specialty goods, while still another closes its doors for good. This would be a different form of chaos forcing the adaptation of the structure to mutate or even "un-structure" into a virtual networked community, administered creatively with software scheduling and curriculum.

If real chaos theory were applied to the education sector by policy makers, chaos would be allowed to grow and even be enabled as a first step. We do this when we first allow our children out of the nest to become young adults. In the education sector, this step has happened with the introduction of charter schools and school choice. Yet this small step towards chaos did not really give way to an "un-structure" with technology to allow greater freedoms at the learner level. This is hard for Americans to envision, because the world of education has for so long been a closed system without a feedback loop. All ingenuity about education has been absorbed or suppressed into the greater system. Ideas like charter schools and online or distance education have been tightly bound by ideas of existing structure and measurement. Real chaos has been disallowed for so long that it is hard to imagine what it might be like to be given free reign and funding, for there to be open competition.

Most administrators consider that a sort of Wild West of education, where learning is happening willy-nilly, any-old-where, with anyone or anything doing the teaching, would be very, very bad, and learners would be given inferior educations. I have had education executives actually tell me that children *can't learn without a teacher.* Maybe this is true for some children, but certainly it is not true for all of them.

The history of all public education is one long experiment of its own. It is easy to argue that much of it has already failed, so finger pointing at any other idea, like an online consensus network and various outposts for projects, arts, sports, and experiential learning, is somewhat bad form.

Right now, in other industry sectors, change is fast and moves across the greater systems of those industries at the hyper-revolution rate, or "rev rate" of technology – based on computer and communications networks. The introduction rate of new technology is so fast that the rev rate is almost impossible for humans. While many of us can barely keep up with the number of new iPhones every year, high tech industries thrive on this speed of change.

The rev rate is chewing away at all other industries, flattening and transforming them, but the incredible size in bureaucracies of education have remained. The myth of a "closed system" of education is with us, because there is still just enough strength in the similarity of one school to the next such that, when you mess with one, it is apparent that another whole part of the system can see unintended consequences. Because there is not a diverse enough ecosystem for dispersal to push out into, there are few sprouts of innovation to build ancillary units, and there is no dissipation of contrary efforts. The contrariness sits in the works and sort of stagnates there, souring one and then the next entity by contagion and gossip. You can readily observe this by the rather dysfunctional adoptions of technology without an ecosystem view. For example, thousands of computers bought by a school without a view to what software would be being used on them. Many stories of still-boxed devices sitting in classroom closets are still happening nationally.

Unfortunately, with technology so ubiquitous, the high speed of communication and news further enable mistakes. The closeness of cause and effect, the continuing uncomfortable pin-balling of consequences after any move from any level of education governance observably can lock up the whole works. In recent years, teachers have tended to try to just ignore the latest edicts and hope some of the new demands will blow over and be forgotten. In a burst of dissention with policy, they set out on their own, becoming innovative superheroes.

As we look at the state of education nationally, the reason it seems more natural now to consider an un-structure is that the ability to maintain any sort of commonality across systems throughout all fifty states, nearly 14,000 districts, 97,000+ schools, and now numerous charter schools is increasingly impossible. There is no equilibrium in the national landscape like there was only fifty years ago. A fracturing of social, economic, and political realities has led to a lack of an effectiveness in centralized education policy mandates. Even while trying to minimize central mandates and push more local control, governments in the U.S. still manage to issue more disorder – largely because in a representative system, whose numbers of representatives have largely remained level politically over a great many years, there are far more people to represent than any politician can effectively serve.

There never was great central control in education, but technology and human organization have sought to exert themselves and draw together a single masterwork. Ideas about everyone using the same textbooks, everyone having the same type of computer for every use in a single district, everyone having the same Learning Management System, are attempting central control. Such ideas have been pushed, and yet, have not seemed to work, at least not for any great length of time to create any significant lasting reform in education. Some of them are very needed, while others are merely control for the sake of control and national statistics.

Consider this: the "Greatest Generation" was the first one to have a few members of every family make it through to a high school graduation. Those people are now in their 80s or are dying off, so the significance of this has been recent and did effect a great national boom, the golden era already described. The "Baby Boomers," who are now in their late 50s through to 70s, were the first generation to have a significant number of college graduates. Now the Millennials are mostly college educated but not finding work at the same rate. There is an apparent dwindling return on investment for ever-higher educational achievement and higher volumes of achievers.

Ideas about how learned you have to be are shifting yet again, morphing in the direction of higher degrees on the one hand and self-directed educational mixing on the other. Other ideas that have more to do with *what* is the most imperative to teach are finding fertile fields of interest – especially the "soft" skills and social-emotional learning long ago left largely to parenting and the field of religion. As is talked about in other parts of this book, this is perhaps part of the needful thing in the face of chaos in digital transition; a need wrought specifically by a functional superiority of technology that is outstripping the humanities' ability to keep up. Education needs a corollary of superior humanity, including all things related to manners, social environmental and ecosystem dependencies understanding, and faith.

Colleges are under heavy pressure to deliver value but are delivering straight into the gaping maw of commercial industries that look nothing like they did just ten years ago and are changing so rapidly that no specificity of courses could possibly be a perfect fit. The fall back to basics and some small tweaks is the survival strategy for many, leaving wide open the just-in-time training that is now a requirement of most businesses. This, along with its high cost to those businesses, is not doing higher ed any favors. The lack of synchronicity of formal education with the rev rate of the commercial world is resulting in a lost opportunity for schools as that burden shifts to industry. If schools were custom-built to respond to their environments with great precision using superior human and tech understanding to deliver just-in-time learning, the burden would shift back to education, and businesses could get back to building national income – what they are supposed to be doing.

Look, from a business view, at what is being done to streamline production and fulfillment of learning in business. Consider this in relation to where we can take education and the education industry in this new age of consumerized learning. What if schools and districts could deliver learning at high efficiency, meaning less time, while still being of the highest quality? That is usually nearly the exact opposite of the intentions of schools who make their income on orchestrations to take longer than absolutely essential.

Here is some evidence that time and efficiency for things that have never before been made efficient can be done from industry:

- Amazon Prime has organized such powerful web shopping interface and logistics that they can offer same-day delivery service in some cities. In some cases, they can deliver within hours.

- Food box services, like HelloFresh and Blue Apron, have sophisticated fresh food options with recipes completely pre-measured and ready-to-cook, available by subscription and cheaper than eating out or shopping, because there is less waste in spoiled food.

- Dollar Shave Club and related services offer an update to routine grooming in a newly simplified product at lower cost. This is in an industry that had been over-building for decades in order to charge so much money that razors are held behind locked cabinets in some stores like jewelry.

- Crowdfunding sites like GoFundMe and Kickstarter have raised hundreds of millions of dollars with so little overhead as to be a sort of efficiency nirvana.

These trends show what can be done when you combine internet access with a rethinking of the product and distribution mechanisms. This sort of thinking promises a far more efficient educational system with better outcomes.

Reference Material:

Carter McNamara, *"Thinking About Organizations as Systems,"* adapted from the *Field Guide to Consulting and Organizational Development.* 2006.

Chapter 11

Disruption: The Sum of the Effect

What's the sum of all this semi-invisible disruptive force known generally as the technology transition running over and through our education system? Is technology villainously ruining the idyllic word of educational institutions?

Besides everything already mentioned about the changed world due to technology, teachers are also experiencing a skyrocketing workload. Teachers are exhausted. There are shortages because many new teachers give up too soon. In fact, our own Learning Counsel research found that 25% of instructors' time is now spent on 1) searching for digital curriculum, or 2) custom building a digital lesson plan. Additionally, many of these same teachers claim to be spending a lot more hours working.

> *"Of the 4,450 respondents to the Guardian teacher network and Guardian jobs survey about teachers' lives, 82% stated that their workload was unmanageable, with two-thirds saying that expectations had increased significantly over the past five years. And 73% of respondents said their workload was affecting their physical health and 76% their mental health. Almost a third of teachers reported that they worked more than 60 hours a week."*[1]
>
> – Rachelle Banning-Lover, *The Guardian*

In addition to stress from managing the technology revolution, the Washington Post summarized

Key Points

- Total disruption is due to what's really missing: not enough tech sophistication that is truly student-centered, teacher, and administrator levered as well as a needed open incubation arena for a consensus network "un-structure" of personalized learner paths.
- As learning moves into consumer-grade online experiences, the software systems for it may never be "done," but will continue to get grander.
- An un-structure in our form of educational distribution gives the individual the freedom to use tech to learn and compete against tech and their peers via tech.

a number of studies indicating general low morale with teachers, a situation few Americans would consider abnormal.[2] With an epidemic of school shootings, violence against teachers anyone can see on YouTube, and mass and repeating changes to policies, it is an acknowledgement to the passion and integrity of teachers that more don't give up.

> *"In Chicago and elsewhere, the reason public school students in major cities are suffering so much is because union leaders don't want to focus on making concessions or prioritizing funding for the classroom, at least not if it means they would have to reform their compensation and retirement benefits. When it comes to school negotiations, arguments among adults have taken precedence over educating kids,"*[3]
>
> – Hilary Gowins, *The Huffington Post*

The sum of the effect is clear for anyone to see, because we are hearing about it everywhere – failures. Where prior to the tech incursion altering all the other industries we had reached great highs of literacy and graduations and were fairly pleased with ourselves, statistics are falling in our existing public structures.

The other result is growing awareness of a consumer-direct tech-alternate route – a bypass of the public system because it's "not working."

What's Missing?

What's wrong with the current state of technology incursion into education is actually that *there is not enough of it* in education, and the not-enough-of-it is orders of magnitude above what is currently there. Most non-technical teachers and administrators cannot see what's missing; they only see what is there now.

What has been happening with industry products is the same stepped approach that has occurred with the education side, purchasing first projectors, then TVs, computers for labs, interactive whiteboards, then computers for everyone, and finally digital courseware, apps, and possibly even a Learning Management System and Student Information System. Companies are making digital things that replace what were once textbooks and workbooks, systems that replace grade books, and digital rosters to replace attendance sheets. Of course, there have been some real new innovations but these have still been adapted to the existing structure. Companies, as a matter of necessity, have to sell to what is there, what they can earn revenue on, what schools will rip-and-replace with a digital alternative. They are in a constant juggling of trying to push what's new while actually selling more of what's old.

What's missing is an autonomous digitally oriented alternative with full coverage of all subjects that has learner centricity as its very first and only relevant precept. This does not exist yet, to my knowledge, in its entirety. Of course, the vision is the same level of dazzle as the biggest online shopping sites, media hubs, and consumer games mixed in with the best of machine intelligence and online chat or telecommuting teachers-on-demand. There are some pockets of excellence and new apps arriving, but the entire journey through the academic standards, and beyond that for tangential learning interwoven with projects, is not totally crafted yet. Travel planning the individual student's journey itself could be a whole programmatic area for software and for the tie-in with institutions, creating an inter-weaving of the online with the offline experience.

As learning moves into consumer-grade online experiences, the software systems for it may never be "done" but will continue to get grander.

The Goal: Student Centered Learning in a Digital Age

Properly implemented technology allows for the individual content and lines of questioning to build from foundations around an individual, dictating, therefore, the governing form, the human interactions required, the time, any physical convening space, and speed of delivery.

This type of learning would be a full leveraging of tech directly, without consideration of the existing institutional or teacher-learner structure. Yet build it, and consumers will come. That is evident from the mass followings online by learning apps and sites.

There are just a couple of tricky parts. The most significant of these is the burgeoning capability of intelligent learning engines. Although not truly "A.I.," or artificial intelligence, machines are starting to get pretty close.

For example, instead of using the brute force of *Deep Blue*, as in the IBM program that defeated chess champion Garry Kasparov over twenty years ago, new programs go beyond encyclopedic databases of potentialities and strategies that use superior code-crunching aimed at overwhelming with sheer power. Now, intelligence engines are built in a layered approach analogous to how the human mind operates. Each layer is an artificial set of algorithms that recognizes patterns, similar in theory to a neural network using a lot of big data, and when layered on each other can form constructs and evaluations. Each layer passes up to another layer in a decision chain that acts like a brain. These new capabilities are known as "deep learning" because of the layering. Super-fast computing makes the massive crunching of ever-more layers of data easier than ever before. This is the up-and-coming age of teaching and learning in just the next few years. The current IBM version is called *Watson*, and, like some of the programs emerging in the education field, leans on this idea of machine learning.

The Administrator's Role

Leaders look at these shifts as they see "techie" teachers using new tools and understand that their role and function must change. They see they must harness this new power but have little knowledge of how to really do that. Many do not have the idea of tech being ubiquitous, a sort of "it's-everywhere" in the function of education. They do not even yet expect it, but leaders in the field are now starting to talk like that, at least from an infrastructure viewpoint.

> *"Technology in a school needs to be as simple and expected as light when you flick a light switch. Nobody thinks about it. When I walk into my office and I hit my lights, and I want my lights to come on, I want them on, and when I walk out the door*

> *and I'm not using it, then I don't care about it. We need to be that invisible, and if we're not that invisible, then we are absolutely impacting teaching and learning. I think here at Houston ISD we're well on our way to becoming that invisible to the organization. The way I see it, you get your seat at the table by supporting teaching and learning by being invisible and always on. In fact, it's above and beyond even that because you need to also redefine ways in which you're improving and making more efficient, the teaching and learning process."*
>
> – Lenny Schad, Chief Technology Information Officer, Houston ISD

Most of the time school leaders are far from the view expressed by Schad in the quote above. They are missing the attitude of dominating tech administratively. What's also missing is the software tools leaders *should* have to hand with a set of algorithms already built for every human assessment, every sense, and every perception point, so that a simulation of actual intelligence is accomplished, such as we are starting to see with smartphones and online ad tracking.

This seems like a long way off for the education market. What is missing for administrators inside software are evaluation points, buttons on the screen, and feedback loops that make it really clear automatically what is going on with a student's learning by inference, including emotionally and experientially. Presently, they must struggle along with tools that do not present those distinguishable insertion check-points with machine logic that involves the best of teachers very simply – as simply as using their smartphone apps. When that day comes and all the software is that good, administrators will see every teacher shine as beacons of tech integration. And the tech will give teachers back their power, because they will have real assistance, not just tools.

What's Unavailable?

What's unavailable so far is a full digital transition in education with the real heritage of American democracy – open country to incubate the networked system that will work and an experimental playing field divorced from most common structure but fortified by public funding and a quality promotional campaign. Alternatively, the private sector could do this just as well. Some of this has been done with fully online charters attached to the state levels as in California, but those do not seem to have a social support structure into communities that engage instead of completely replacing the public schools. Those students enrolled are opted out of all physical local interaction and have literally "left the building" to join a sort of unschool that is still a school but totally virtual with remote teachers-by-Internet, although not necessarily highly immersive intelligent software environments. The online virtual school is still a bit "flat" in terms of the technical software sophistication. Additionally, a trade-off of sports, arts, and social interaction is made to go fully online that is perhaps unnecessary.

The thing being semi-proposed with consumerization of learning – a highly actualized digital learning journey completely customized to fit a student with a high degree of quality digital experience, but not necessarily with physical or social experience – will also miss the point that many online charters miss.

The next thing needed is a real strategic plan that would encompass a role and responsibility shift for everyone in a gradual enough scale that all the current players in the education scene can follow the path to give the best of both worlds, blended together in a wonderful orchestration. This is entirely possible with the right planning on a national scale. This is not "blended learning" the way it is commonly thought of today, as just a technology embedding inside the classroom, but a blending between the worlds systemically at the institutional level.

The war for the survival of public schools is here. We can know it is here, because the number of people arguing about public education and whether charter schools should be allowed to survive and people experimenting with alternatives has never been greater. The number of opt-outers of various types has never been higher or growing as quickly.

Many people believe that public education is so embedded that it is on the same plane with death and taxes. But as more people discover alternatives, and especially the simplicity of a tech-delivered alternative, a sort of negative momentum will build. The negativity has the power to kill public education or force ever more brutal reforms. Again, you can know the war for public education is already engaged because of the fierceness of the discourse. [3]

Leaders who are entirely comfortable with their reign in schools fear no one and pretend they would never drop down into petty defense, but that's precisely what is happening to some of the largest districts.

Public education must plan a way through and out that acknowledges with clarity a new economy and creates a workable structure – or "un-structure."

New Forms and Structures

What's indicated now in the Age of Experience is a consensus network structure similar to those that are already evident in other industries. For education, such a network would knit together the best subject experts, curate knowledge, and facilitate individual students to maneuver amongst the basics they must know and all else they *want* to know. And it should have an eye to the creation of real experiences, digitally and otherwise. It could be a placeless and virtually structure-less modality. Buildings would not be a key factor as telecommuting teachers is a high probability already working in some places, just like tele-medicine.

Using courseware, teacher guides can put the student as an individual at a completely individualized point of entry with a personalized path. The important point would be the freedom of "un-structure" – a fully personalized learning path.

An "un-structure" gives the individual the freedom to use tech to learn and to compete against tech and their peers via tech. This is a novel but important distinction.

Less human interference in things that are common points of knowledge that can be taught by tech, and more human interactions on being human, being moral, and social, will balance what is currently missing from the existing structure.

Interestingly, it probably won't matter if no one changes the current structures and they continue to collapse, because the market is already forcing the issue with the consumerization of learning and alternative schooling. What will matter is a survival bridge-to-somewhere for the increasingly marginalized existing institutions.

[1] Rachel Banning-Lover, "60-hour Weeks and Unrealistic Targets: Teachers' Working Lives Uuncovered," *The Guardian*, March 22, 2016.

[2] Valerie Strauss, "Yes, Teacher Morale Really Is Low – Despite a Report to the Contrary," *The Washington Post*, February, 2014, https://www.washingtonpost.com/news/answer-sheet/wp/2014/02/05/yes-teacher-morale-really-is-low-despite-a-report-to-the-contrary/

[3] Hilary Gowins, "'This Is Our Story': Chicago Public Schools Are Failing," Aug. 2014, *The Huffington Post*, http://www.huffingtonpost.com/hilary-gowins/chicago-public-schools-are-failing_b_5488973.html

Chapter 12

A New Base: Standards

Let us now dive in to the proverbial chaos and cascading failure more deeply, philosophically speaking, and try to understand what is going on within the educational community to bring order to it.

For chaos to exist means there has to be some basic determining equation. Chaos has a "base" and an impetus that starts it in a direction.

As mentioned earlier, the Common Core Standards and other enumerated Standards are the new equivalency to a determining equation, a single algorithm that will be deterministic from the level of an individual student all the way up to a means of measuring the outcome of whole schools and the whole system. The Standards are constructed in such a way as to allow for disparity in interpretations and a degree of chaos, but still with the initial condition of a stated core of ideas, a defined set of things to know. This is a sort of reset to a new base.

It is beyond fascinating that the academically-oriented Common Core Standards have emerged at such a point in our history. They arrived at nearly the precise point when chaos is also arriving to usher in a new un-structuring of education. Both standards and a new chaos in structure are aligning to match or adapt education to the greater rev rate of all other industry.

The initial condition of an earlier great orderly system, with classrooms and hallways and teachers and principals and grades and graduations,

Key Points

- Standards are the new equivalency to a determining equation, a single algorithm that will be deterministic from the level of an individual student all the way up to a means of measuring outcomes. This is a sort of reset to a new base.
- Both standards and a new chaos in structure are aligning to match or adapt education to the greater rev rate of all other industry.
- Fully embracing and fortifying these ideas, extending the chaos rather than protecting the old structures, is the leadership challenge of this generation.

Types:

- Academic Standards
- Technical Standards
- Technical Models
- Meta-Data Standards
- Commercial Combo Standards

underlie the burgeoning education chaos. Why? The chaos is sensitive to that initial condition but is ever further from it. The Standards atomize the "things to know" and have furthered the potential to untether the structure from itself. This makes possible many different potential outcomes that we had come to expect in earlier education patterns. The former system, while orderly in most respects, never did have any great national order in what was being taught – that is, the subjects and topics.

Using the backbone of Standards like a sort of DNA of knowledge, the mixing of ingredients around it could create entirely new patterns. For example, specialists in the action-sense of achievement could emerge.

Scope and sequence of parts of the Standards for a single grade with some sort of integrated story woven between them all could be a new publisher brand of content.

Items that match each Standard could be marketed to consumers individually.

New online courseware with distinct virtual reality could be created to cover the discovery and exploration of new worlds while, at the same time, meeting certain sets of Standards.

Ideas like teachers-as-freelancers with global connections, a distribution network of resources and aid for any individual or group seeking knowledge acquisition, a lessening of "place" significance, and a democratic openness as to what constitutes knowledge are all elements with seeds in the present age. Fully embracing and fortifying these ideas, extending the chaos rather than protecting the old structures, is the leadership challenge of this generation.

The Standards, Re-ordering the Chaos

The understanding of all of the types of Standards and where they are going is the first stage to understanding the remodeling going on. Right now whole companies have come into being to keep track of the academic Standards. Yet this is only one of the parts of the new standards in education. There are many more sophisticated things that will happen as open-market consumerization grows. Things have really only just begun in terms of a backdrop of standards academically and technically.

The enablement of an exchange for digital resources tagged for what standards they purport to meet has been being worked on disjointedly by various organizations. Adoption of the Common Core Standards is an incomplete landscape, making it even more difficult for schools to move to better student personalization. The incomplete adoption puts more on all schools and teachers to find or build their own digital learning objects. The burden on industry to build against a multiplicity of academic standards is so high that most of these companies do not even try. They sell their objects without tags to the Standards in hopes the districts and schools will sort it out for themselves.

The DNA of Education, the Standards

In mapping the solutions to the chaos of education, we must take a look at the many standards. To help in understanding and to order my thinking, I've attempted to classify the various standards by main types.

Academic Standards: These are like the Common Core with their little numbering schema and short descriptors, and TEKS for Texas and various others.

You can find out more on government websites and www.corestandards.org.

> "While I hope and believe that OER (Open Education Resources) can pave the way for open practice (learner choice and flexibility, collaboration and sharing, and transparency and open access, 'in the open'), it is not at all obvious that the use of OER is a necessary condition. In fact, some of the most vibrant classroom exemplars of open practice in action that I've seen have not involved OER. It is possible to have open practice with proprietary content. While this may skirt the gray edges of copyright law, this has long been the case in education, and most don't want to talk about it or simply don't care.
>
> "My concern about many efforts to make OER 'mainstream' in K-12 education (work that I should say I have long been supportive of) is that it may not lead to open practice or in the (worst) case, any meaningful change in practice."[1]
>
> *Karen Fasimpaur, EdTech Blogger*

Government-originated academic ideas are their prerogative, but what they cannot do under law is cause "discovery," which would give advantage or disadvantage to companies. America itself was discovered when voyagers were looking for a faster route to the Orient, after all.

With a federal focus through the new Every Student Succeeds Act (ESSA) on free Open Education Resources (OER), schools are supposed to employ the funds to use technology but not pay for content, apparently. This act and others in individual states pushes them to *prefer* OER. Those digital resources are things offered free or non-copyrighted, open to alteration, usually made by teachers. They are effectively disadvantaging all private industry from selling digitally created objects to a degree. It's totally great that there are free resources out there and schools can and should use them – but almost universally, the free and open resources are at the very lowest level of technical sophistication. Teachers are not developers or animators or designers. They are not creating a highly designed user interface and user experience. Effectively, this OER preference by government is a trust that can't be fought because of government's anti-trust immunity, but the body blocking of content commerce by OER is definitely an inhibitor of tech advancement. It has been weakly protested by the Association of American Publishers (AAP). It will not ultimately inhibit consumerism because good marketing and good products will find a way commercially. But it has and will slow public school progress, so instructors don't go out and look online or use the better technical designs and so are further disassociated from consumer realities.

In watching the industry over the last five years, more and more small innovative companies have either gone out of business, sold out to the bigger publishing conglomerates, banded together into small working operations with shared marketing and sales operations, or – and this is the clincher – turned their attention to the broader consumer market and bypassed schools, selling to parents and students directly. Extremely few companies have strategies that only to sell schools. They must go outside to survive – so the strategy of OER is forcing two things:

- Largely technically inferior content that might still be rigorous but isn't truly "digital."

- The set up of a direct-to-consumer reality of education.

In addition to the academic standards, there are also things happening on the technical side.

Technical Standards: These are standards created to be in the realm of learning object interoperability with systems and repositories. Movements by groups like IMS Global are creating interoperability technical standards with a little bit of the "what" that goes inside those things in the data table fields. Mostly it's file standards. These standards, like the "LTI" and "Common Cartridge" and "OneRoster," are standards that help the technology of the learning content objects fit like puzzle pieces inside Learning Management Systems and other repositories. These are not necessarily commercial-grade standards acceptable to the major platforms, like Apple, Android, Microsoft, and others, who appear to think of technical standards as actually the foundational languages, not the articulation of the sequence of code in an existing language. Those types of standards haven't been yet created. In the meantime, those by IMS are ideals of orderly field structure and filing so that everyone's files match and are interoperable and understandable, a lot like the Dewey Decimal System familiar to educators.

Technical Models: Another dimension to standards is a model that is quasi-technical called SCORM, which stands for "Sharable Content Object Reference Model."[2]

SCORM is all about creating units of online training material that can be shared across systems. SCORM defines *how* to create "sharable content objects" or "SCOs" that can be reused in different systems and contexts.

SCORM also isn't actually a *technical* standard from a language viewpoint. SCORM tells programmers how to write their code so that it can "play well" with other e-learning software. SCORM does not speak to instructional design or any other pedagogical concern; it is purely a standard of how to render something in a way that it plays well with other similar things. The utility of some of these standards for some school districts has been that the standards have caused publishers to render their objects into those formats for easy ingestion by districts in their Learning Management Systems.

The origin of SCORM is the U.S. government, particularly the Department of Defense (DoD), which realized that it was procuring the same training many times over but couldn't reuse it across departments, because each department had its own Learning Management System (LMS). In those days, each LMS had its own proprietary content format that encouraged vendor lock-in. In 1999, an executive order tasked a small research laboratory named ADL to "develop common specifications and standards for e-learning." Rather than starting from scratch with a whole new language standard or method, ADL harmonized the work of existing standards organizations into a cohesive reference model. SCORM was released in 2001 and was quickly adopted by both government and industry.

Meta-Data Standards: These are schema for how learning objects should be tagged to make them easily discoverable on the Internet by major search engines. Standards in this area offer field normalizing. These come from groups like the Learning Resource Metadata Initiative (LRMI), which is now the Dublin Core Metadata Initiative. According to the LRMI website, the origin of this meta-tagging standard was:

> *"Co-led by the Association of Educational Publishers – the 501(c)(3) division of the Association of American Publishers – and Creative Commons, and funded by the Bill & Melinda Gates Foundation and the William and Flora Hewlett Foundation,*

> *the LRMI has developed a common meta data framework for describing or 'tagging' learning resources on the web. This frame work is a key first step in developing a richer, more fruitful search experience for educators and learners... The LRMI was spurred by the announcement in 2011 of Schema. org, a project by Bing, Google, and Yahoo! to create a standard way of tagging online content... The metadata schema developed by the LRMI was adopted by Schema.org in April 2013, meaning that anyone who publishes or curates educational content can now use LRMI markup to provide rich, education-specific metadata about their resources with the confidence that this metadata will be recognized by major search engines."* – Learning Resource Metadata Initiative, "LRMI Today"[3]

Commercial (Combo) Standards: These are, or will be, academic standards and/or technical standards and/or technical models and/or metadata tagging standards. One that crosses technical with academic (what fields are used) is the Mozilla badging standard.[4]

The industry lacks a complete arsenal of Combo Standards akin to the UPC bar codes on all consumer products, which in the process of adoption, also incorporate other laws and capacities to ensure quality, acceptability, and alignment.

Work by the Learning Counsel is currently focused on helping a new enterprise work to build combo standards acceptable and mutable by states to accumulate a greater use of digital learning objects that will allow schools better orchestration to compete with straight consumer learning. These include the work to provide an evaluation in technical object maturity (how it is created to be high-engagement and rigorous).

This is important differentiation work for the consuming public, teachers, and schools, who know well the differences between a ringtone, a song, an album, and a movie, but encounter real consumer barriers to differentiating between an app and a full textbook, or a single course and full courseware. This is needed because of lack of standards and basic understanding of the capabilities inside software types. Commercial grade standards are planned to emerge in the next couple of years through the work of already active committees made up of both senior education executives and industry experts working with the Learning Counsel.

While talking about standards is potentially a very boring conversation to be having and likely to cause arguments about what they are and how important they are from others, it is an essential one to be had by education's leaders.

They are the building blocks of education's future in terms of the distribution of knowledge, a potential boon for everyone.

[1] Karen Fasimpaur; credit- Gurmit Singh, "Granularity," *K12 Open Ed: A blog for reflecting on the opportunities and challenges in open education*, May 2016, http://www.k12opened.com/blog/archives/2193

[2] *Rustici Software*, "SCORM Explained," http://scorm.com/scorm-explained/

[3] *Learning Resource Metadata Initiative*, "LRMI Today," http://www.lrmi.net/about

[4] *Mozilla*, "Open Badges," http://openbadges.org/

Chapter 13

Introducing Screen Learning

How could learning ever be "consumerized?" It starts first with what has happened to books, may they rest in peace, and ends with the brave new world of "screen learning."

Oh, there are still books out there, and plenty are being used in the education sector for teaching and learning. It's not that the books are *all* going away. It's about modality and the way the delivery of knowledge is mutating because of technology.

Books had a certain structure and paced learning through chunks known as chapters. Each chapter typically had a formative assessment, a little test for understanding. Or there was an accompanying workbook for practice, depending on the subject being covered. Books can deliver ponderous amounts of information and plenty of nuances using the bridge of language. A novel draws out readers to exercise their imaginations and shows them a train of thought sentence by sentence. That alone is very instructive and could be one of the things we now see missing in the TV and video-game generations.

Videos and games convey a lot of the same things as books, but they do so, many times, at the expense of imagination, which is perhaps the *one* thing most needed today. There is no doubt that people learn from videos and games, but the holy grail of learning things that are not easily story-formed, such as all mathematics, is something that fits between the book and the

Key Points

- Screen Learning is learning built for the computing screen, specifically toward the individual user. It can teach, and it's not the same as other terminology, like "blended," "online," or "virtual."
- The most interesting thing about the burgeoning new world of Screen Learning is what it's doing as a form and how fast it is propagating, which leads to a ripple effect in other aspects of education. The objects are in a trend pattern of more discrete, individual, and highly mobile bits.

full video or game world. That something has come into being and is rapidly populating the learning landscape.

It's called "Screen Learning." Not to be confused with online learning, which is defined very loosely as an online course that requires guidance by a teacher and may have recorded lectures in it along with documents and instructions; or distance learning, which is even more loosely defined as learning, across a distance from an instructor-led course. It's also not "blended" or "personalized" or any of the other terms the industry has used to modify the existing classroom scene.

Screen Learning is both in and outside the context of the classroom and teacher-learner paradigm.

Screen Learning is also both simpler and more complex than other terms related to imbuing education with tech.

It is learning built for the computing screen. That's it. It doesn't care where you are as a learner or if a teacher is even there, necessarily, although it doesn't replace a teacher in every sense. It's straight up *built for the user.* For example, see how Microsoft's *Minecraft* is built, marketed, and sold to kids who learn elementary code concepts from using it.

Screen Learning is a content delivery mechanism which a teacher has had as only one of many functions in the past. It usually combines reading and video embedding and can get as deep as a full virtual world with interactivity of most of its elements. It could be built to talk to you and be personalized by the student, and sometimes individualized by the teacher so that the student view to lessons is narrowed or "gated" in order that a particular student gets a precise set of lessons. It may require certain teacher inputs and teacher creativity within the framework of its master conception.

Being built for the *user* is where Screen Learning is abruptly, but subtly, turning learning into the next big thing for commercialization. Because it also exactly matches the goals of customized learning so that every student gets exactly what they need, it's also dovetailing into what institutions want to use but are not quite sure how to leverage in their current context.

The most interesting thing about the burgeoning new world of Screen Learning is what it's doing as a form and how fast it is propagating, which leads to a ripple effect in other aspects of education. Consider that there are an estimated 7,000 digital curriculum and content companies or publishers, and that's before adding in all of the one-off app builders that are sometimes one-man shops. These companies, along with teachers working on their own, have already created tens of millions of learning "objects" or bits of learning. Think in terms of "chapters" or "chunks" of knowledge, like how to add and subtract fractions, or perhaps the Declaration of Independence. The objects are in a trend pattern of more discrete, individual, and highly mobile bits.

"The industry of education itself has long been in a dialog about what the small bits are, be they "artifacts" or "concepts" or "elements," and whether or not they are performing technologically (doing something) in order to qualify for "object" status versus being lifeless words or pictures, which would be mere "content" or "resources."

For our purposes, we are using "object" in the *computer programming definition of objects,* which stems from: "In Object Oriented Programming (OOP), the word 'object' has special meaning: objects are defined as a specific way of organizing source code." [1]

In an attempt to define the characteristics of what a "learning object" is, I've created this summary list, if for no other reason than to sort the subject out in my own head:

- An object may explain a single part of knowledge such as understanding pyramid structure.

- An object can be interactive in and of itself.

- The objects can be multi-sensory, incorporating touch-screens and sound.

- Some objects are found in collections of like things, like videos and short games, and e-books or e-chapters.

- Some objects are knowledge artifacts built into full courses, with a scope and sequence pre-built for those individual bits until a pinnacle or totality of knowledge in that topic is achieved.

- Some courseware objects are single lesson and others are full-coverage of a subject with multiple lessons that can be spread out in incremental amounts of time, mirroring a daily classroom need.

- Some objects come tethered together with assessments, and some are teaching *as* an assessment.

- Many times the objects in courseware have intersection points where teachers can interact and set controls for the student.

- Sometimes the student self-controls the sequence in a randomized pattern, such as book collection sites.

- Many times, the courseware and collections of objects offer analytics showing how a student is doing to the student and/or to the teacher. These are sometimes called "solutions" by the software industry.

- Sometimes the learning object is a game, offering all the typical game maneuvers, like rewards, penalties, and achievement levels.

- Learning objects can even be highly stylized with actions, animations, mechanisms, aesthetics, controls, individualizations, instructs, and more. Using developer and designer skills, they can include ideal user interface/user experience (UI/UX).

- Some of the learning objects are apps just like consumer-side game apps. Most of them are one-offs, like downloading a single song.

- The objects may be accrued just like consumer-world shopping cart technology or iTunes libraries and cut-up and rehashed into a new object for new "playlists" of knowledge or "mixes" of learning.

- The learning objects are increasingly meta-tagged as aligned to a myriad number of Standards in the K-12, higher ed, or professional learning certifications world. The higher education world and some of the K-12 world *require* learning objects to have meta-tags or they're not even considered an "object." This is because, unlike

> the K-12 market in the U.S., which has largely been creating learning objects to fit into the existing classroom model where teacher and learner are physically together. The higher-ed world is already more solidly into consumable learning objects that operate nearly independently of the context of communication between teacher and learner.

That final point, that the learning object provides instructs in such a way that the learner knows they know the subject at the end (i.e., accomplished a standard) is a growing trend. This is perhaps one of the most significant redirects away from how teaching and learning has been in the past. When a learner knows they know, intermediation by another, as in a teacher or institution, becomes irrelevant *for them.* Testing becomes irrelevant *for them.* They already know and may or may not care to prove it to others, especially when demonstration of mastery is on-the-job or enhanced contribution.

In fact, one of the constraints of the consumerized learning trend is a perceived requirement for grades, diplomas, and degrees that require institutional accreditation. This may be solved when trusted software says via built-in summative assessment that a grade or credit has been earned, and it does so in a publicly consumable way on behalf of the learner that can be displayed at will. Since ultimately the utility of a grade, degree, or diploma relies on the trust of the inspecting party, the college, or employer, so the rise of trusted third-party issuers could become a normal and necessary reality.

Major brands like Cisco, Microsoft, Disney, and many others already have certifications that have meaningful value to anyone.

Places like Houston Independent School District in Houston, Texas have a Learning Management System that houses *over two million digital learning objects*. Other districts are similarly situated or well on their way. The textbook, while still important in many places, was almost never used in its entirety, and those unused chapters were considered wasteful. In the transition to digital, teachers wanted "chunked" content so they could mix and match at will. The industry responded with delivering exactly what was asked for, in large volume. Industry also took the opportunity to envelop that content into scope and sequenced courseware and sell it as "remedial" to schools and parents online.

That was an easy entrance into schools: offering extra practice and help for students falling behind. Screen Learning was a perfect fit. It did not require much teacher intervention and solved a problem. As education became ever-more complicated with new standards and accountability demands, increasing reliance on Screen Learning allowed schools to start thinking about it as core learning, not just supplemental. Now the high-engagement coupled with multi-sensory interactions of Screen Learning meets digitally native students exactly right, and increasingly has the heightened scores to prove it.

Commercial World vs. Education World

The problem is that the uptake by schools has been too slow for the commercial world. Upon invention of these costly learning objects, publishers have had to try to earn in any way that they could. Many of the largest have been nearly gutted, as non-spending of billions of expected dollars by schools to publishers caused cutting of staff and resources. Many times the talent who were cut simply went out and started new software companies, now using superior knowledge curation skills coupled with new programmers and software architects. In the meantime, schools almost universally went with their own teachers, building homegrown learning objects, the vast majority of which are mere documents, links, or recorded lectures. While these may be pedagogically useful, they aren't necessarily meeting students with what they expect given all their other exposures to consumer-grade technologies.

In fairness, with the content world in fractured small bits, publishers weren't ready for a while, and no educational institution was structured to curate and sequence every one of thousands of standards, plus build all the tests. The ordered world of education began to fall into chaos and is still falling, with leaders and politicians struggling to hold together a semblance of the old "workable" structure.

While the consumer world keeps gaining ground – and companies and products like ABCmouse, with its billion-dollar market valuation, LeapFrog, PBS, History Channel, Disney, Amazon, and others suit up for the coming takeover – teachers and schools using no Screen Learning, or no tech at all, are not only behind, but many have little understanding of the quantum shift that is coming their way.

Definitions of Terms

With lessons learned on the road, there are a lot of terms bandied about concerning the new modalities and new pedagogy. Here are some definitions of terms which tend to be used interchangeably but do need clarification as we move forward.

Screen Learning: Learning built for the computing screen to deliver content for a user with fancy digital aspects. It doesn't necessarily use or fully replace a teacher, but could be used in a classroom or outside of it as an individual learning object or full courseware for mastery of the content. Screen Learning assumes an "objectized" or "chunked" view of subjects and topics much like a single video, short-form game ("gamelet") or app that might be on the history of the Gettysburg Address by Abraham Lincoln versus a whole course on the Civil War or America's Founding Fathers. It may be a digital journey through multiple topics within a subject in a virtual environment that may have game and animated, storied features, taking students through multiple lessons that are presented based on that courseware's sequence. The screen learning may even be adapted to the individual student via an intelligent learning engine that understands that student's level of need, presenting alternatives to the same lesson for reading level or practice to ensure mastery.

Screen Learning Time: Refers to the classroom time dedicated to the use of Screen Learning of digital curriculum, content, or courseware on devices.

Blended Learning is a broad definition pertaining to doing both in-person and online learning in a mix custom for a class by a teacher. Also called hybrid learning and mixed-mode. *It assumes a teacher.*

Online Learning may be a part of a course syllabus or the entire course, but it generally *assumes a course* context, not a single-object or discrete knowledge lesson as Screen Learning can do. It may be from an outside institution or entity as a requirement for part or all of a larger learning journey such as Udemy, Coursera, or Khan Academy courses while attending a K-12 school.

eLearning assumes any digital object and is a term also widely used in the corporate training industry.

Distance Learning *assumes geographic distance* between the teacher and learner and *assumes a teacher-led* model.

Flipped Learning *assumes a physical environment locus* and is a teacher-led model.

Individualized Learning *assumes teacher interposition* within the learning inclusive of levels allowed into within the software. This is a trait of some Screen Learning.

Personalized Learning *assumes self-direction*, which is a trait of Screen Learning, but teachers can also interpose as guides by individualizing the software view. **Personalized Learning Environments** are software structured to allow a student to self-direct. These are different than **Virtual Learning Environments** in that the Virtual ones typically would model traditional education, just in a web-based virtual environment but with a teacher/instructor.

[1] **Source:** https://en.wikibooks.org/wiki/A-level_Computing/AQA/Paper_1/Fundamentals_of_programming/Object- oriented_programming

Chapter 14
Consumer Awakening

Most educators, along with growing numbers of families and students, are aware of screen learning options. They've been seeing advertising on television. They have apps. They see ads pop up when they do Internet searches for "back to school" and see things like "Not-Back-to-School-Camp" – an annual *camp* for unschooled teens in Oregon. Finding a course, finding a piece of content, downloading an app – all of those things are for the truly earnest, but increasingly the not-so-earnest at digital learning are seeing intrusive ads as they surf, shop, or pick up email. The great default is simple search engines, which is the same for shopping any consumer product.

> **Key Point**
>
> Consumerization is beginning. The advised route is to know, in detail, what is really happening and develop a brilliant strategy as a school, teacher, student, or parent, to embrace the shift and use it for greater gains.

Yet it didn't start with the average parent and student. Consumerization started with teachers.

According to the Learning Counsel's national 2015 Digital Curriculum Strategy Survey, in which 540 U.S. Schools and Districts responded:

- 58% of teachers already spend up to five hours a week just on web search for resources. Approximately 12.5% of their work time is consumed in web searching. (Do the math; this is a huge shift that has happened gradually over the past ten years or so, at a phenomenal countrywide cost.)

- One-third of teachers spend up to 10% of their workweek building digital curriculum. (Which typically will be a lesson plan

> built on top of some Internet resource shown in the lesson with a link to some discrete piece of knowledge in a document or site, or a video.)

In fact, teachers themselves have built a huge portion of the available consumable digital curriculum. Most of the industry content vendors have had trouble in the last ten years making digital sales because of this, although total spend in 2015 on digital resources topped $7.2 billion in the U.S. The faith in the textbook model, or do-it-yourself by teachers, was hard to overcome initially, and the distribution of computing devices was not what it is now at 77% of all students having a device for a significant portion of the day, if not a full one-device-per-child model. But now the paper-versus-digital trade is happening at a phenomenal pace.

Learning Counsel research indicates that 2016 was the first dramatic shift, popping the digital purchase side up to a total of $9 billion (a $1.8 billion increase in a single year!) to educators and institutions, while diminishing the textbook side by at least that much. At the same time, the overall market has lost at least $1.8 billion in worth due to the fact that some spend has actually left the market for teacher-created or free and open resources. From the outside, the curriculum resource market looks like it hasn't gone up in four or five years, remaining relatively flat but shifting from one foot (paper) to the other (digital). What growth there could have been to coincide with nominal population growth never happened, because the market instead chose non-purchase and has put in place a significant portion of home-grown or free digital resources.

Industry players have long been aware that their entrance point into selling schools was initially the supplemental resources space, things like math games, videos, etc. Administrators in schools were usually not the purchasers; school principals and individual teachers were, at a rate of 3 to 1 in local small purchase versus institutional. This meant that companies had to sell in a nearly pure-consumer-marketing model to reach the bulk of the buyers who had been teachers for the starter years of digital transition (the nation has 3.3 million teachers). This cost-to-market for industry has therefore been built-in to most companies who are using tactics that completely skirt the old textbook district or school board levels.

Now that schools are at long last taking inventories of all that their teachers are using and establishing strategies to get full-coverage models of digital curriculum and content, they are making short work of saturating the school landscape with all things digital learning. In addition, the industry of paid professional digital resources is gaining some minor efficiencies now reaching whole districts, resulting in lower costs of marketing overall.

Meanwhile, the seeds of consumerization had already been sown, with many for-profit and non-profits continuing to bypass the existing governmental structure and sell learning directly.

The seeds have grown so much that companies are selling digital learning objects to consumers at a pace that's faster and growing more quickly than that sold to schools (currently at \$10.44 billion and growing at 20% annual growth rate versus school/teacher purchase, which combined was at \$7.2 billion last year and predicted to jump by

25% this year. Hereafter, it will level off to about a 5% growth rate due to 2016 being a major adoption and new purchase year because of pent-up demand to utilize the computers and tablets purchased). Ultimately, indications are that consumer-based learning purchase will outstrip institutional spending by a factor of at least 10, and rise to assume 10-15% of all mobile market purchases whereas it is currently .08% of a $1.4 trillion industry. That promises industry a potential gain of some $100 billion in the next ten years. It may go even faster if it catches a strong consumer trend pattern.

The major digital learning objects, the "**Three Things of Digital Learning**" are:

1. Discrete digital learning objects – video, apps, eBooks, documents, sites, games and courseware (iTunes, Teacher Created Materials, YouTube, Overdrive, Scholastic, Waggle, Amplify, Tenmarks, Macmillan, Disney Interactive, Lumosity, ABCmouse, ReadingKingdom, Rocket Group, HMH, Discovery Education, and thousands, if not millions, of others)

2. Discrete Online Courses (The Great Courses, Khan Academy, Udacity, Coursera, Florida Virtual School, Fuel Education, Lynda.com, LinkedIn)

3. Online Schools & Distance Supplemental Services (Fuel Education, Florida Virtual School, Presence Learning)

The intermixing of these into existing schools is part of the blending of education today, and the growth of all these learning things is now saturating teacher, administrator, and consumer consciousness with big media messaging and socialization online.

The design basics of the *Three Things of Digital Learning* reflect the internet modalities of other things, like the single-song sales on iTunes and one-off game apps downloaded onto tens of millions of phones worldwide. The *Things* are commonly all grouped into the terms "learning objects" or "learning resources." As a trend, the *Things* are all attempting to be:

- Shorter form
- Participatory
- Multi-sensory

The "Long Form" *Things* are attempting to be the same as the "Short Form" but additionally:

- Book and textbook replacements or whole libraries (collections of Things), now typically coupled with pre-assessment for reading Lexile level

- Mastery games complete with all gaming stylizations

- All-inclusive immersive environments, covering standards by grades and single log-in

- Embedded assessments with analytics

- Provisioning teacher controls

The "Long Form," a gaming term, is not typically seen in the straight-to-consumer world if the item is educational. Only recently did Amazon start to include long-form games for sale on its consumer web platform. Most teachers and schools are actually going the consumer-oriented route of short-form purchase, especially free. This means that rather than the form the textbook took of a collected and scripted knowledge masterwork, they are following the internet modality which atomizes things but also adds dimensions like sound and interactivity, and ultimately allows for a re-collection into a customized and branded learning experience.

This is real consumerization now at work, knowledge reorganization across a newly globalized neural network for mankind. True personalization possibilities are endless. However, curation is a bigger burden on teachers.

"Apps can bring a portable solution to every learning style which can suit different language learning skill requirements: grammar, vocabulary, reading, listening, writing, or speaking. A combination of apps (app mashing) that covers the different skills will help language learners engage, any time, any place, and at any pace with a variety of teaching styles, from the repetitive grammar drills, to the gamified all-in-one solutions," said Fernando Rosell-Aguilar, Lecturer in Spanish at The Open University.[1]

Commissioned studies are showing vocabulary and literacy gain for young children with app use.[2]

Arguments may be raging for a few more years about whether the *Things* of consumerized learning will continue to make relentless incursions into the education landscape. Or whether they will tear down the status quo, put teachers out of work, and rip up the bureaucracies. Or if these "digital natives" with their apps and games will be made powerless and ignored by all consumers everywhere because educators launch an effective challenge as to whether the *Things* teach anybody anything or are mere amusements and a passing fad. This is doubtable.

It's doubtable because the proverbial cat is "out of the bag" already. People see learning online and they are using it. A bald-faced order to just "get back in class and learn" won't hold out for much longer now that nearly everyone has a device on them all day anywhere they go. The advised route is to know, in detail, what is really happening with consumerized learning and develop a brilliant strategy as a school, a teacher, student, or parent, to embrace the shift and use it for greater gains.

[1] Fernando Rosell-Aguilar, Lecturer at *The Open University* "How Smartphone Apps are Revolutionizing Language Learning", *The Conversation*, April 29, 2014.

[2] Cynthia Cheong and Carly Shuler, *The Joan Ganz Cooney Center at Sesame Workshop*, "Learning: Is There an App for That?" 2010.

Chapter 15

The Face of Consumerized Learning

What does the face of consumerized learning look like? What's it like to experience it?

The fact is, it's a lot like watching a great movie or documentary that has commercial breaks and the people around you are slouched with you on the couch making various comments and asking questions about whether one character is doomed and another one destined for greatness before the end.

It's also a lot like playing a game – a board game, like Monopoly, with your friends. In fact, the "gamification" of learning is not creating violent or silly games; it's creating games that challenge you intellectually and may even be co-played by others in your global class. You might be the game assigned "banker" in a math schema teaching you to think in denominations of drachma (the old monetary standard of Greece before the Euro and the European Union). The game may be studying international finance and have open discussion going on with fellow players.

There are three ways to consumerize learning and try to sell it on the open market, and each has a major effect on what the learning objects look like.

1. Create digital schools and courses.
2. Create digital objects.
3. Create digital solutions (things that put multiple objects into a sequence of learning).

Key Points

- Consumerized learning looks more like a great documentary or video game than a lecture captured into YouTube and a scrap of old textbook that has been digitized.
- The face of consumerized learning is as varied as the app world with its millions of options. Beyond apps is an even larger-sized universe of online schools, courses, digital learning objects, and solutions.

Each of these ways can be seen morphing into the others within the broader education market. It's confusingly complex.

The main considerations by those in the education market, business-to-business consumption, is around what *they* will *use,* and they are seeking first and foremost a replacement technology to prior resources. They seek cost efficiency and immediacy. As the distributor of the learning objects, certain schools could be buying them in bulk to retail out to students.

Schools don't think of distribution of learning objects this way; they normally think of the digital objects as the elements they must work to build into something interesting, a course or whole subject area coverage model grade-by-grade or within a single school inside a university.

They want to custom curate and then manipulate and personalize the digital objects themselves. This is a lot of work and may actually be duplicative work better left to the pros of digital instructional design. If not, it may be building things that will not "compete" against similar learning objects in the consumer world.

Creating Digital Schools and Courses

Online schools are typically course-centric. They are not retailers of digital learning objects except in the sense of courses. They are increasingly commercializing those, selling even without regard to enrollment in their school (if there is an actual physical school). This is a sign the U.S. is at the early stages of consumerization of learning. Why? Because the early stages of any major industry started with sales to existing lines of business.

Consider the car industry. The earliest resellers of the first cars were the horse-drawn buggy makers who had for hundreds of years been the go-to source for people needing faster transportation.

Virtual online schools such as Udemy, Khan Academy, Fuel Education (K12, Inc.), Florida Virtual School Global, Open Culture, Ed-X, Lynda.com, and Coursera are proof positive that course-purchase and use is hot and continuing to grow. It is only a matter of time before they are also widely accredited, and perhaps accredited-in-context, or each course is its own accruable unit regardless of diploma or degree plan. "Badges" are more and more acceptable as evidence of training on resumes.

The consumerization of higher ed in the long run will necessarily need to include its willingness to disaggregate into consumable digital learning objects or solutions to aid the consumer. A complete disregard of past forms and a favoring of the consuming student will be an enabler for life-long learning and new revenue paths for higher ed. It directly supports the greater business and economic model that needs rapid training on new tech for staff.

Digital online schools by every K-12 school will be problematic unless it is a local flourish to other consumerized learning objects and courses created independently. Such constructs full of customized digital curriculum will quickly be seen as a massive duplicative effort and wasteful.

Creating Digital Objects

Governments and schools love to create various meta-tagging schemas and giant repositories for learning objects, especially the "free" ones their teachers create. Unfortunately many of which often have internal copyright infringements.

Creating a digital object is a piece of cake with a few authoring tools or just Word documents or maybe a presentation tool. It's maybe "doing something" technically, but more than likely it is not.

Who likes individual digital objects the most?

Students. Individual apps, books, videos, and other sorts of disaggregated content are the way consumers are used to getting their content. It is a normal thinking pattern to seek out elements to teach themselves "X" and to cut right to the chase with *only* that thing they want to know. This is the great legacy of search engines, which have taught nearly everyone that a thing we want to know is only a search-engine entry away.

It's also a great thing for the enablement of learning-by-discovery.

Teachers, again, are huge proponents of objectizing learning. Most teachers like individual learning objects and discrete elements more than courseware for the simple reason that an element can fit into a lesson plan, whereas courseware *is* the lesson plan.

Publishers that are app creators, lesson-plan distributors, and for-profit or not-for-profit repositories love individual digital learning objects or elements. The reduction of an entire subject into bite-sized pieces or individual books or individual apps, lessons, or tests allows for a perceived low cost to each. This allows for all levels of students, teachers, and schools to acquire without feeling like they've spent all that much.

The problem with elements is that they are even more disconnected from the everything-you-have-to-learn than the single-subject textbook was. In some instances, they are not even *chapters* in coverage for what a student needs to learn in a subject. One example might be Adaptive Curriculum's free sample entitled Mathematics, 2D Views of an Object Formed by Unit Cubes 1. This allows students to draw different 2D views of the 3D object formed by unit cubes. This is nifty, but does it do anything for the meeting of all the school's goals for student learning? Well, *this* one element does meet a couple of Common Core State Standards, so it is a good find, but not all elements have any notation of what they do to help. Adaptive Curriculum's website is gracious enough to offer a means of checking their elements against any Standards in the U.S. – a very cool feature.

There are thousands of other resource sites and government repositories to go and check out, but one example is SAS Curriculum Pathways, which is unique in that it promises all of its digital learning objects are *interactive*.[1] Each of the elements are "free" and certainly cool. However, they are one-offs from a company with hundreds of other products that are also for sale. It is up to a teacher to search the site and incorporate them and then test on them and see if students learned anything. In addition, the school needs to determine if this is going to feed into curriculum goals overall, or if it's just a fun side activity that teaches some important concepts.

Other services like Knovation and Overdrive offer pre-curated digital resources that are otherwise scattered across the Internet and freely available but now can be consumed en-masse in one place with a subscription model.

The individual objects, while not always fully digital but only "digitized" documents, are put into an efficient consumerized model to serve teachers and learners with low-cost resources that are still pre-vetted and continuously refreshed. The reason for this type of work is that an estimated 60% of all links for free resources fail annually and a new resource must be found or the pathway to the original reestablished.

Creating Digital Solutions

Publishers love whole courseware solutions, because they are whole systems with lots of individual learning modules in them and can be sold and supported for large numbers of users, often at different grade levels. There are two general types of courseware solutions: learning object repositories with management functions built around them (Learning Management Systems) and guided courseware systems, which are a combination of digital lessons with the functions of managing and analytics around those. These later ones, the courseware type, are not objects individually but whole journeys through a subject or many subjects that typically have gamified elements.

A courseware "solution" is by definition beyond the simple digital learning object or even a single lesson or course. It can be an entire subject like math from simple addition and subtraction all the way through various topics up to calculus.

Take for example Triumph Learning's Waggle platform, which offers students a "scaffolded" or pre-architected lesson structure they step through autonomously with some teacher interaction. In addition, teacher training and other benefits all tie together. With courseware solutions, publishers also gain from predictable subscriptions that are renewed often. Other full solution vendors, albeit sometimes for single subject areas, include Edmentum, Myon, Brainpop, Edgenuity, Thinkcera, Curriculum Associates, Scientific Learning, Redbird Learning, Inspiration Learning, Accelerate Learning, TenMarks, Odysseyware, Renaissance Learning, Imagine Learning, Lakeshore Learning, Britannica, Stride Academy, Reading Kingdom, Achieve3000, Copia, Active Learning, Amplify, Apex Learning, Tiggly, and hundreds of others like them which seem to usually have named their company "*Something Learning*," and the "usual suspects" in the group of big publishers, like Pearson, HMH, McGraw Hill, Cengage, Follett, Voyager Sopris, etc.

District administrators and teachers love courseware solutions, because they often come with measurements and log-in counts, and they can "see" what's going on with learning, right in the system.

Information Technology Directors like courseware solutions because there are less loose elements around to keep track of and provide support for. The only drawback is the complaints from teachers and students who don't like to keep track of upwards of 50 different log-ins for various publisher solutions.

Another problem with courseware solutions from the school viewpoint is that they require a lot of vetting and can be pricey. They also require a lot of agreement amongst a lot of people to the solution, which is like trying to find the Holy Grail for many schools. Publishers have sometimes admitted that, while they do sell a lot of subscriptions, use is sometimes questionable unless tied to some metrics. Often this is a result of the solution not being properly introduced, but it could also be lack of a simple user experience.

How consumers choose digital learning objects, schools, courses, or courseware solutions is the topic of many studies yet to come. One thing is a sure bet, though – consumers will seek the best value at the lowest cost. Making a learning object something that is hard to find, making it related to having to enroll in something, or making it obscurely require something to happen, like a paper transcript getting mailed in, are all things that will derail getting learning to be consumer accessible.

Schools choosing digital learning objects, courses, or courseware solutions are an important *tactic* and could be an enormous part of their marketing plan and success.

Hiring a virtual school and "white-labeling" them, or basically slapping a logo on top of their courses, is a fast way to get things going for existing schools. If buying a lot of digital objects, a school has to set up means to vet every app or lesson plan or video, etc.; this is very important to note because of student data privacy and security issues, as well as potential exposure to inappropriate advertising.

Some other important factors to consider:

- Make sure teachers align their lessons with apps they choose to download so they also don't overburden the students.

- If teachers are downloading a bunch of digital learning objects, you're going to need a repository Learning Management System or virtual server in the cloud with a single sign on solution.

- If it's a solution that runs on district or local servers, there needs to be tech support and storage.

- If it's a solution that is in the cloud, you're going to need some vetting security-wise, because you'll be having students access the system as a requirement.

- Who's going to manage all the passwords kids are sure to lose constantly or mistakenly share, thus creating some level of instructional design flaw for things as serious as testing results? If you *do* take this on, how will you explain to the State that you have adopted some acceptable level of cheating potentiality that will affect reporting because of possibly shared passwords?

- If it's an individual digital learning object like an app, lesson, game, video, or something else, who owns it? Who is making sure there are no copyright infringements or non-licensed copies? Who keeps it if students can bring their own devices (BYOD)? Who pays for it?

- If a school is going to bring in consumer learning objects and use a tactic of sending students out to "get the Shakespeare app," some will get the "Complete Works"

> from Google Play, and others will get the "Sonnets" from iTunes. Having a view to different ecosystems for apps is important.

The face of consumerized learning is as varied as the app world with its millions of options, a tiny percentage of which are widely used. Beyond apps is an even larger-sized universe of online schools, courses, digital learning objects, and solutions.

The ultimate sophistication of all of these on a technical scale regarding how well designed and interactive they are will be changing as the industry matures.

[1] Curriculum Pathways, Free Learning for K12 and Beyond, https://www.sascurriculumpathways.com/portal/

Book 2

The Solutions Arena

Chapter 16
The Grand Scheme

Thus far, some of what might be a grand scheme for a revitalized and restructured education sector has already been hinted at – an unstructured form that relies more heavily on direct delivery online with a sort of a virtual networked community administration of parents and students and local schools delivering new roles and redefined functions.

Functions of the digital courseware have already been discussed, so the issues of the grand scheme include:

- How it could be set up
- How it could work in practice, and for every age of student
- Impacts on parents
- Impacts on learning
- Transition costs
- Transition time
- Workforce modification
- Professional development stages
- Cost factors

Those are the biggies. How it could be set up is a matter of taste once the concept of unstructured form has set in.

Key Points

- School administrators need to think without preconceptions, meaning trying to start at the place they are really starting from regarding fully digital and mobile education reality – nothing.
- The grand scheme is a virtual community network form that relies more heavily on direct delivery online with a consensus network of parents and students and local schools delivering new roles and refined functions.
- A software-driven enterprise of schooling could allow for great efficiencies in education, including great gains for families, provided it is carried through with that in mind.

Avoid Preconceptions

For several years, education has taken technology on at its front lines in the teaching and learning arena. This is not thinking organizationally, seeing the finished product and how it will be arrived at from the top in the executive suites like companies more typically do. It could be said that the thinking by education administrations so far has been with a preconception of delivery mechanism, *via* or *at* the teachers, and not even necessarily *at* the learners. It has been as if the identification of the target to change by the executives was *their teacher as delivery mechanism* more than the structure with tech as the delivery mechanism. Administrators seemed to have been considering that the structure could all pretty much stay the same and only the troops needed to fight with some added attention from the back-office tech guys. This is not sufficient.

School administrators need to *think without preconceptions,* meaning trying to start at the place they are *really* starting from regarding fully digital and mobile education reality – nothing.

Actually, this is important no matter who you are, from superintendent, to state administration executive, to teacher. Think first about the goals of learning and the students – *that* is student centricity. It is also the same mentality that the commercial consumer delivery mechanism will operate with.

Direct consumerism will think that way; it is the primary appeal – custom personalization without all the added inapplicable regimentations that are sometimes given with an air of authoritarianism presently by our brick-and-mortar schools.

To think without preconceived notions is to do one's best to deliver a quality, personalized experience for the individual *without regard* to present realities of buildings and staff but via an extremely well-informed digital reality. Such a reality would have a care to the finesse of digital distribution and all the nuance of successful user interface and experience. Well done, the new reality would be one that allows students to take ownership in themselves. The way this is done in the consumer world is to give the individual, and their parents for the very young, a role as a member, someone who has "skin in the game" the same as having purchased something. Their "agreement" to their highly personalized journey in the open market will be a financial buy-in, typically. With that comes the expectation that it will be that much more quality than anything found "free." Imagine a school that drives online "membership" and guides achievement and schedules arrivals at certain activities and events in a seamless interweaving of meaning into the whole learning experience, and refers students to individuals as mentors both inside and outside the current teacher and administrator paradigm. This is well more than a focus on attendance and classroom dynamics.

That is the challenge for schools who want to deliver for free on taxpayer dollars – compete with what will be a highly marketed, crafted user experience, just like consumer choices will offer, except as a school, now with an *absence of any negative.* There are plenty of negatives in the present structures. Restructuring is not impossible; it just requires an understanding of what technology should really do to transform the end-user experience. Putting the existing structure *first* just won't do.

A first step is for state governments to allow a lot of experimentation and alteration at the school level, even across multiple schools and multiple districts, to consider the learner first, and the learner's life, before other requirements. The age-old "must be present" physically for everything should go. Learners will still *want* to go when there is a truly good reason.

Local schools must start with a strategy that encompasses how they can facilitate *full* mobility for learning as a foundation. It may not all be done that way, but having it as a founding goal allows an assumption that all other things can then rest on. An initial program will be to collect all digital inventory and start mapping out how to deliver this in a direct screen-learning model. Make a list of things that just *can't* be delivered fully online, such as subjects, projects, or activities. Question anything on the list repeatedly, of course. Note as you go which ones are specialties, perhaps so engagingly delivered by a teacher who dresses up as Abe Lincoln and affects so convincingly his famous Gettysburg Address that this particular lesson gets on a separate list of planned in-person delivery at a physical location as an "Expositional" lesson. It's a performance, so it fits with the idea of creating a highly engaging experiential learning that it might even make it onto a separate list the school keeps regarding top bullet points about the school's marketing identity. It might be that students of different ages are at different stages of their learning, so signing up for the annual lesson by Abe is part of student scheduling boards, run off of a software interface that alerts a student that he should calendar it because he's close to that part of his journey. Attracting or cultivating "talent," like Hollywood and radio stations do, or porting those individuals in via live webcam, are things that could be a major part of administrative work.

As part of this initial strategy, survey parents of the younger children about forming local parent-run bands of oversight for their own kids in a rotation the school helps figure out; perhaps each parent in a group of five families takes one day of the week for oversight. All families get a monetary credit and more quality time with their kids. They can "rent" facilities like a classroom from the school if need be. The school gets an overarching insurance policy for parents. Note this is fraught with obvious worries, such as whether or not parents can be trusted with each other's kids or even with their own kids! The idea is not at perfection but a matrix of alternatives, a virtual network.

Also as part of the initial strategy, investigate the options for managing all the digital personalization for every learning objective and the scheduling and time management of any of the responsible party(s) for everyone's learning. This may in fact include signing up grandparents and neighborhood matriarchs who keep watch and shuttle the younger children, in fact extending the current relationship beyond kids to communities in a much more meaningful way. To be a virtual networked community administrative structure, potentially gaining great efficiency by work distribution, it's important to keep in mind that the effort is a giant community network. Going digital means concentrating on *engagement* of your whole audience in as many ways as can be delivered while staying focused on your specific

> "Schools need a renewed focus on arts and extra-curricular activities including drama, speech, debate, sports, all things you can't get online while in your slippers at home, as a survival tactic. With kids getting their information elsewhere, I think that we also need rich human contact now…and help with teachers remaining positive, so much so that kids will be asking 'can we cancel summer break?'"
>
> *- Clay Stidham Jr., Director of Curriculum, Instruction, Innovation & Assessment, Federal Programs Director, Blue Ridge School District, Arizona*

core competencies and purposes. Your educational community network has at its center the individual student.

In this strategy, ignore the ideas that someone else could do this better, some already-operational online school. That's not true. You have things and people that do some things well, perhaps better than anyone. Maybe you take those certain teachers and set up a bank of on-demand expertise in offices that administer personalized journeys through all the software and intersperse that with fantastic and memorable activities to punctuate learning. Some of these activities might be purchased assets including actual physical travel, although virtual travel could do just as well.

Your strategy needs to keep a focus on the end goal – leveraging consumerized learning for deeply individualized educational paths. This could mean that one of the programs you put into your strategy for later execution is a set of teachers re-dedicated or hired to be the on-boarders of the student into an individualized learning plan, and then actually do the mixing and tracking of those plans across time. This is sort of like a combination of teacher, counselor, and digital curator all in one. It might be done that way, or it might need to be done with a separation of duties in a sort of chain-of-delivery unlike what has been done in the past – a chain akin to the way stores both online and offline interact with speed and precision of service.

Second, this strategy will take some serious "selling" by schools to engage communities in different ways, to evoke personal responsibility in each learning plan and to gain grandmothers and grandfathers and neighborhoods and cross-neighborhoods who adopt each other. There may have to be penalties for flunking out of participation in a primarily online type system being administered, one that reverts to a single central location of old-line professional schooling. Or this is simply looked at as a method more appropriate to that one individual who seems to need more structure.

The setup would also include laws and regulations and normal procedures changing, of course. There is, though, in most states, a lot of flexibility for schools, sometimes more than they know.

What Does It Look Like?

Simply, it looks more like online colleges than it does the primary schools for kindergarten through high school across America.

The individual learner joins a school or some a la carte offerings of the school since they will be buffet-like offerings marketed online, just like most higher-ed institutions. The issues of administration are ones of *scheduling* and putting in place program leaders, ones who will run certain activities. Historically, those leaders were coaches and teachers.

The student chooses, usually in coordination with the advice of school leaders, their mix of online learning and activities. They accrue credentials along the way.

Parental Involvement

In practice, the big stumbling block that comes to mind for most people is how to handle the younger children. People are very concerned about kindergarteners and primary grade school children. It is perhaps the one point, in my opinion, to worry

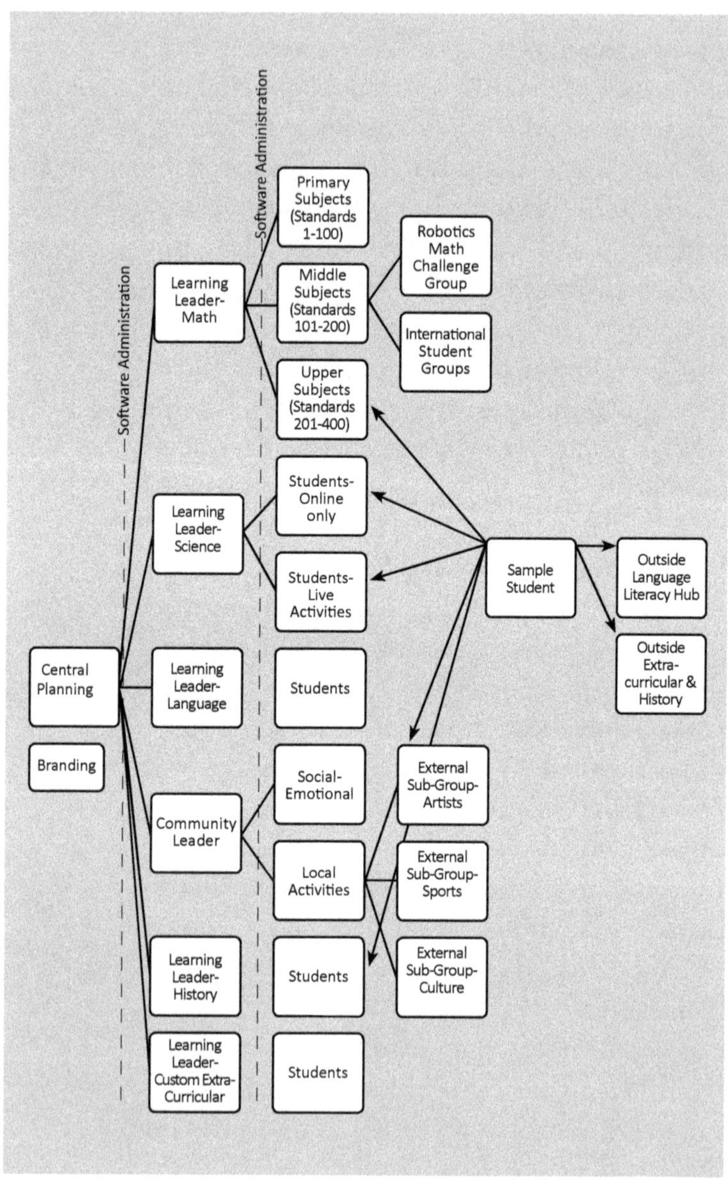

A hypothesized new structure for a school's staffing and functions:

- *At the top is a central planning and branding function*
- *Second-layer leaders organize by function and major subject area to service the end ideal of personalized learning for all students.*
- *The individual learner joins a school or uses marketed offerings al la carte because they can be chosen buffet-like.*
- *Some "live exposition" of lectures, labs, sports and collaborative projects can be scheduled by a teacher-leader or opted-into by students.*

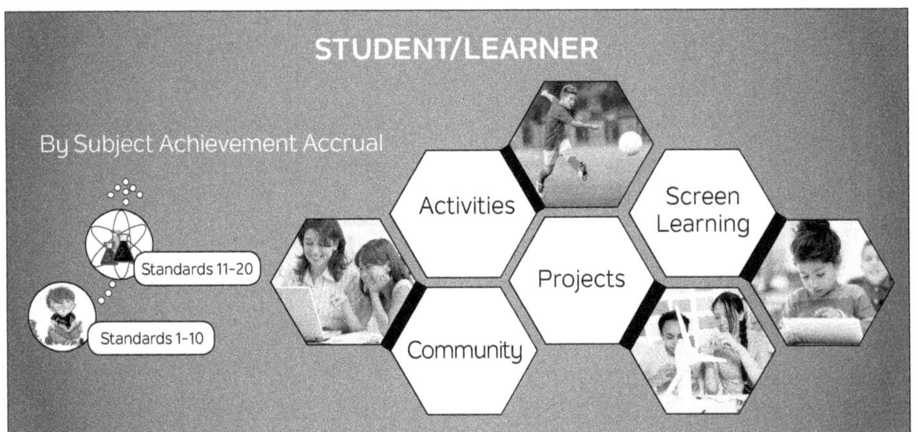

about the least regarding the software. The best software and most consumerized space are already the earliest lessons for reading, writing, counting, and more. It is the structure of administration of this that is the issue. If parents are all working, how does a school help them? There are myriad ways to engage a community to reduce overhead costs and also cause more learning by leveraging software that is already there that does a large portion of the teaching. The hugging and caring and making sure the work gets done, those are the factors to concentrate on.

To personalize for every student, all curriculum is divided into different learning assets – activities, screen learning, projects, community (which includes class-like lecturing and meet-ups of any kind.) The teacher-leader or student chooses the mix of assets that make the most sense for that one student, including scheduling time for each part of the curriculum. Students accrue credentials along the way.

The impacts on parents have the potential to be enormously positive. Some parents, with proper scheduling, can have children with them for periods of the day while they are working

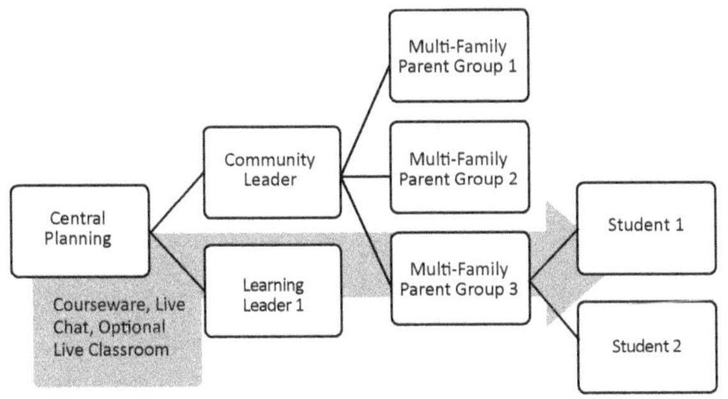

Schools have the potential to incorporate, and lean on, their field of responsible parents to take over some of the pushing of students to complete assignments, especially if parents can be paired or made into sub-groups so that peer pressure and reporting keeps everyone contributing.

and the child is doing their own digital work. There is great promise in that for families. There is also, of course, potential for negatives. I think it is best to consider that a change will go positively because mobility is such a driving force for improved life experience – focus on this, not the negatives.

An actual tax credit or flexible spending accounts are some things that may evolve into being for parents, while also saving enormous amounts of tax money.

All the Rest

The transition costs should not be considered to be nothing, as they have largely been considered thus far. A reworking of budgets in the direction of technology and simply dropping paper textbook purchase will work to get a great distance into the transition. There needs to be incentive money and capital expenditure for the software, but learning gains and administrative efficiency are the prize. An estimation of budget to pull off a complete and fast transition should be put above the $100 billion range for the nation, which is interestingly close to the $100 billion recession bump up of the 2009-2011 federal awards. Those monies, unfortunately, were tracked as having been spent largely on building massive numbers of new buildings, perhaps precisely the opposite of what should have been being done.[1] Schools and districts across America still have an opportunity to do things incrementally.

Workforce modification is another matter, and perhaps this is where things really fall down. How *does* one restructure the work effort into a new model that will work, whose central structure is software driven? A software-driven enterprise of schooling could allow for great efficiencies in education, including great gains for families, provided it is carried through with that in mind. This is worth studying for the next several years.

I am convinced that a grand transition plan would *retain* and perhaps *expand* the number of teachers who may not still be *called* teacher but would be something they could enjoy fitting into – just within a digital reality. It would not necessarily be a dramatic shift to still do some whole-group-type teaching, while also doing a whole lot more office work running digital learning. Ideally this might free a lot of former teachers to work remotely from home for a far greater portion of time. They would just meet up with individuals and "classes" in the schedule as needed. This is exactly like higher education has been operating for decades.

The professional development stages schools should go through will be complex, to say the least. The one piece of advice in this must be to focus attention not on the transactional model of teaching and learning as it has been, but on the model of services used by commercial industries. A service-level-type model works with onboarding, service plans (the educational learning plan), agreements for service levels and extras, help desks, and in many cases has physical outposts that support consumers. This is much like how telecommunication companies operate with mobile phone plans. Transfer plans to other carriers using an underlying technology of SIM cards (Subscriber Identity Module (SIM) card is a portable memory chip that goes with you if needed to another phone if your old one breaks). A school that offers a service-level agreement to learners based on usage will help all students and families achieve the time and utility efficiency they seek in the modern age.

Ultimately, the model for delivery with technology needs to go to what industry calls the "C-suite," or the Chief Executive Officer and others at that equivalent level in schools, like superintendents, school boards, and states. *They* are the ones who must understand the new model completely. Keeping local control while building some sort of underbelly of support administratively for state reporting is going to be an issue. Then, doing real professional development is going to require boot-camp-like timed major immersions into systems. Repetitive staging of these types of things would have to be a new normal.

In all, the new trend will be to "flip the administration" of learning, similar to the prior trend that resided at the teaching and learning level of flipping the learning so that reading and taking in the lessons were done outside of school, and then in class students engaged in discussion and projects. We need to now take that trend and expand it out to the entire scheme of education – the whole enterprise must now "flip" so that the entire administration mirrors the changed actions.

This is a job for everyone and a grand scheme that could give education a second life.

[1] Dupor, Bill, "Stimulus Grants and Schools: How Was the Money Spent?" *Federal Reserve Bank of St. Louis*

Chapter 17

A Model Architecture for Schools

A solid digital curriculum strategy and planning architecture can guide a school district through the transition into a fully digital education age while managing potential pitfalls and risks.

While computers and devices have been extant for many years, the price point was often too high for wide-scale implementation to be practical for school districts. During the 1980s, 1990s, and 2000s, when every other industry was making the transition to a digital-centric environment, the educational system was left behind. For a long time, the best they could do was computer labs and single computers for whole classrooms. It is interesting to say that the lack of *real* transition to a wholesale change in the distribution mechanism of education, such as been had in other industries, is *more* due to a lack of sophisticated curriculum and administrative software than hardware or teacher follow through. Blaming lack of technology infusion on teachers is, and always has been, a wrong target.

Everything changed a few years ago with the introduction of low-priced tablets such as iPads. The lower price point made it possible for a superintendent to afford to begin placing numbers of devices into classes, if not into the hands of every student. Except there was still the problem of what the student was supposed to do with their device. Often, the device became an auxiliary tool that was only used occasionally, given as a reward for students who had completed something else to

Key Points

- Schools need to take inventory, plan their digital house, have real strategies and not mere tactics, write new policies, and transition through great professional development.
- The game-changing software is screen learning and something more – digital administration.
- It's important to understand the difference between tactics and strategy. A tactic is an individual action that is taken in the implementation of a larger strategy.

go and play some games in the back of the room. If not that, various one-offs were employed such as using video conferencing to "visit" other places, with all other structure and materials remaining the same.

Missing was a model architecture for schools. It takes the lead from other industries that have successfully made the transition to being tech-embedded. With the right game-changing software, computers that were once secondary tools became the central method of getting work done in the office. Adobe graphics products changed the way publishing and creative tasks were done, and CAD software pushed the drafting tables right out of the engineers' and architects' offices. When it comes to education, that game-changing software is screen learning with all sorts of digital curriculum and something more – digital administration. The very human-transaction-intensive education world has never been rethought with a high understanding of what software can do to process and method.

So, while getting devices into the hands of all of the students in a district is a good step, it's only setting up the classroom and, very often as the education industry has seen, it is a classic case of "putting the cart before the horse." Digital curriculum is needed to take full advantage of the devices and in a way that changes the interrelationships within the tasks. For a shift to technology to be as effective as possible, the right strategy and digital curriculum architecture must be in place for schools.

In the past couple of years, I have advised schools to take these steps first in their transition to digital.

Step 1. Start with Inventory

I have found that, almost universally, schools do not know what they have. Inventory controls are minimal when it comes to digital curriculum for a very good reason. The content industry blew up and atomized into millions of pieces when it used to be consolidated into a few mammoth publishers that pushed out lines of books with an internal structure and consistency to learning that was all mapped out for schools.

Step one, therefore, is inventory collection. Currently, there are some 7,000 publishers in the field with various levels of tools and curriculum. There are many sites, some government supported, for free and open resources. The volumes of digital files and objects in the teacher ranks are massive–for some schools in the millions by count. For some schools, taking inventory can take years and is largely an un-automated area. It is important to mention that the Learning Counsel aided in building a new free social media site called Knowstory, which has inside of it a tool to "invenstory" teacher by teacher. It's the most modern, algorithm-based inventory tool on the market to simplify this potentially mammoth data collecting and processing task. Knowstory allows a merging of inventories by each individual teacher into a collective as each teacher associates with an institution and gives a school their list of learning objects. This, then, can provide a view to a data story about that inventory, also known as a "gap analysis" of what curriculum pieces may be missing.

Step 2. Organize

Most schools to date have given the task of digital asset tracking to their technical staff to collect the major system software, the devices, and network information. They typically leave the information as to what files and what apps to all the individual teachers. This is no longer a sufficient strategy due to the high cost inefficiencies and labor intensiveness behind curriculum work. A good digital curriculum strategy starts by organizing all of the pieces available, and there are quite a few in play for school districts. These include:

- Portals
- Devices
- Networks
- Professional Development
- Apps
- Videos
- Courseware
- Online courses
- Lesson plans of any digital flavor
- Office suites
- Collaboration tools, such as video conferencing
- Virtual reality and field trip tools
- Paid subscription services
- Free subscription services
- Digital/digitized elements (such as documents, video, e-books, lesson plans)
- Resource services, such as plagiarism checkers, online chat staffing, and special needs resources like speech therapy distance educators, YouTube, and more
- Drivers (for printers and 3D imaging)
- Learning Management Systems (LMS)
- Student Information Systems (SIS)
- Instructional Management Systems (IMS)

- Library Management Systems
- Talent Management Systems
- Financial Management Systems
- Procurement Management Systems
- Device management
- Technical skills software, such as Adobe Illustrator or AutoCAD
- Project based hybrids, such as software to run a robot, science instruments, and calculators
- Other tools, such as clickers, polling, testing devices, whiteboards, portfolios

Collect as much detail as possible including what platform the software resides on and all other details about it technically, as well as descriptive tags and any standards it meets academically or technically for easy use and sharing. For major systems, discover and map out how each major system integrates with others, and whether there are application interfaces prebuilt.

A thorough system of managing digital objects and the learning within them, an architecture to hold a ll of this for a school, is what has been missing. Leaning only on a Learning Management System (LMS) is nice if you have a ton of administrators who will centrally manage every single thing. An LMS becomes unworkable for inventory when it is so large it cannot be managed centrally well and must have a decentralized local authority that provides updates to teachers themselves. What will need updating on an almost continual basis is the internal list of what is allowed to be used or is working for teachers. As new publishers provide more digital curriculum and tool choices or refine the systems that deliver them, the five-to-seven year "adoption cycle" of new textbooks is a thing of the past. A strategy needs to account for these pieces and speed of change and figure out how they're going to be used within a distributed system.

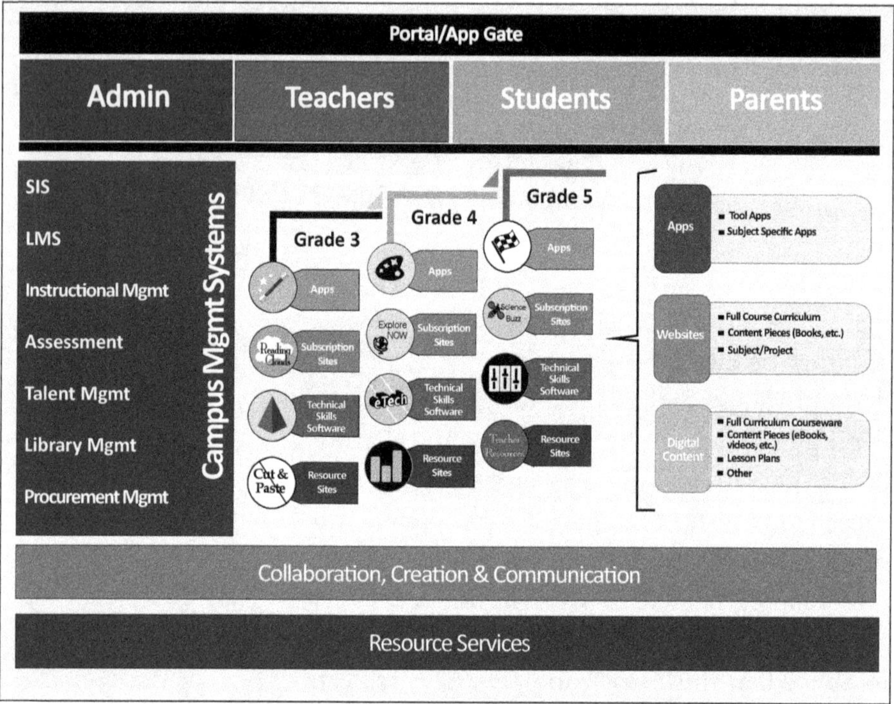

A Model Digital Curriculum & Systems Architecture

One way to visualize these pieces and systems is with this Model Architecture showing:

A. At the top, the portal layer, where the institution relays and displays communication about stake-holder groups, including all administrators, teachers, students, and parents.

B. Along the side, any of the major systems.

C. Then, by grade, and perhaps by subject, all the various apps, websites, courseware, digital content, and the lot.

D. Along the bottom, as a universal layer, the collaboration, creation and communication tools, such as Microsoft Office 365, Google Docs, videoconferencing tools, and every variety of communication app. Resource services would also be a universal pool used by all teachers, and this same pool may carry some of the larger multi-grade and multi-subject online courseware and web book collections.

One other item could be the various pilots run by the school as side attractions; these are used by a few until they make it out of pilot and into the larger pools.

Step 3. Recognize the Difference Between Strategy and Tactics

During planning of a school's architecture for screen learning with all sorts of digital curriculum, it's important to understand the difference between tactics and strategy. A tactic is an individual action that is taken in the implementation of a larger strategy. An example is the distribution of iPads to all students. This is a tactic, and a perfectly good one if there is a strategy backing it up. A good strategy will provide the oversight and direction to use those iPads to change the students' approach to education. And that is one of the strengths of having a thought-out architecture strategy. When digital innovations were previously offered to students, like a computer in the classroom, the decision of how to use it was often made on a teacher level, such as what programs might be on it. Fully implementing digital curriculum is simply too large of an issue to be decided on a classroom-by-classroom basis exclusively. To be effective, a strategy will lay out how every part of the curriculum goes together. Take the straightforward task of taking notes. There are many note-taking apps out there. Deciding on a single note-taking app that students will use through multiple grades means they don't have to learn a new app with every new grade level.

What's interesting is that many school districts are set up via school boards to oversee curriculum selection, but not at the scale needed by schools today. Choosing a few textbooks is one thing, but overseeing every app and every lesson plan is full-time work for several people, even in small districts. Yet a good selection process should be applied to new digital curriculum materials if only to ensure the materials are not rogue and outside basic curriculum maps, as well as ensure that they have security and protect student data privacy. Rather than simply letting students use any app, or letting teachers select the apps that they like, a well-communicated plan can ensure that every app available fits the overall strategy and architecture.

I should note here that this type of higher level strategy doesn't preclude savvy teachers from trying new things, like coming back from conferences and piloting a piece of software. But those *must* be pilots and then proposed to higher levels for broad acceptance and implementation if a new tool's effectiveness in teaching and learning is agreed upon. Consider as well that good ed-tech companies will utilize conferences to announce improvements for their tools and train teachers on their use.

Step 4. Policy Refinement

Now that a school knows where it stands with inventory and a rough architecture has been made known, a refinement of policy is in order. It's important for administrators to write institution-wide policy that makes sense for everyone about what their strategy is so that tactics can be employed by all. Teachers could also implement their own policies and ensure they are not overwhelmed by technological change.

Typically, some policies are made known from the beginning, such as "only buy apps that fit the Android platform," but as schools find out more and more about what is actually happening in detail at the school and teacher level, a refinement or a full shift of policy is going to be self-evident.

Step 5. New Professional Development

As mentioned before, once a school has a change in administration and a technical, model architecture is running a strategy well through policies and all teachers are implementing viable tactics, there will be a need for some new kinds of professional development. The new areas of professional development are also new areas that aren't typically had inside schools. The typical professional development sessions are related to how to teach, how to turn on and maneuver in any new computing device or classroom machine, making accounts in systems, writing digital lesson plans, and the like. For one, a thorough indoctrination on the architecture and policies will be a necessary element for professional training. For another, teacher training is needed on the types of acceptable digital learning objects that comply with all policies, including security, the technical standards, and the aims of the curriculum management teams. Other professional development will be required as to how to truly personalize to one individual student and how to use a lot more human touch to balance the vastly increased tech. There are skills teachers will need professional development on that we are only just starting to see schools talk about – including managing live online teacher chat to help students.

To build the new digital administration of learning, it will be necessary to visualize an ideal scene of blending together the full experience of associating to an institution as a learner, the individual tactics for different types of learners who access different teaching modalities, and an entire community of activities scheduling.

Chapter 18

The Characteristics of Digital Curriculum

When something is defined, you can get multiple people agreeing and building a conversation around it. Since I had spent the years of 2007-2013 visiting many schools and getting on innumerable "demo calls" where publishers would demo their software to me, at one point it became obvious that I knew more about what was going on inside software than most folks. In 2014, I started to keep a list of what I thought of as "the things going on inside curriculum software," and then discussed this growing list over the next year with numerous educators and publishers. In conversations with my staff programmers, I had been making more and more sense of the details of digital curriculum.

While it is true that there are tens of thousands of options right now with the types of digital objects – apps, websites, courseware, eBooks, eTextbooks, assessments, loose content pieces in PDFs or word documents, games, and more arriving in schools – there is hope that it can be mastered from the inside out. More simply put, understanding the inside helps as a first step. I had already looked across the industry to see how the market was fracturing into various publishing types, the view of the *outside* of the transition, so to speak, and had been planning out how to bring some order and understanding to all the commotion with Knowstory.com.

Now with a new "Characteristics List" of digital curriculum evolving from looking at the *inside*,

Key Points

- Low-value versus high-value digitally sophisticated objects make a difference in how much teacher planning versus automated learning goes on.
- How much teachers focus on the learners versus the business of selecting and curating is a balancing act that should be weighted towards quality time spent with learners. Few teachers build highly engaging objects that can compete with ones that are professionally animated and intelligently designed from a software development perspective, but you only really know that when you really know the software capabilities today.

there was another aspect of developing to share with educators. I expect that this list will develop arguments from some, some exclamations of delight from others, a few confusions, and some comments that I have probably missed some important items.

I got to thinking about what's inside curriculum software during my travels across the U.S. with our Digital Curriculum Discussions tour, when I noticed that the national school market typically lands in one of two major camps:

"Organic" schools, where the digital things can run wild at the teaching and learning level.

"Repository" schools and even states, where a central office builds a master repository, usually with a Learning Management System to hold all the "things" or to be a switchboard mechanism into the username/password access of publisher websites.

Both camps have been eager to know more about the developments within digital content and curriculum. Why? Because some of the things are flat and fairly uninteresting digitizations of what was once in the analog-paper world of educational resources. Others are very deep into a foreign world of instructional design crossed with code development, user interface/user experience (UI/UX) high design, and the automation of functions like assessments.

Throughout 2014 and much of 2015, I was looking at what was going on *inside* software, turning digital content *into* courseware. This was what a lot of companies were then starting to get really good at. A lot of discussions with developers, a lot of research and asking what the software mechanisms were trying to do, brought about an ever-expanding confusion of terms. The terms list was attempting to describe what the various digital curriculum was trying to do, and a lot of work went into making sense of it. The Characteristics List became a set of six categories and 71 "characteristics" of what learning software is doing descriptively.

This list of characteristics became the "71 Characteristics of Digital Curriculum Special Report" published in 2015, and then republished because of high demand several other times. The report was not a comment on the rigor of the digital things, but it sparked a new conversation as to how digital curriculum could be changing teaching. It explored the creative ways learning was being evoked through *software* and not just the typical hardware conversation that had priorly dominated.

The reason for this was that printed content is printed content. It is static. It changes only when reprinted. Even in a digitized format, it is still "flat." It cannot talk, convert to a different language on the fly, become interactive, be searched internally on keywords or phrases across multiple of a document species in some instances, assess the ability of the user, or remember where you were when you quit interacting with the content, like the age-old bookmark. Yet when it comes to digital content, this list is only the beginning of the capabilities that can go on and on depending on the digital content, where it resides, how you access it, if it is a singular piece of content or part of a bigger collection, if interaction with the system causes an intelligent learning engine to adapt the digital environment to deliver a more personal experience, or if you can know how your skills rank alongside others interacting with the same content. Digital is "unflat" and that makes all the difference in a changed paradigm to teaching and learning.

Is it important to understand what is happening with the change in content? Resoundingly, yes. Not only is the form of the "content" changing, but the delivery, presentation, interaction, scope, sequence, and adaptability, too. The results of use can also be significantly different. The new capabilities do make the days of textbooks look obsolete. Both traditional and innovative new publishers are racing to put digital curriculum and content in the hands of students. All students can be accommodated through various mechanisms.

There is a real challenge in investigating and implementing digital content. This challenge is partly due to an incomplete understanding of the capabilities and characteristics of digital curriculum. A deeper challenge is the fact that merely digitized or "low technical value documents and videos" *seem* like a transition to digital but are an augmentation to existing pedagogy. They don't bring the promise of going digital, and worse, they add to the overall amount of work teachers have to do. As noted in the original Digital Curriculum Characteristics Scale, at the low end of "going digital" is just documents and single-loop animations. These are things anyone can do if they have a word processing program or can use the embedded animations inside Microsoft PowerPoint to do "single-loop" animations. These take a lot more work by the individual teacher to create than the use of textbooks.

This scale starts with things that could be considered low-technical value with way more work of instructional planning and rises to highly sophisticated software that has more automated learning. Envisioning where virtual reality and "touch screen floors and walls," as well as holograms, will go, it is conjectured that at the very

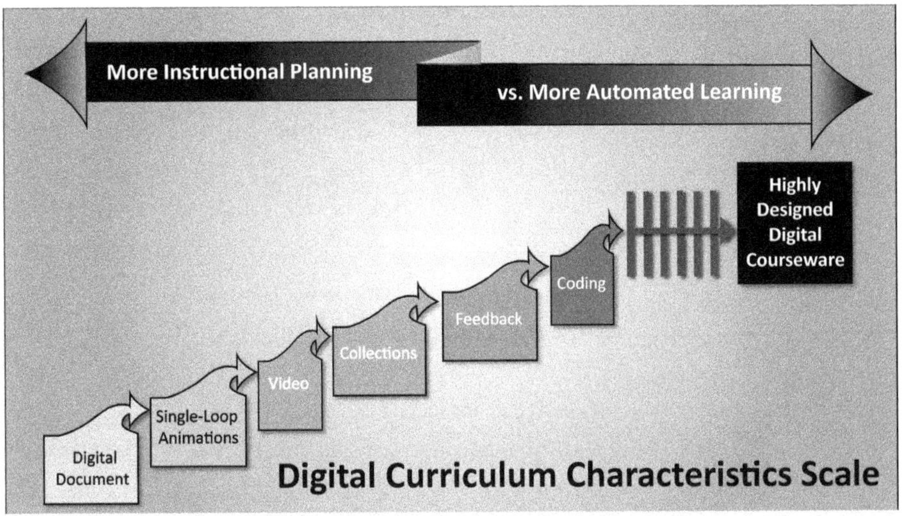

This above scale shows a progression of low-value technical objects up to the more sophisticated objects in terms of the complexity of their programming. At the height of the scale is software that is known as "courseware" and requires very little in the way of instructional planning, because it is the learning plan within a gaming type environment of scope and sequenced learning. A "single-loop animation" is a function like those in PowerPoint or Prezi where any user can do a single-loop action layered on any object to allow it to "swoop in" or "appear" in a timed interval after the slide is already up. A "collection" is often multiple eBooks or videos or objects with a website or App that serves them all to learners by assignment or by user choice. Feedback is something software does to give users the ability to input answers or receive answers on text, pictures, or video. Coding is something done to use a multiplicity of computer code mechanisms to craft a whole learning environment or a simple app to do a function – but by a coder. The range of characteristics in between this and the highest-level of digital object, designed digital courseware, is a wide arena of coding characteristics defined in our "71 Characteristics" Special Report.

highest levels of sophistication, there will be immersive virtual "worlds" that a student enters, which have been called serious gaming spaces. Think of the famed Star Trek "Holodeck," where an entire 3-D world exists holographically, or the "Room of Requirement" of the also-famous Harry Potter books, a magical space that gives you what you need.

The now ever-growing list of "Digital Curriculum Characteristics" describes the capabilities and options. After the 2015 release of the first list, education executives from major school districts began work in 2016 to edit, expand, and find more examples of what is going on inside commercial software to share it with peers nationally.

It's important to understand that "low-value" and "high-value" digital curriculum is a valuation of its *technical rendering,* on a continuum scale based on engagement capability and other user-interface/user-experience considerations. The subject of user interface and user experience is typically considered to be only the domain of programmers, but understanding how humans engage with machines is quickly becoming of high factual importance to teachers and administrators everywhere. A good learning experience from screen learning can only be wrought when the curriculum planner understands, selects, and implements a mix that, by its internal workings, will necessarily achieve the ends.

At the top of the scale is what is considered the "fully-adaptive-immersive-virtual-environment-curriculum-courseware" or shortened to courseware. This is not the same as adaptive curriculum or learning, which may or may not be a full course with scope and sequence along subject or topic lines, but for sure uses intelligent learning engines to "adapt" using pattern recognition and logic to give the right questions to guide the student into paths of learning appropriate to their level and style of learning automatically. The fully adaptive, immersive courseware will be even beyond that, creating a "world" for achievement across a multiplicity of subjects and, of course, including machine learning to adapt to the individual. This is no different than major gaming platforms and products like Siri or Cortana on smartphones or Echo from Amazon, all of which use machine learning to deliver greater and greater value to the individual as they "learn" your preferences.

Many of the new commercially available paid professional resources (PPR) and some free open education resources (OER) offer these leaps ahead with automation.

These characteristics do not address *rigor,* only the character of the digital learning object's development or programming within six categories. By the time this book is finished, there will be seven or more categories to include security and student data privacy and more characteristics, such as creative inception mind-mapping, back-up for self-review, timers, and more. The list in this chapter is the original and updates will be available at LearningCounsel.com.

Understanding this list is important in that how much teachers focus on the learners versus the business of selecting and curating is a balancing act that should be weighted towards quality time spent with learners. Few teachers build highly engaging objects that can compete with ones that are professionally animated and intelligently designed from a software development perspective, but you only really know that when you really know the software capabilities.

The 71 Characteristics are just that – how the software itself manifests utility. These are *not types of software*, but what is going on inside much of the software available. Of course, all digital curriculum and content is assumed to also have actual instructional value, something to learn, a lesson, a bit, chunk, or wide amount of knowledge. That's the "given" in the entire list.

The six major categories for better understanding and differentiation:

Actions:
Functions of the code that do things, generally, singularly, and discretely, without involvement with other processes.

Aesthetics:
Design or dressing or engagement-oriented elements.

Controls:
Administrative capabilities or reporting.

Individualizations:
Means of making unique, keeping in mind that "individualization" is something you do for someone else and "personalization" is when it is something one does for oneself.

Instructs:
Lesson-giving qualities.

Mechanisms:
Processes or techniques, generally longer

71 Digital Curriculum Characteristics by Category

Category:

Actions – Functions of the code that do things, generally, singularly, and discretely, without involvement with other processes.

1. **Audio Enhancement**
   Interaction with the content or even the delivery system includes sounds to provide audio cueing to help direct the student to respond. Buttons, clicks, appropriate and inappropriate responses, and music are just a few examples. Specifically, downbeats might signify an incorrect attempt or trial, while upbeats signify a win, and music tracks provide drama and more.

2. **Live Chat/Instant Messaging**
   Live chat or instant messaging is the ability to synchronously chat with another person via a text-based communication tool(s). This type of tool can be a stand-alone app or a built-in ability of a larger platform. This tool can allow two or more persons to communicate at one time and teachers to guide learning from a distance or even in class during individual study.

3. **Live Video**
   Live video is the ability to synchronously communicate with another via video with audio. This type of tool can be a stand-alone app or a built-in ability of a larger platform. This tool can allow two or more persons to communicate at one time via video with audio.

4. **Annotating**
   With a cursor, mouse, or digital stylus, students can place notations, highlights, comments, etc., into the body of the content presented. These annotations can be stored, and even possibly organized and manipulated, for later use by the student.

5. **Accessibility**
   On or offline access to strong digital content is a must. For example, the requirement for constant internet access to read and work on assignments, as well as in-school internet bandwidth pressure, is still a struggle in many places. Apps like HMH Player™ allow students to upload and download materials, including interactive features such as videos, when online, enabling off-line access to digital content.

Disabilities Access – In 1996, the U.S. Department of Justice clarified that the Americans with Disabilities Act (ADA) requirements apply to all programs offered on the Internet, which include all educational digital materials for students, as well as all digital professional conference materials. This means that web page materials and formalized online courses and programs must be made available to qualified individuals with disabilities and apply the Universal Design for Learning (UDL) framework to the degree possible. Understanding this in its entirety is starting to be addressed nationally for all areas of disabilities.[1]

6. **Social Gaming**
   Social gaming includes online games that may or may not be educational. These games can be for students of any age. These games can be played individually or with others in groups ranging from small to large. Results of

the individual player can possibly be posted and viewed in comparison to others playing the game.

7. **Spell Checkers**
   The ability to check the spelling of words, definitions, derivations, live-pronunciations, and parts of speech.

8. **Spatial Temporal-Reasoning**
   Intentional non-use of language or lecture-based instruction in favor of interactive, symbol-manipulation animations that visually represent mathematical concepts to improve conceptual understanding and problem-solving skills.

9. **Dynamic Definitions**
   The ability to access the definition of a word or phrase instantly from the immediate screen. This allows the student to go back to an earlier chunk of content to better understand that foundational definition. Definitions can be open for modification by students or curriculum leaders wanting to change them because of some new development. For example, if the content is about a science concept, and if there is a new discovery made commercially, the definition can be shifted. Additionally, if there is a reason for the leadership to shift a definition because of beliefs, advanced digital curriculum allows for an administrator-level user to do so.

10. **Probeware Viewing**
    Probeware hardware viewing is an action of software (i.e., microscopes displaying their

magnification right onto laptop screens). The software interfaces with and graphs incoming activity from scientific probeware instruments, such as digital microscopes, sound sensors, motion encoders, spectrometers, and more. This is not the same as device input which includes the incoming data within a lesson plan or project.

11. **Social Interaction**
    The embedded capability for students to synchronously communicate while learning but beyond one-to-one within a social environment. For example, students might share what they are getting out of materials with others in their classes. This makes use of the texting and social media that is already so familiar to students.

12. **Sketching**
    The ability to write, draw, or illustrate within an application as part of the practice or response process.

13. **Gambling**
    Gambling is something that can be done inside many commercially available games and on many sites, and it is banned in some areas of the U.S. There are some groups who would contend that the use of "coins" is representative of "gambling" within learning tools where the student is "spending" to purchase some device in the hopes of winning some at the end. Even if the learning tool is not using actual money but merely showing something symbolic of money, like gold coins, such a device could be construed to be teaching the

student to gamble and should be avoided based on potential conflicts with religious preferences or legal constraints.

14. Touch Enabled

The experience of interacting with a digital device through touch. The interaction modality has become second nature to most students. Their interactive preference for mobile phones and tablets is definitely touch enablement. The expectation is that the software experience takes advantage of touch regardless of form.

Category:

Aesthetics – Design or dressing or engagement -oriented elements.

15. Character(s)

The use of animated or actor characters within the content. The character could be someone of significance to the topic covered in the lesson or unit – for example, Abraham Lincoln – and dressed up in period costume or rendered in period outfits. Period costume or authentic dress would be utilized to make the character appropriate for the information being conveyed.

16. Voice

The use of recorded reading of text for playback on-demand. For example, an audio book.

17. Virtual Reality

An artificial 3D environment, such as a maker lab or "world" that consists of images and sounds created by a computer and is affected by the actions of a person who is experiencing it, including editing it or using manipulative interactive gloves, a stylus, glasses, an extra monitor, or other specialized holographic image creators.

18. Animations

From single-looped (like those anyone can do in a simple presentation) to full-motion cartoon animation, the use of animation today is unlimited. Higher value digital content and curriculum necessarily will have high-value animation embedded. The value of animation is that it can be played and replayed as needed for mastery learning.

19. Visual Advantages

The use of non-animated infographics, such as a backdrop photo of a landscape being discussed in the unit, or an image that shows a concept or person being discussed in a lesson, is similar to books and may be interactively linked.

20. Video Embedding

The inclusion of video as part of the content. An example of this is HMH's HISTORY®. HMH's core social studies curriculum infuses HISTORY® assets, bringing history to life with anytime, anywhere mobile access to videos and biographies that can be used to enhance classroom instruction and add a visual element to the teaching and learning of history and politics.

21. Avatars

In computing and digital learning, an avatar is the embodiment of a person or idea. In the computer world, an avatar specifically refers to a character that represents a user online. Avatars are commonly used in multiplayer gaming and online communities. When combined with intelligent learning engines, the avatar could take on a greater level of importance to the student in their learning.

Category:

Controls – Administrative capabilities or reporting.

22. Dynamic Curation

Dynamic curation is the ability to take individual "pieces" or chunks of content and place them into a repository for use. The closest thing to this vision is a Learning Management System, which is more of a repository for building out an inventory. That inventory may be full digital curriculum courses or it may be a lot of content pieces and lesson plans. We see the future as adaptability for dynamic curation by administrative users for subscription systems much like current customer relationship management systems do, such as Salesforce.com. Industry standard-setting organizations, such as IMS Global, are aiding in making digital curriculum and content "curate-able" by promoting interoperability standards for content. Dynamic curation may also apply to individual digital courseware wherein a function allows students to drag and drop in elements or chunks to their own collections to create portfolios or reports.

23. Plagiarism Checking

The ability to check the originality and authenticity of a student's work is the purpose of advanced plagiarism-checking sites and services.

24. Interoperable

The capability of a product or system to interact and function with others. Open and interoperable learning management systems, longitudinal data solutions, and digital content are becoming increasingly important in the education sector. Common cartridge compliant solutions and programs that align with IMS Global Standards can be used in open environments and provide educators with greater choice and flexibility.

25. Project-Based

Digital curriculum is built or can be linked in a manner to allow for projects to be assigned and tracked by teachers as they are being done by individual students or groups of students.

26. Gating

Gating is the ability of a teacher or adaptive learning engines incorporated into the curriculum platform to determine the progress of a student through learning. The gating controls would allow a student to move ahead or be redirected into remedial material based on their performance. Gating makes digital curriculum much easier to individualize for each student.

27. Analytics

Analytics based on student achievement for lessons takes old-style grading to a whole new level. With embedded analytics capabilities and screen learning, teachers can see exactly how students are doing with each lesson. Multiple data points, such as time spent, accuracy of response, or number of solutions can be collected, measured, and reported without paper. The efficiencies of digital analytics are great, and the enablement of individualization and personalization even better. Feedback can be as timely as needed to inform instruction.

28. Self-Contained Learning System

Digital curriculum and content, and all its associated tools for access, management, and reporting, contained within one learning system.

29. Metrics

Metrics are calculations performed on data from the data collection infrastructure to describe what is occurring (depending on what data you are collecting). These can be rendered with or without analysis, allowing the end user the ability to choose when making judgments about what the data mean.

30. Grouping

Grouping students per levels or by interests helps students grow in ways that maintain their enthusiasm for what they are learning. This may occur at the direction of the teacher or through the recommendation of intelligent or adaptive learning engines based on the analysis of student data.

31. Data Collection Infrastructure

A system for warehousing data generated by interaction with a delivery system of the curriculum and content. Digital curriculum publishers and learning management system providers are collecting information to make inferences, provide suggestions, or draw inferences. With the application of learning from statistics, intelligence learning engines, machine learning, and neuroscience, publishers are working to mine the databases and infrastructure to provide useful feedback for teachers and students that was never available with textbooks.

32. **Enveloping/Pull Mechanisms**
    Enveloping and pull technologies address the need to protect intellectual property rights of specific content. To maintain control of the content, mechanisms for delivering a "protected" version to users are being developed that let the administrator of that system control how that content is then consumed. The end-user device can use the content only as prescribed, and the system administrator can remove, or pull, the content from end-user devices on demand.

33. **Favoriting**
    The concept of "favoriting" something has become commonplace in online commerce sites and social media thanks to feedback mechanisms designed into these platforms. "Favoriting" serves as the method for promoting items or topics that are useful or of interest. This ability within dynamic curation repositories, discussion boards, etc., provides a way to crowd-source what is potentially better or most useful in the teaching and learning process.

34. **Administrative Personalization**
    Teacher ability to manage student access to and progress through the curriculum to maintain motivation and attention and ensure mastery learning. For example, student progress through

learning activities can be manipulated by the teacher in the best interest of the students' demonstrated learning or need for extra support.

35. Second Screen

Second screen learning refers to the "syncing" of the content to be viewed. Rather than students independently viewing material, second screen refers to content that is asynchronously viewed from teacher to student. The teacher controls the pace of the material viewed by all students on their individual screens or one shared by a small group.

36. Projection

The ability to share content on one or more screens. This can be asynchronous or synchronous projection, depending on the need. New device management also allows teachers to control all screens in their class at once, a form of projection that keeps everyone on the same task. In addition, the "projection" within the software has options to show part but perhaps not all of what is on the teacher or student's screen at that moment within that app, system, or site.

37. Portability

The ability to access and interact with content across multiple hardware devices of different screen size, input method, and operating system platform. Standards institutions, such as IMS Global, work to ensure that digital curriculum meets standards and can be delivered over any device.

Category:

Individualization – Means of making unique, keeping in mind that individualization is something you do for someone else and personalization is when it is something one does for oneself.

38. Feedback

Feedback opportunities allow the end user, in this case educators and/or students, the ability to provide written comments to the publisher or creator. Feedback may also include a rating scale that the end user may complete to share their level of satisfaction, from which an average rating for display can be calculated.

39. Student Personalization

The personalization of student learning allows the student to adapt the software to their preference of topics, outcomes, and pace. Digital curriculum by many publishers is built in this adaptive way. Students can be unleashed and gated forward to complete more than one grade-level equivalent of material in a single year. Others can choose more remediation that bolsters their mastery of the material before going ahead. Preference can be determined in consultation with a teacher, who in turn makes the necessary settings within the learning system (i.e., teacher individualization).

40. Multiple Languages

The capability of digital content to be quickly converted from one language to another, with both print and audio.

41. Collections

Software "libraries" of multiple assets, like books, videos, and other learning objects, usually wrapped with gradations such that a student is placed at his or her "level" by pre-assessment and continues from there.

42. Work Product Curation

The ability to store student work product for retrieval and review over a period of time within a digital learning system.

Category:

Instructs – Lesson-giving qualities.

43. Chunking

The process of presenting the curriculum and content that, 1) takes smaller pieces of information/benchmarks and combines them to make a unit of material for learning unified by a common theme or big idea, and 2) then presents the "chunk" to fit the screen size of the device of choice. Paper textbooks have always "chunked" material into chapters, but new digital materials are doing this in a different way – chunking even smaller and then using other new characteristics like clip or video embedding to demonstrate a concept. Students can follow directional arrows and pictures to interesting tidbits and quizzes. The benefits of providing less, as in curated-down minimalist text and more digital characteristics, give audio learners, text learners, visual learners, and explorers-of-tangents a different experience.

44. Intervention

Intervention programs are built to meet the needs of students performing below grade level. Tools that utilize adaptive technology can support teachers working with struggling students by providing tailored assistance that helps raise their achievement and abilities.

45. Training

Embedded "How-To" or professional learning in order to maximize teacher productivity and student achievement using the device, system, or content. This can be embedded training modules that help teachers be able to incorporate and deliver content effectively or that train students on how the system will work for them.

46. Project Mastery

Through a project as an individual or as a small group, the student has a computer-based project that culminates with the demonstration of mastery of one or more skills or knowledge sets. For example, a complex coding problem, illustrative challenge, writing exam project, or a combination of skill elements that are selected and then demonstrably mastered.

47. Distance Live-Lab

When physical distance or geography prevents the use of laboratory settings in order to perform exercises required for a class, a "virtual" lab can be used to facilitate the learning. In this scenario, the environment used by the student mimics as closely as possible all steps and manipulations that need to occur in order to perform a lab exercise. Recent advances in holographic and virtual reality computing will greatly enhance this type of environment simulation soon.

48. **Content or Course Authoring**
    The software provides a framework for building an eBook or lesson or lesson plan.

49. **Terminology**
    The better digital curriculum and content keeps a terminology reference list as part of the program that is reachable as a tab or link, and all newly introduced words in the material are linked with either a pop-up or drop-down definition.

50. **Interactive Queries**
    Student or admin originated multi-layered queries are embedded or enabled through the system. Unlike flat texts or jaunts to the library, students can reach resources instantly and also do interactive queries of major data repositories to know the state of things in real-time.

51. **Programming Practice**
    The ability for students to practice programming for things like manipulating robots. Through their own programming input, they are achieving the objectives of specific digital curriculum targeted at teaching math or scientific concepts.

52. **Inference**
    Guided by the data collection performed as students interact with the digital curriculum system, inference can be made about the progress of the student. It is the job of the inference

engine to apply knowledge based on the knowledge base of the current situation. These inferences can be based on unbiased analysis of the data to help the teacher better understand the needs of a student. These inferences generated by pattern recognition could possibly be a superior method to evaluate students. Common biases, such as race, sex, socio-economic status, personality, and ambition (attributes that might consciously or subconsciously bias analysis) can be left out of the interpretation of student performance.

53. Clip Embedding

A clip is a short animation of a single, simple concept. Clip embedding is a multi-media addition to the material of a very short duration. It may be an animated cycle or graph. It could also be an excerpt from a historical address with a picture of the speaker. A clip is not full-motion video.

54. Standards Alignment/Attainment

With the advent of the Common Core State Standards, many schools have scrambled to try to find and organize appropriate content and adapt their pedagogy to fit the demands of mastery. New digital curriculum has been built specifically to address standards and remove a lot of the work of hunting through older materials. In addition, as mentioned prior with mastery, new digital curriculum provides practice for students with embedded capabilities.

Category:

Mechanisms – Processes or techniques, generally longer than actions.

55. Machine Learning

The following definition of machine learning comes from Wikipedia: "Machine learning is a subfield of computer science that evolved from the study of pattern recognition and computational learning theory in artificial intelligence. Machine learning explores the construction and study of algorithms that can learn from and make predictions on data. Such algorithms operate by building a model from example inputs to make data-driven predictions or decisions, rather than following strictly static program instructions." What does this mean for education? Think of learning platforms for knowledge learning that require scaffolded skill sets to keep advancing in knowledge attainment and understanding. The application platform could continuously monitor and adjust to the needs of the student, accelerating them, refreshing them, or remediating them as necessary based on the performance of the student. The key differentiator here is that this level of software builds its own adaptations.

56. Practice Microgames

Short, single skill, or object learning games of short duration. For example, a link to a puzzle to show some concept rather than merely adding a note or source, allowing kids to play to learn.

57. **Social Experimentation**
Safety alert! These are games that can be found online that are really collecting data in a social experiment as to how humans react to things and could be tracking computer IDs of students, which isn't disclosed to them. Even if the site or game is not asking for identity, it could possibly obtain the identity of the individual whose machine is being used through a triangulation of other available commercial data.

58. **Formative Assessment**
Assessment conducted during the instructional process designed to monitor learning as it occurs. Conducted in a variety of ways depending on the type of learning, formative assessment provides just-in-time feedback to adjust the pace of learning via either teacher monitoring or adaptive learning engines.

59. **Pre-Assessment**
The evaluation of what a student knows or can do prior to learning occurring.

60. **Coding**
Computer language code or an order of logical operations created as part of the learning.

61. **Game-Based Learning**
The practice of and demonstration of learning using a game or game-like environment. The elements of a full game (one with purpose(s), freedoms, and barriers) can culminate in real challenges and recognition of accomplishment for students who can play simulations utilizing learning related to one or more areas of study.

Performing well by demonstration of mastery of abilities within the game can be rewarded with systematic recognition (for example, leader boards or rankings) as well as social recognition.

62. Gaming Rewards

Games are often engaged in because of the competition or rivalry between one or more persons. This competition is the motivation to play well in order to achieve a positive outcome. Rewards for successful game play do not need to be an outright "win," but can also be performance at various levels. The ability to replay and receive higher value rewards is the motivation of students to continue in the game play until a more satisfactory outcome is achieved. In digital curriculum, the concept of gaming rewards can be applied in many different ways in order to maintain student motivation to complete the desired course of learning over time.

63. Real-Time Attention Data/Neuro-determinism

Uses keyboard or eye tracking to adjust lesson developments or evaluate comprehension. By monitoring combinations of various physical response and/or brainwave data, digital curriculum software can monitor for such variables as time to answer and more. This input is analyzed in real time to make the curriculum adapt in even more precise ways to that student, depending on the need for such adaptation.

64. Device Input

Probes, sensors, or other single-purpose devices can enhance learning by collecting data being used within experimentation or a project. Sensors that can measure acceleration, three-dimensional movement, and temperature are plugged into computing devices to interface with software for data capture during student assignments, can provide an element to an overall lesson or project. For example, advanced calculators can provide added value alongside math software. Video capture allows for teachers to see students demonstrate understanding of an idea or concept or curate the completion or outcome of a task.

65. Intelligent Learning Engines (Pattern Recognition & Adaptation)

This is a capability in what is known as the "adaptive" sorts of curriculum software in that, in a certain lesson with a certain objective, if the student keeps getting something "wrong" in a certain pattern, the learning engine adapts with a new track of questions or alerts the teacher to intervene.

66. Gesture Controlled Data

The detection of physical movement and gestures by devices created to sense these activities has become highly reliable. The gaming industry is already commercializing this industry as part of the game playing experience. But when gesture control is combined with information systems that allow the manipulation and display of data in original ways, the ability to explore the relationship of the information takes on new capabilities.

67. Collaboration-Ware

Those software tools and platforms that enable multi-student authoring of content (documents, spreadsheets, presentations, etc.). Communication between individuals or groups may also be an integral part of the tool or platform. Versioning, reviewing tools, and change-management can also be functionality included to further enhance the ability to collaborate.

68. Assembly

Think puzzles, pictures, diagrams, or operations that when assembled would show a sequence, visual elements that are required to be assembled in a specific manner. The components of each could be manipulated with a cursor, pointer, finger, or stylus by the student in order to complete the proper order of the assembly.

69. Manipulative-Object Interplay

The use of a separate physical object in conjunction with a digital device that causes interaction between the physical object and the application on the digital device.

70. Summative Assessment

An assessment given after a period of learning to determine the mastery of knowledge and/or skill by a student.

71. Artificial Intelligence

Per Wikipedia, artificial intelligence is: "The intelligence exhibited by machines or software. It is also the name of the academic field of study, which studies how to create computers

> and computer software that are capable of intelligent behavior. Major A.I. researchers and textbooks define this field as 'the study and design of intelligent agents', [1] in which an intelligent agent is a system that perceives its environment and takes actions that maximize its chances of success, and [2] real A.I. is above machine-based learning by definition in its perceptivity. Machine-based learning is greater than Intelligent Learning Engines, which are pre-determined pattern recognition, which then shunts the learner down a pre-built additional path or alert loop."
>
> It is important to know and understand this definition to know what are and are not accurate claims by digital education content providers as to the true capabilities of their learning delivery systems. Artificial intelligence, as it has been defined by preeminent mathematicians, is not something the Learning Counsel has yet been able to find in learning software – yet.

So, there you have it.

71 Digital Curriculum Characteristics for digital curriculum and content – so far. In coordination with leading educators, we are currently working on an update due to be published soon.

When looking to introduce new curriculum and content into the teaching and learning process, especially if it is the first-time digital curriculum and content will be implemented, a holistic inventory and audit is not only advisable, but imperative. Look at what is available commercially or even free and look at your pedagogy – ask "Why?" The new software available may change the dynamics at the classroom level, and consideration must be given to the teacher's time – time to plan, time to teach, and time to take care of the logistics of both.

Digital curriculum and content that would be the core curriculum should be inspected closely against your class or school goals. Why? Because if there is a goal to individualize student learning, it will require that the teacher plans out a multitude of digital learning objects for each student, not just a single plan for the whole class or small group – unless a full curriculum software is chosen to do much of the individualization itself. Planning for each student in the digital realm will typically take more time than writing the "whole-class" lesson plans of old. Even supplemental curriculum will require a greater level of attending-to from the teacher to be meaningful. It is not fully adaptive, immersive-environment-type software with tons of the above characteristics embedded in it, but bits of video, apps and pieces.

The road to building your digital curriculum and content story as a school, a district, or a teacher is a wide open one – but becoming knowledgeable about what is going on in it may save many schools from becoming irrelevant while they pick things that only digitize the old ways and are not truly "digital."

[1] National Instructional Materials Accessibility Standard (NIMAS), *National Center on Accessible Education Materials*, http://aem.cast.org/creating/national-instructional-materials-accessibility-standard-nimas.html#.VhcqhWvVuql http://www.setda.org/wp-content/uploads/2014/03/SETDA_PolicyBrief_Accessibility_FNL.5.29.pdfhttp://teachinghistory.org/issues-and-research/roundtable-response/25092

Chapter 19

Evaluating Digital Curriculum

Discernment between curriculum materials has always been the job of educators. Today it is important to discern whether digital learning objects are granular or systematized, where they are at on a scale of curated free document-type lesson plans and home-built learning objects via build-curriculum-yourself customization software (authorware) versus professionally coded courseware, and whether either one has all the elements of rigor. Here we will delve deeper into how to think about digital resources and how leaders and teachers alike can create a method to evaluate all their options.

> **Key Point**
>
> In evaluating digital learning objects, it is important to discern whether they are discrete, granular objects, like a single word document, or systematized, where they are on scales of home-built via customization software (authorware) versus professionally coded courseware, and whether they have all the elements of rigor.

The Digital Scene

The power and depth of digital curriculum and its ability to reach and engage students continues to evolve. There are tens of millions of digital learning objects, including the massive numbers of items that are in the free and open education resources sites. There have always been seemingly tens of thousands of books and options, but now in the digital arena, the number of *companies* seems to have massively expanded. Now the trend is to build in virtual reality languages.

Hunting around for digital learning objects and inspecting them once they're found is a nationwide undertaking being played out in every school and by every teacher across the land. There is hope in the construction of Knowstory.com, where a personal inventory against requirements, standards, lesson time used and more, and the sharing of those inventories with others who might want to copy parts of it to use in their own teaching or learning, can help bring order to the great sifting and refining of all these digital things.

Educational leaders want to differentiate various digital learning objects. They also want to have some stability and workability in their digital resources. A new problem of *digital* continuity of operation is at hand as files and lesson plan storage is not the same as handing a substitute or new teacher a textbook that has already been in use. The complexity of operation for digital stewardship is an important new consideration of leaders.

Digital Object Sophistication

What is essential for educators to think with is the **degree to which an object is digitally fashioned**. How digitally sophisticated is it? As content started to go digital, the initial learning objects were static bits of knowledge. Examples of such content include links to sites and excerpts from books, loose videos out on YouTube and unsophisticated databases of text-based information. As network speed and capacity improved, these objects evolved to be more sophisticated, such as full courseware with embedded video and virtual reality.

Many of the free Open Educational Resources (OER) came out of greater academic works that were "atomized" into little bits that could be mixed and matched up with lessons as needed. Think about ripping up a whole textbook into chapters and the chapters into the individual concepts inside each one, and you get a picture of how many objects live now on the open Internet. Initially, a lot of the work of curating these "chunks" of knowledge into a meaningful scope and sequence for learning occurred manually by educators for consumption by students. They must be meta-tagged and filed and the path to finding them well traveled. Even after all that work is done they may still be disassociated from larger contexts of learning, like how textbooks were planned works with defined scope and sequence.

Chunks & Lesson Planning vs. Courseware

Compared to courseware organized into a sequential progression of chapter-type elements with quizzes at the end, all the various chunks of video and text are non-sequential little bits of knowledge that require the work of contextualizing from teachers to make them into something meaningful. That curation and sequencing is called digital lesson planning, and while the objects themselves may be copyrighted or open-licensed, in many instances the lesson plan framework around them is automatically the intellectual copyright of the school or district and not the teacher's, although this is rarely known by most teachers. There are still arguments that could be had about whether the act of creating a framework around other licensed works is itself a "work" to be copyrighted or simply a compilation effort, like collecting movies of a genre together in a reference library and critiquing and comparing them one against another in a blog about the whole genre. The ideological difference between this sort of library-plus-blog and a lesson plan framework is minor, and the Learning Counsel predicts the future copyright issues around what text or framing was uniquely created versus simply curated will be numerous, because the mixing-and-matching is a growing new area of art for digital teaching.

Since many times teachers never used the entire textbook for a subject in the past, the chunking idea is great in some respects. It allows a certain freedom, but it is more work than buying the equivalent of a textbook or the new digital textbook that has been re-modernized into the "full courseware" idea.

One courseware provider, Dreambox, has this to say on their website about courseware:

> **Courseware**
> *"Our innovative technology captures every interaction a student makes while working within and between lessons. As it dynamically adapts and individualizes instruction in real time, it provides millions of learning paths tailored to each student's unique needs. It is a ground-breaking, student-driven learning environment that leverages gaming fundamentals to inspire and empower students to build 21st century thinking and problem solving skills, master key concepts, increase achievement, and boost long-lasting confidence in learning."* – Dreambox Learning (http://www.dreambox.com/company)

Courseware has programming aspects that deliver the most appropriate type of object in sequence for learning, just like teachers do. This is critical for good digital lessons, along with individualizing that object so that it's the right one for that specific student user. Courseware is simply log-in-and-go-through-the-lessons, pre-built and structured in some instances to offer "levels" much like games do so that faster or slower students go routes unique to them or are looped back into multiple avenues of remedial learning.

Choose with a Consumer Attitude

The ability to distinguish a digital learning object that is "flat" (for example, a text document that does not do anything – the lowest level of object) from an entire program of courses that are animated and contain internal logic requires a different mindset. In fact, the consideration would need to be more than an academic attitude – it would require a *consumer attitude* and a designer view about the user interface and user experience. Such an attitude would guarantee a higher level of user appreciation and therefore have a heavy impact on learning. But beware! Just because it's glamorous does not mean it teaches. Early software was more glitz than substance.

Consumers are drawn to appeals promised by software that are usually very simple. A game like Candy Crush allows a player to do exactly that, crush digital candy. It is also *only* doing that. Courseware is changing this over-simplification of appeal with a consumer appeal to *accomplishment*, which is an implied appeal in game apps but usually not emphasized because it is only a game, so getting a high score is not an actual achievement level in life like finishing a course or graduating. The more sophisticated courseware is a game world of options and sometimes allows teachers to assign or "lever" learners into certain routes within it.

Whether an object is just one concept or a collection of concepts incorporated into courseware is an issue for educators to come to grips with by actually looking inside and experiencing all the routes of courseware. The same is not as true for direct learning courseware consumers who have typically had experiences with e-commerce and gaming worlds online which have already raised their level of expectation for learning objects. They expect the software to navigate them. Educators typically do not expect this, but the K12 market is now smaller than the open consumer market for learning. Therefore, we see publishers creating awesome digital courseware and massive collections of digital objects that have suggested meta-tags for student reading levels and more with the navigation consumers expect. When schools use courseware, it is an adjustment for the teacher who must learn two things:

1. **How to use it.**
   The full breadth of the courseware and how it is structuring learning, where it allows the teacher to interject, and what sorts of analytics it provides.

2. **How to supplement it.**
   How the use of the courseware will replace old pedagogy and allow the teacher to use it as core while the teacher now *flips* the learning and focuses on supplemental activities, projects, and some lecturing. This is one of the real revolutions in digital. However, it is *no different than the days of textbooks.* Textbooks had to be considered for how to use and how to supplement, but in the early days of digital

publishing, the learning objects were the dead opposite – supplemental and not core. Teachers already know how to do this well.

What's also interesting about courseware is that the consumer/learner can see it fit itself to them as they use it. This is the same way that our intelligent assistants like Siri or Cortana on our phones work. It is also the true definition of "personalization" in the software world. For consumers and high numbers of screen-learning students (in-class activity or out of a school), curriculum software products need to be highly systematized and courses that contain preset programs that can be personalized will be expected. An everyone-is-the-same experience and a whole lot of odd navigational quirks that cause large amounts of user questions will fail, as some publishers experienced in their early forays into online sales and customer support.

Again, when learning objects are only discrete concepts, they present more work for teachers to curate and frame. However, and this is one of the more interesting things to consider, when students themselves curate, discrete learning objects that are not systematized represent a rebirth of *discovery* as part of the learning process. Allowing them to do that is the tricky part if the school's system is built to only allow teacher discovery, manipulation and assignment of learning objects, and the student is still a passive receiver-only of the pre-determined set of objects.

Optimum Digital

Teachers tend to do better with optimally aggregated digital learning objects, full courseware, for at least 60% of their materials. These should be used for a maximum of 40% of lesson time used in screen learning with the rest being active discussion, lab, and other activities, projects, and the like. Full courseware or collections that function autonomously give teachers back more of their much-needed classroom time to individualize learning and give their attention to students. The promise of the emerging industry of digital courseware, both for-profit and free, can return teachers to greater time spent on student interaction and the "human side" to balance the screen learning.

EVALUATING DIGITAL LEARNING OBJECTS

Evaluating any digital learning object is complex, because, like textbooks, it can't be done based on just its title or marketing claims. It must be done with each of the concepts inside the software, and sometimes there are a large number in any one learning object. Unfortunately, being a "software guru" and knowing what you are looking at in terms of how well something is designed for interface and rigor is not something that any research or ratings firm other than the Learning Counsel has a handle on.

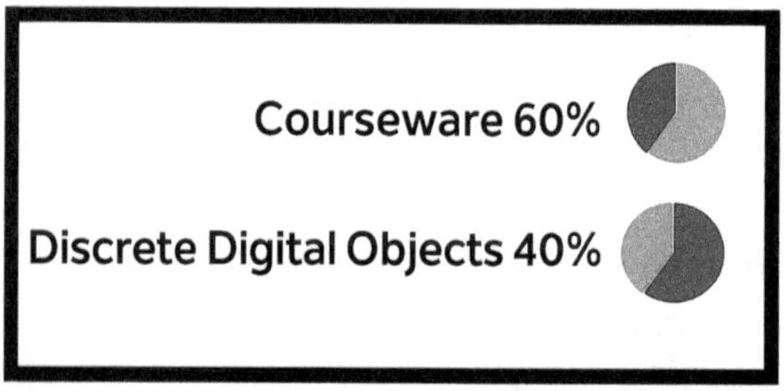

Courseware 60%

Discrete Digital Objects 40%

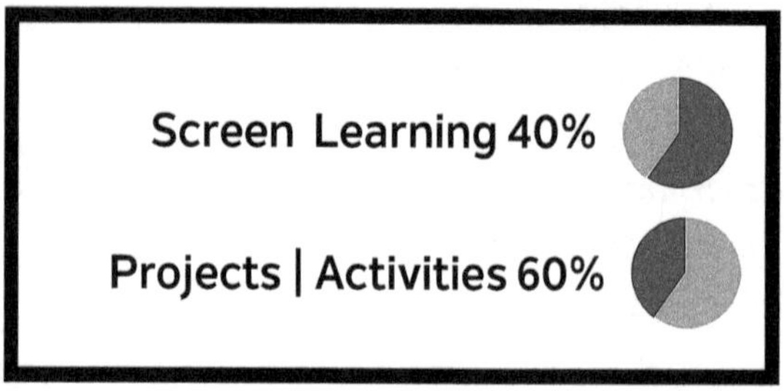

Screen Learning 40%

Projects | Activities 60%

Merriam-Websters defines the noun "concept" as the "idea of what something is or how it works." When that definition is used for evaluation, the digital learning object is either a single concept or can be partitioned into multiple concepts. Evaluators are then analyzing objects in the same way that developing software is done – by each concept being coded individually.

To do this you must look at and validate each part of the digital learning object *by experiencing it.*

The Super-Hurried Evaluation

Evaluating digital learning objects *by concept* is arguably the best way to evaluate what the worth of a digital object is because it can be broken down into three things.

Example

Concept: Identifying Past Tense in Language Arts – 1st Grade. (Example lesson from IXL Learning, see: https://www.ixl.com/ela/grade-1/form-and-use-the-regular-past-tense)

1. Technical and **design** sophistication.

By looking at the application, there is clearly a single focus on each web page with a practice question for fill out that is clear to see and centered, without any distraction, and it is offering feedback of how much time is ticking off per each practice question. It could perhaps use more stylizing with a digital character guide appealing to different age sets, like Mickey Mouse greeting software guests as they enter some Disney Interactive lessons.

2. Completeness of knowledge coverage (actual **instruct**).

The software is dynamically giving practice but does not appear to give lesson context for what past tense means as a lesson – it is therefore most probably something to classify as supplemental and not core curriculum.

3. The combination of the first two in the digital realm that results in the ability to *cause* learning, a.k.a. "**rigor**."

The software appears rigorous from the definition of being right in each practice question and the design is functional and not distractive. So, in summary, this one concept of all the IXL Learning lesson concepts appears to be 1) technical design appropriate, 2) supplemental instructional (practice), and 3) rigorous – at least upon cursory review of that one lesson within the total number of lessons in their website collection.

People are already generally using these simple 1-2-3 steps of concept evaluation when looking at digital learning objects. Design-plus-instruct-plus-rigorousness are the major points and comprise the "super hurried" evaluation.

Scoring an object across these three most important things *in detail* requires a sort of "matrix" to evaluate, and that is what we are presenting to you here in this article.

Regular Hurry – Overall Evaluation Using Level 1 of the Matrix

If you're in a *regular* hurry, you can use the comprehensive new Digital Curriculum Evaluation Matrix to do a rapid evaluation using just the "Overall" points. You would only get into using the entire matrix if it's a major adoption. Teachers or committees of curriculum experts can make rapid analysis just on the Overall points.

Schools can figure out their own specific number score for digital learning objects for overall value using the Overall section of the Matrix. Highly sophisticated programs can take a short amount of time to evaluate by looking at each characteristic of the software and experiencing it from a user point of view. Using the list of just the items in "Level 1 – Overall," anyone can make a quick mental calculation of those things for that object. These are listed below in numbers 1 – 7.

This ideology of how you would take a quick-look or go deeply into inspecting any piece of software for what it is and does as a learning object is a work-in-progress.

Level 1– Quality of the Knowledge Object

At the simplest levels, the most critical things for any evaluation are the things that have always been critical for instructional design, but now with a digital twist.

Note that we suggest a scale of 1-10 for *each* of the areas and all of the 71 Characteristics. The-highest score, then, would be 81 for each area.

1. Quality knowledge concepts or artifacts (a fancy word for things like pictures, video, and primary sources that have been scanned in – still usually a picture). Watch it! This one is more subjective and opinionated than the others. 1-10 value per concept. It would be wise to number how many concepts there actually are in the learning object. It's extremely difficult to evaluate all of them if there are hundreds or even thousands, so a random sampling is usual.

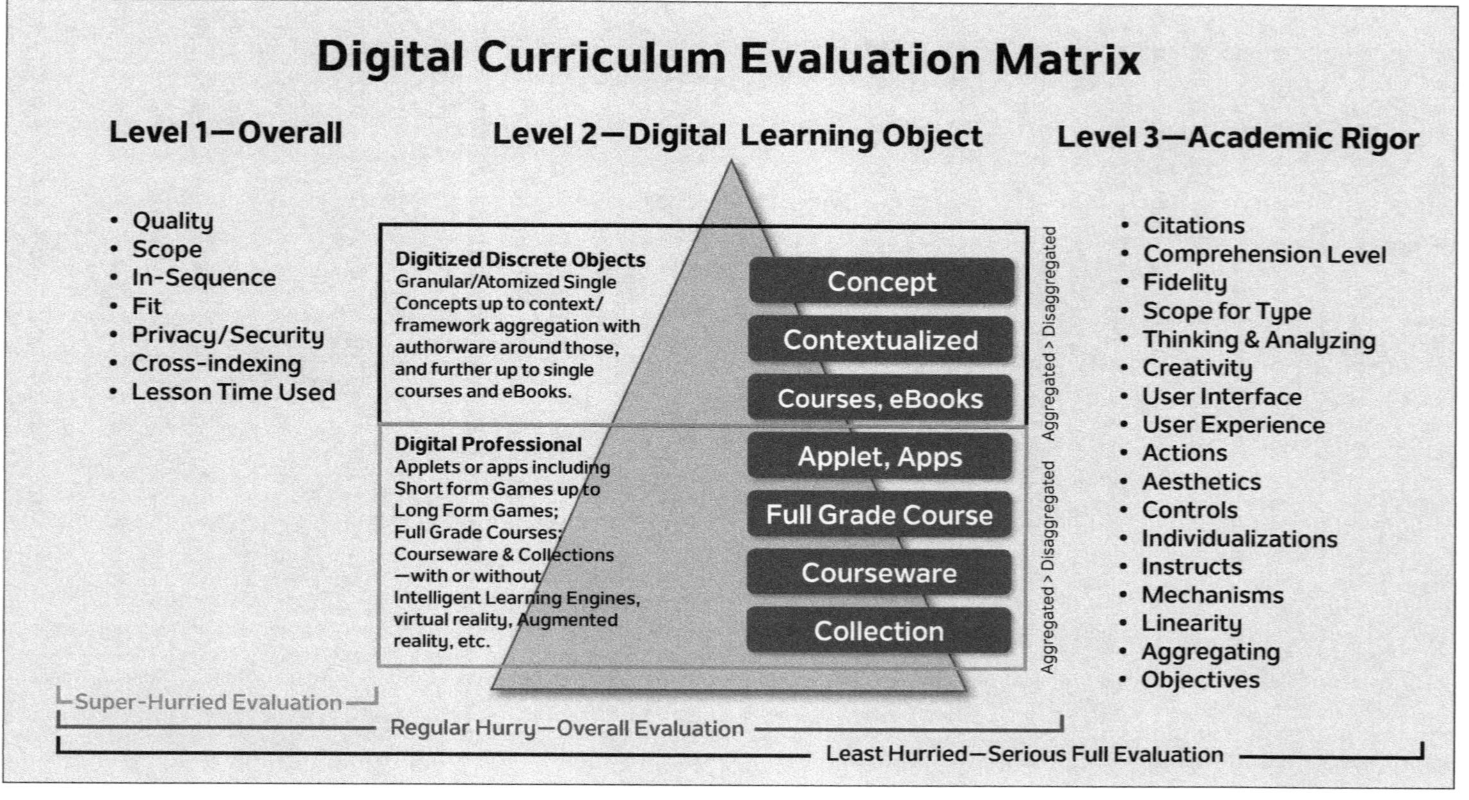
Digital Curriculum Evaluation Matrix
Level 1—Overall
• Quality
• Scope
• In-Sequence
• Fit
• Privacy/Security
• Cross-indexing
• Lesson Time Used
Level 2—Digital Learning Object
Digitized Discrete Objects
Granular/Atomized Single Concepts up to context/ framework aggregation with authorware around those, and further up to single courses and eBooks.
Digital Professional
Applets or apps including Short form Games up to Long Form Games; Full Grade Courses; Courseware & Collections —with or without Intelligent Learning Engines, virtual reality, Augmented reality, etc.
Concept
Contextualized
Courses, eBooks
Applet, Apps
Full Grade Course
Courseware
Collection
Aggregated > Disaggregated
Aggregated > Disaggregated
Level 3—Academic Rigor
• Citations
• Comprehension Level
• Fidelity
• Scope for Type
• Thinking & Analyzing
• Creativity
• User Interface
• User Experience
• Actions
• Aesthetics
• Controls
• Individualizations
• Instructs
• Mechanisms
• Linearity
• Aggregating
• Objectives
Super-Hurried Evaluation
Regular Hurry—Overall Evaluation
Least Hurried—Serious Full Evaluation

2. Taking one or more of the concepts, individually, next in importance in instructional design is a reasoned scope that takes advantage of the things that are of high quality when the content is digital: visualizations, animations, scaffolding of information, content levering, pre- and post-use formative assessments, audio, and all other enhancements that are useful for the chosen subject and topic. (See Chapter 18 for the 71 Characteristics.) 1-71 Value.

3. Next, in-sequence delivery of that concept through the digital mechanisms that support mastery of what is being taught. Once mastery occurs, the learner can then be exposed to a multiplicity of in-sequence concepts building on the original topic. These extensions of the original topic can go in various directions in ways that are themselves instructional because they are non-linear and serve to create more learning. 1-10 Value.

4. Fit (alignment) with requirements and standards. 1-10 Value.

5. Privacy and security of student data. Note that this is an entire subject of its own and best left to the experts for right now. The Learning Counsel will be releasing important national data and analysis points on this that can be asked by non-techies in the near future. In the meantime we suggest you ask of any software what data it takes that might potentially compromise student privacy and see what the publisher's terms of service include. 1-10 Value.

6. Beyond those, and what makes digital delivery unique, is a cross-indexing of the concept with other concepts in a greater ecosystem of knowledge. This might be as low as simple meta-tagging or correct filing. If the object doesn't have this quality, it will be hard to find again. 1-10 Value.

7. Lesson Time Used (LTU). Total LTU is a single numerical value per year. You can figure out LTU by asking approximately how much time it takes to learn or do one learning concept in any learning object, or the average time of that concept if the object has many different features and functions. This is most like one chapter in a textbook or one lesson or section or quiz or one book (a book being usually themed around one major concept.) Apps and courseware might break down into different concepts as lessons. These are typically individual concepts attempting to be taught. What's important about this is that it is very hard for teachers to assign a digital object to be completed by a learner if they have no idea of the time involved to complete it.

One concept might take 15 minutes for a learner or more.

The basic thing to ask is what number of concepts are covered? The second basic thing to ask is how much time do the concepts take on average? Then multiply those two numbers to get the total.

LTU CALCULATION

50 concepts x 10 minutes Average = 500 minutes or (divided by 60 minutes in an hour) = 8:33 hours

Example #1:
A digital collection of books with 3,000 total books has been purchased. Each book typically is one major concept (particularly for fiction; non-fiction might have multiple concepts like textbooks.) So we're using one (1) as the number of concepts per each book, and we're going to say that one book takes 10.5 hours on average to read.

3000 (total number of books) x 10.5 (average time) = 31,500. This means the total *Lesson Time Used* (LTU) is 31,500 hours.

Collections are like whole libraries, so this should not be a surprise.

Example # 2:
An app has been purchased which covers math for both addition and subtraction, two major concepts.

To learn the concept of addition in the app takes 2 hours of in-app screen learning. To learn the concept of subtraction takes 3 hours of in-app screen learning.

With one concept taking 2 hours, and the other one 3 hours, the total is 5 hours of lessons in that App that teaches just two concepts.

The total Lesson Time Used (LTU) is 5 hours.

Later on, you may want to find out how much time is *actually* being used of total LTU by any one user for courseware that has been purchased if you are not sure it is getting enough use to warrant the spend.

Least Hurried – Serious Full Evaluation Using Levels 2 & 3 of the Matrix

A full evaluation looks at all of Level 1 *after* using Level 2 and 3. So you start with "What is it?" which is Level 2, then move through each part of Level 3, grading as you go, and end with an overall evaluation of Level 1.

Level 2 – Object Scale

This is the "*what is it?*" level. You must understand the quality of the digital object you are looking at. This is not "quality" as in being *better* necessarily, but in terms of *its having a quality that can be defined.*

The two major quality categories are:

1. *Digitized by a non-developer* – Usually developed by teachers with support from the school or district. This could be build-curriculum-yourself software (authorware) that uses pre-built parts of development to make a lesson or a course and might be pretty cool, but the object is not professionally coded by some developer.

2. *Digital professional* – Developed by designers and programmers with testing for the education market. Again, this doesn't necessarily mean it's totally awesome or even more rigorous, just that it is professionally built by someone who is a code writer.

Within those two categories are the granular, disaggregated objects at the top of the scale and the more aggregated objects at the bottom. Schools may need to decide to target some ratio in their mix of all objects of professional versus non-professional to lessen the expense and inefficiencies of custom creation and upkeep. This is especially true if the discrete learning objects are found via links for their use in lesson plans and the links break. They may also want to have a care to how much is purely granular versus systematized and aggregated objects. Potentially, paid professional industry work can more efficiently spread the cost of creation and upkeep across many schools and keep accurate track of what is working.

At any level, each object can contain various digital characteristics. "Scoring" in this area is non-professional versus professional (developer), and the quality and quantity of added characteristics in the software. In addition, how granular versus aggregated is another area of scoring. The question of what a school or teacher scores an object is a question of what percentage of their time they want to spend on building all home-grown materials versus professionally built. Schools may have signed pledges to be fully free and open education resources, so their score model would be weighted in favor of more granular because that is more typical to the free resource world. It may also be more typical to the older grades where discovery of what object could be a part of the learning design.

As a comment on the all free open education resources, it is important to note that originally the train of thought for focusing attention on free and open resources was very pointed at money savings. That was when schools couldn't conceive of buying all their computing devices *and* high-value digital courseware. That is just as it should be, of course, but presently the market has shifted, and more schools are realizing they can achieve full, or nearly full, coverage models of high-value digital curriculum with a mix of their own materials or outside courses if they stop buying paper books and shift over. The Learning Counsel's 2016 Survey showed that fully 80% of schools have not yet reorganized budgets away from paper purchase into digital purchase.

Other considerations on the technology side of *what is it?* include the deeply technical ideas that would require the ability to inspect inside the actual program code for syntax, data structure, control structure, and how well it's all documented, organized, and labeled.

Whether any digital learning object "works" and is "easy or difficult" in terms of user experience should be evaluation points of the technical sophistication of the user interface/user experience where it intersects with the academic rigor of the concept.

Level 3 – Academic Rigor

The following list can be used with a point system to evaluate the rigor of digital learning objects. It would be used in combination with the other two levels of the scale already noted and is adaptable for teacher or school needs. It combines the concept of academic rigor with the digital qualities that are instrumental in delivering that rigor. It should be used against every individual concept or minor aggregation within a digital object, as in one section of courseware teaching something like addition and subtraction of fractions.

Rigor Scale: one point per each (1)

1. Citations
2. Comprehension difficulty level as in reading (lexile) or mathematics level (quatrile), if applicable.
3. Fidelity (The instruct inherent in the learning object delivers its concept in the way it should be to achieve learning with the software, or in a way that is a true assessment if it is a test.)
4. Individual object, for its type, has an appropriate scope – not too broad or too narrow.
5. Elicits higher-levels of thinking and analyzing in the learner.
6. Elicits creativity in thinking and responding.
7. Uses an appropriate user interface with proper navigation.
8. Provides an overall positive user experience.
9. Has appropriate Actions. * (one point per each of audio enhancement, live chat, live video, annotating, accessibility, social gaming, spell checkers, spatial-temporal reasoning, dynamic definitions, probeware viewing, digital social interactions, sketching, touch enabled, storied)
10. Has appropriate Aesthetics.*(characters, voice, virtual reality, animations, visual advantages, video embedding, avatars)
11. Has appropriate Controls.*(dynamic curation, plagiarism checking, interoperable, project-based, student personalization, navigation)
12. Has appropriate Individualizations. *(multiple languages, collections, work product curation)
13. Has appropriate Instructs.* (favoriting, administrative personalization, second screen, projection, portability, feedback, programming practice, inference, clip embedding, standards alignment/attainment)

14. Has appropriate Mechanisms. * (machine learning, intervention, training, project mastery, distance live-lab, authorware, terminology, interactive queries, real-time attention data/neuro-determinism, device input, intelligent learning engines, gesture-controlled data, collaboration-ware, assembly, practice micro-games, social experimentation, formative assessment, pre-assessment, coding, game-based earning, gaming rewards, manipulative-object interplay, summative assessment, artificial intelligence, recall mechanized [selection or matching from memory], dimensional)
15. Uses appropriate linearity, as in the presentment of one concept or one question or one answer for any one True/False, fill-out field, or buttons.
16. Uses appropriate aggregation tools, as in the way shopping-cart technology allows learners to collect and build artifacts into a portfolio that demonstrates understanding, if appropriate.
17. Sets and meets objectives.

* *See Chapter 18, The Characteristics of Digital Curriculum*

This new Digital Curriculum Evaluation Matrix is the start of how to *look* with a bit more sophistication in mind, using our eyes and ears and sense of learning engagement, at digital learning objects. Within Knowstory, the ability to rate objects as a broad community for "Fit," "Worked," and "Easy" has the promise of creating a coordinated national and possibly international sorting of the good from the unworkable learning objects, the poorly crafted from the finely wrought, the biased from the unbiased.

As commercial programmers step up to build ever-more sophisticated digital courseware, the consumerization trend in learning will continue to increase. Teachers and schools knowing what they are looking at, and how to think about it, evaluate it, and apply it in meaningful ways for teaching and learning, is one of the first steps to co-opting consumerized learning resources.

Definitions

Key terms as we speed into digital curriculum tactics.

Concepts are single discrete knowledge objects and could be called just "content" or "resource" but are more accurately a concept. These are artifacts, like photos or videos. Also called "granular" and "atomized" bits of knowledge. Examples include Word documents, PowerPoints, notes, short videos, pictures, etc.

Contextualized concepts are lectures, stories, articles, lesson plans, or assessments/tests and are usually meta-tagged. These could be elements made with authorware of various types including animated objects. May have minor goals or objectives. A part of this category are systems that are contextualizers, or Learning Management Systems (LMS) that frame and hold such objects in repositories. Some LMS's contain analytics on use of objects and connected grading, but are not by definition creating object internal intelligence adaptations – the objects themselves are not coded with algorithms. However, they could give single-sign-on into independent professionally coded adaptive learning courseware.

Courses and eBooks contain multiple concepts. This category includes non-coded courses made inside LMS's and eBooks, which can use non-programmers to author them. Such objects are often bundled with directions for activities. These have short or mid-range goals or objectives to achieve and include defined scope and usually sequence.

Apps are whole programs that perform small, short-form (applet) operations or large operations like long-form learning games.

Courses that are professionally coded are composed of a set of lessons and goals to achieve that take longer than a single 50-minute class period. Professional courses have a defined scope and a workable sequence towards learning goals. Some courses include intelligent learning engines so they can be adaptive to individual learners and provide analytics back to users and instructors.

Courseware is like courses except it may have a much wider scope with multiple subjects and topics. Once logged in, the student uses the navigation to go from lesson to lesson without further interjection by an instructor. However, the courseware may give some levers to the instructor to gate or ungate progress (as in hitting a digital lever that allows freedom to surge forward to new lessons), and at times provide analytics to the students and teacher.

Collection(s) are typically many eBooks, lectures, courses, apps, or videos that have a management framework around them. This may include other functionality like testing for the entrance level of the learner.

Note: This list of terms does not include "tool apps", which are usually single-function like note-taking, or authorware like Adobe Illustrator, or technical software like computer-aided-design programs (CAD), none of which have knowledge concepts already embedded.

ORIENTATION TACTICS

To speed along without major problems, here are questions to find your own answers to what will help you and your schools work out quality digital curriculum transitions.

1. What is happening as learning objects become consumerized – built expressly for the individual? What will this mean for professionally developed digital courseware?

2. How many digital learning objects do you have? Are teachers aware of what they each have?

3. What is your overall digital transition strategy to provide for digital devices that use curriculum that takes a lot of bandwidth like video streaming? (Consider the devices, student access when not at school, what's allowed on the networks, filtering, and security and privacy.)

4. Will you be using a Learning Management System? One or many?

5. What can your networks handle? What if every student brings multiple devices and then crowds into three rooms instead of twelve for some project work – can those three rooms handle the load?

"With digital learning, the network has never been more important to improving student outcomes. Would an Indy racer perform better on a race track or a dirt road? You need a quality race track for your students."

–Richard Nedwich, Director of Education, Ruckus Wireless

6. What sorts of curriculum things could be services you can have other organizations do including technology support? Language pathology help via distance teaching? Foreign language courses?

7. What sort of curriculum "mix" do you want by grade? All discrete, granular objects or more systematized? Why? What are the repercussions of that?

8. What is the pedagogical use of any one tactic – concentrated in whole group teaching, project-based learning, individualized learning, or…?

9. Are the tactics extensible to other teachers in that subject or grade?

10. Are the tactics subject-specific as a learning object, or is it a "tool app" that is a cross-subject asset for learning?

11. Are you carefully avoiding just "niftiness" (digital things that are nifty but may have little rigor) to focus on substantive digital learning object tactics?

Chapter 20

Consumerism's Current Constraints

The full-scale leap to consumerized learning is at present constrained by forces as thin as gossamer. There isn't much holding it back as we can see by societal factors. First of all, consider that many families today are dual-income and rely on public education for occupying the time of school-aged kids. This is a positive only when parents are convinced the time is usefully spent. If it is considered irrelevant, which is happening increasingly, then this consideration is potentially at risk. Merely occupying time can be done by other constructs.

Then there is the idea that there have to be accreditations and degrees and "seat-time" for how schools get paid. Since the arrival of MOOCs (Massively Open Online Courses) like Udemy and Khan Academy, the stance of having to be accredited for learning to have occurred is observably a baldly protectionist stance around revenue generation. People can and do learn without a regulator standing over their shoulder. The posturing in this area, while having some merit, associates once inviolate institutions with money-grubbing, and so quickly puts them under the glaring lights of competitive posturing that have heretofore been reserved for corporations. The public, seeing this sort of behavior, is prone to then *look* for directly purchasable alternatives and skip the pretensions. Consumer behavior does not always go towards the most costly and prestigious stores – in fact, the majority of it goes in the opposite direction.

Key Points

- Consumerized learning's constraints include beliefs, seat-time, accreditations, full-market coverage of subjects with good user interface and design, and deep marketing.
- Once through the transition to consumerized learning on its own terms, education could be the bright economic and achievement differentiator long sought for the U.S. and the world.

Another constraint is the last vestiges of hope from the educational establishment that our 200-year-old system will keep running. Leaders say the general public is not yet ready for a full-scale shift. But change hangs heavy in the air and the statistics say otherwise.

In a visit by Learning Counsel staff to the Santa Ana Unified School District's Advanced Learning Academy, Deputy Superintendent of Educational Services Dr. David Haglund mentioned that students presently don't typically comprehend that they can find and consume learning on their own. They may know games and social media, but consumer-based learning online as an acceptable replacement of the institution is a new idea for many.

Schools like the Advanced Learning Academy have already seen that a heightened personal responsibility in the individual student to take ownership in their own learning has caused a chain reaction in parent involvement. Students make reports and recordings weekly that parents can check and that students are enormously proud to show. Parent responsibility is highly questionable in our present age and could be another factor holding back change.

A shift in parent involvement could be the change agent that fractures the current public education system, as parents pull their kids out to "unschool" or homeschool. Parent cooperatives like Crestmont School are already emerging but are not necessarily taking full advantage of digital learning. However, with social media and some public policy shift to administer a network model, these constraints could easily be overcome. In fact, they are being overcome in some corners already.

Admittedly, the digital consumer user interface and user experience has a way to go. This is another constraint to change. A home-schooler working online can be distracted by pop-ups, advertising, too-small text, "flashing" peripheral animations, ineffective graphics, being branched to the wrong information or exercise, or getting confused as to where they are in the progress through their information or exercises. At times, poor activity navigation or the activities themselves are too bothersome to complete. Needed information may be obscured or too hard to find, screen width or vertical scrolling make comparisons or references too difficult to use, interactions are slowed, or the student may receive crushing negative feedback. Any of these things inject uncertainty, mistakes, and frustrations that may well have been duplicated in the analog world, but can be magnified in the digital world.

More particular constraints include the compulsory nature of the educational system, usually directly associated with physical presence and the "butts-in-seats" clauses of old that will require actual legal change. In the meantime, frustration will mount as learners find exception to being marginalized in an old model, disconnected from the allure of interactive personalized design and exhilarating immediacy of the Internet.

Another constraint, though not easily discernable, is how industry has positioned itself to infiltrate the education system but not necessarily alter the distribution of education. Everyone in the game still considers trained teachers to be the required delivery mechanism. Industry is visibly not "all in" with a direct-to-consumer model, and perhaps that has more to do with the maturation of the consumer side to appreciate all that digital learning offers. Across all companies being funded, the major investment houses have largely preferred companies who are selling to institutions and individual teachers. The vast majority of ed-tech start-ups are configured to sell to schools, either as a direct sales model to the institution or a freemium model with a low-end configuration for teachers that costs money only when premium features are needed. Industry seems to prefer having education institutions as a marketplace, largely because a direct-to-consumer model is expensive marketing-wise, even if a sell-to-teachers model is about the same cost to market budgets as selling to consumers. There are, after all, 3.3 million teachers – a massive market by any estimation.

Another consumerization constraint is the industry's inept marketing and lack of structure. With the sheer size of the education market, similar products have grown to take over small portions of dominion with installs in just enough districts to be commercially interesting. Competitive products take the other geographies or niches, and so the whole of the marketplace looks fractured into various product preferences. When these products are the campus management systems, the learning management or student information or library systems as repositories for much of the data and the learning objects, a market-wide inefficiency is created. One school cannot share easily with another. A teacher leaving one school or one district to work at another must learn an entirely new system.

Simply stated, unfortunately, this is not the Apple world where everything works with everything. In education, all the major operating systems collide and there is a mish-mash of old legacy and new industry. This is the goal of big industry's digital evolution, to bring everything up to co-exist smoothly in one ecosystem – preferably *theirs* if you are Google, Apple, or Microsoft.

Additionally, there are numerous standards bodies, each with a different view as to what constitutes a necessary standard. Some are academically focused on "what" is learned, the actual idea. Others are focused on the technical files being interoperable between major systems, while still others on the meta-tagging of each of the learning objects. And the fact that there is no commercial-grade code structure to allow direct consumption across multiple publishers other than for books, loose lesson plan objects, and videos evidences a missing consumerization link.

Certain types of tags and differentiations of digital curriculum are also missing, such as one the Learning Counsel identified as "Lesson Time Used" in 2014, now known as "LTU," which has a minimally agreed-upon definition as an equivalency to one class period or 50 minutes. Another is "Cost Per Unit," shortened to "CPU," which needs industry and institutions to come to a consensus as to how to think of units whether they are apps, full immersive-environment courseware, subscription websites with a multiplicity of objects, single lesson plans, etc. A single measurement would allow for all teachers and learners to understand what they are getting, at least by a cost factor.

The New Market

Commercially, with tens of millions of learning objects out there roaming the Internet, a new sort of retail market could emerge on the digital plane, creating new mixes of learning content along with hardware. Colleges and universities themselves could have digital bookstores, but the commercial enablement of this reality has yet to occur. Knowstory was constructed with this vision in mind – a hopeful place to make it all make sense together, feed the systems and orchestrations of school systems, and harbor the stories and records of students' lifetime learning journeys.

Though the constraints of full consumerization of learning are numerous, they can be overcome. The rewards for individual learners could be enormous. An entire world of knowledge and pathways are presented online and consumable from anywhere, sometimes free and sometimes paid, or offered within the context of a school which may be public and still free. Most importantly, they are navigable and delivering an awesome experience with rewards of knowledge. For teachers, the future of being a content creator or content "mixologist" promises a lot of individual freedom and even a far greater flexibility and income, which exists right now only minimally in an institutionally dominated construct. For institutions, the opportunity exists for reinvention to be a branded hub of great digital mixology, a finely wrought crafting of courseware with real-world social dynamics. Reaching the consumerization of learning could be the differentiator that turns the critics of present-day education away to seek other industries as prey.

Once through the transition to consumerized learning on its own terms, education will be the bright economic and achievement differentiator long sought for the U.S. and the world.

Reference Material:

Parent Cooperatives, http://crestmontschool.org/school/cooperative

Collins, Allan & Richard Halverson, "Rethinking Education in the Age of Technology: The Digital Revolution in Schooling in America", 2009, *Teachers College Press, by Teachers College, Columbia University.*

F. T. Carlton, "Economic Influences upon educational progress in the United States", *1820-1850, Richmond, VA: William Byrd Press*, 1965, (originally published in 1908 by the University of Wisconsin).

Learning Counsel, 2015 Digital Curriculum Strategy Survey.

Cynthia Chiong & Carly Shuler, "Learning: Is There an App for That? Investigations of Young Children's Usage and Learning with Mobile Devices and Apps", 2010, The Joan Ganz Cooney Center at Sesame Workshop, http://wwwtc.pbskids.org/read/files/cooney_learning_apps.pdf

Chapter 21

Full Definition and Critiques

This book is not about the destruction of schools or places of learning. It is about the inevitable remodeling of the system to achieve the meaningful individual experiences sought by students. It is true that schools have been shifting dramatically throughout the past twenty years, and now technology and new academic standards are enabling learning to be a consumable, "at-will" product no different than the way we consume music and movies or shop for shoes online. This difference can change the very fabric of our institutions, allowing them to become places and non-places for student affiliation in any formula schools invent. It also allows for the potentiality of non-institutional paradigms for learning wholly differently than what we now know.

> **Key Points**
>
> - "Consumerization" is the reorientation of product and service designs to focus on (and market to) the end user as an individual consumer, in contrast with an earlier era of only organization-oriented offerings.[1]
> - Consumerization is similar to the ideals of real personalized learning. Critiques of it are easily reasoned away by looking and understanding what software can actually do now.

Let's take a deeper look at this concept of consumerization.

"Consumerization" is the reorientation of product and service designs to focus on (and market to) the end user as an individual consumer, in contrast with an earlier era of only organization-oriented offerings (designed solely for business-to-business or business-to-government sales)[1]. The emergence of the individual consumer as the primary driver of product and service design is the most important new trend in marketing over the last few years. As a trend, it has been most commonly associated with the technology industry, as large business and government organizations dominated the early decades of computer usage and development and focused attention on organizational administration.

Consumerization in the context of education and learning means that the elements and interactions with knowledge are being delivered directly to the consumer at a mass scale and in such a way that new, much higher levels of individualization and personalization are occurring, creating greater market efficiency and potentially allowing millions upon millions of students to win big at learning.

It also has a potential for disintermediation (the removal of intermediaries in a supply chain, or "cutting out the middlemen" of traditional schooling). It is commonly believed that the "middlemen" are entirely the teachers, but that is probably what is most *not* true of disintermediation and new competition from consumerized learning. What is far more probable is a new sort of golden age of diminished ranks of administrators and physical infrastructure because the system and distribution is far better orchestrated and efficient with fewer staff.

> *"Each day at school, students in 21 states will see more librarians, bus drivers, coaches, cafeteria workers and office personnel than teachers, according to a new study that examined school hiring patterns over the past 20 years.*
>
> *"(A) report, released Thursday (February 28, 2013) by the Friedman Foundation for Educational Choice, found that Virginia, Ohio, Oregon, Maine, Indiana and a number of other states – along with*

> *the District of Columbia – employ more non-classroom personnel than teachers, some by a wide margin."*[2]
>
> –Ben Wolfgang, *The Washington Post*

There is no real way to avoid, however, the fact that teacher roles and even their relevancy in context could change dramatically. In that respect, consumerization is the unlooked-for competitor. It is wise to be discerning about *exactly* what is meant by this in lieu of the capabilities of software. Where it, the software, is the delivery mechanism of knowledge and engaging, the roles and responsibilities of humans can change. They can become something else, but not *irrelevant.* The discovery of what is relevant work for human teachers in the context of highly engaging courseware is what must be figured out. I contend that it is the adventure of this Age to figure this out with teachers leading the way – and many of them *are* doing just that.

While it might be easy to consider all the ways this could be a bad thing, it could also be one of the greatest paradigm shifts in history. Teachers, or *anyone* with specialized knowledge, could be rewarded in new ways and become hyper-valuable "services" similar to Uber or Airbnb in the transportation and hotel industries. And what it could do for learners could make the present Age and teaching models look positively barbarian.

It is simplest to consider that consumerization is, in the vernacular of educators, "personalization." Right now, teachers are individualizing many software assets to fit their students precisely by "levering" a capacity faster or slower, higher or lower, within software to fit a learning level and style of an individual student. This is on a micro level, and much of this is now becoming algorithmically determined as more complex software is built. On a macro level, the selection of topics and mixes of subjects in an increasingly sophisticated set of apps and courseware is already what many teachers are doing daily.

Craig Gray, Director of Digital Learning for the Region 10 Education Service Center in Richardson, Texas, said on September 29, 2016 that he felt that the new focus of school administration had left the discussions of devices and networks and "was even not as much anymore on software for the adults (buying systems and lots of content), but had moved on to focus on the learners."

Immunity?

The national education market, particularly the K12 institutions, is full of teachers and administrators who think they are immune to this highly interactive, highly designed software shift paving the way for consumerization. That is far from true, and those who share those beliefs will eventually find themselves obsolete. Higher education institutions have been feeling the pinch of irrelevancy for the past three decades and have been defending themselves with a dizzying rate of change in an attempt to match the shifts in expectations, with little overall success.

The tsunami in global knowledge, now that technology replicates information and distributes it almost sentiently and at an inhuman pace – and offers it directly to consumers – is not a tangible single point. It is everywhere. It is pretty hard to label "everywhere" as an enemy, especially when much of the education sector, in the massive amount of teacher work time spent building millions of digital learning objects, *put it there,* and it is now being bought and sold on the open Internet, sometimes even with the teachers themselves getting financial gain from selling it.

A way to completely define Consumerized Learning (restating from the Introduction):

1. Consumerization is the act of making some thing desirable and consumable *by the individual.* Think of consumerization of *learning* as the personalization of it on computing screens using the capabilities of the software that make it intuitive and highly adaptive just for *that* learner. *It* teaches using highly developed programming. If schools fully discover and adapt around its ingenuity, it has the power to give teachers back time spent custom building every digital resource themselves, time that can now be turned for attention on students, to create more hands-on learning activities, and to guide students in the fullness of a digital learning experience. Consumerized learning is also an alternate delivery mechanism that has the potential to disintermediate on cost, immediacy, and effectiveness. It's time for schools to *co-opt* this trend. To win *with* it.

2. Personalized learning. Example sentence: *"We consumerized it so it would work for the hearing impaired."*

3. Immediately accessible digital learning. Example sentence: *"The consumerization of learning made it so that we could get to our courses on our smartphones from anywhere."*

4. Technological elements that provide a direct-to-consumer learning object, such as eBooks, apps, courseware, digital courses, online interactions (chat, live video online), learning videos, games, and any transactional contextualization of knowledge. Example sentence: *"The company chose to consumerize all their courses and hired fifteen new teachers who work from home delivering live question and answer to students."*

5. The atomization of learning objects, pieces of subjects, and topics discretely exchanged to fit modular lesson plans. Example sentence: *"Where there used to be whole books, there are now consumerized chapters and some formative assessment pieces."*

6. The commoditization of the same learning objects to commercial exchanges. Example sentence: *"The school consumerized the lessons in the new technical standard and published them to a shared directory."*

7. In contrast to institutional learning, the pre-created pathways of digital learning built out of discrete learning objects, subjects, topics, and lessons, sometimes with live-chat or live-teaching in a virtual, completely curated mix to achieve an end, such as a standard lesson, grade, diploma, or degree. Example sentence: *"The student used consumerized learning for most subjects but attended the local institution for sports."*

8. The capacity of the individual learning objects or pathways to individualize or personalize through intelligent learning engines, machine learning, or actual artificial intelligence, the process of achievement digitally. Example sentence: *"The consumerized courseware gave Johnny supplemental lessons on reading Roman numerals until he passed the embedded assessment."*

The critiques so far of consumerization are the same as the general critiques of capitalism or any technology entering the education market. These are some of the interesting critiques and counters:

Critique #1: Teaching and selling (and therefore consumerism) are "inherently contradictory processes." [2] The premise is that "research on how students learn" proves this. The critics argue an extremely vague idealization of academic rigor, teacher-student engagement, and lots of writing assignments as the means proven to gain "deeper learning," from studies that never even looked at new academic immersive digital courseware, but just seem to swing at consumerization rather wildly. On this premise, the critique could be summarily dismissed since it is not considering the alternative of consumerized learning. However, it is further flawed in that it characterizes sales and monetary exchange as an inherent evil that somehow perverts learning. If this were the case, then a logical extrapolation would be that all educators should be unpaid and completely altruistic so that all capitalistically driven incentives could be removed for authentic teaching and learning to occur. The if-money-then-evil argument frays at the point of practicality. If a teacher is paid, then they and what they teach are perverted by money from the inception, just like the purported learning would be. It would by necessity be a two-way street. It also assumes that selling something is somehow insidiously more than what it is: attaching a value to something, which might be merely contextualizing it. This is not a great deal different than what teaching does already when lecturers present ideas.

The counter to critique #1 about consumerized learning being inherently contradictory is that a sales-oriented distribution process is an enabler, not a barrier to learning. It cannot be characterized as an antithesis. It is only a means and can only be biased by its inputs, no differently than teaching can be biased by opinions. The idea that it is anything else than purely an enabler, just a mechanism, is a protectionist stance. *It* is not the adversary, just as the would-be consumers could not be considered an adversary. Saying that the mechanism is an evil because it exists is a simple anti-competitive move. It would guard knowledge as exclusive to a few, rather than broadcast it via the most expedient means for the greatest reach and greatest human good. The stance that deeper learning is only gained with the most expensive human-intensive route is unmasked for what it really is – self-absorption and self-interest by the few at the expense of the many. It cannot be called a more expensive route because commoditization of anything has historically been a great cost reducer.

Critique #2: "Good students are responsible for reflecting critically, exploring ambiguities, and giving and receiving feedback. A customer (meaning a purchasing student) does not have

responsibilities beyond the economic."[2] Such a juvenile understanding of economics and market dynamics ignores the fact that interest and money automatically go towards *value* in an unfettered market – automatically. It is the major precedent of capitalism, the longest-run modern system to work to increase standards of living across the board. Idealization of how the world and students *should be* does not make it so. Consumerization of learning allows consumers to go directly at what is useful for them, and it allows marketing that induces purchase of whatever might be best, including tools to bolster critical thinking skills.

The counter to Critique # 2 is that when education is well-wrought, whatever the form, engagement is a given. To argue that a customer does not have responsibilities beyond the economic transaction of purchasing ignores *why* anyone would pay tuition or purchase any learning in the first place. They are expecting an outcome and will be as engaged as they are able. They have typically bought the idea that either they don't know something or should know something. This is an incredibly wide ocean of potential for any good institution to market into. The customer's engagement *is* the responsibility of the institution or the product, and if it is not good, blaming it on the student is idiocy. In addition, if it is not good, it will be repudiated, and the consumers will turn swiftly to other products. There are those students that, no matter what, will just fail, and consumerization of learning at the very least has the potential to absolve human teachers of blame. After all, the intelligent algorithms will rarely be disputable, whereas it is often a tactic of bad students to blame teachers.

Critique #3: "Learning requires challenging assumptions and paradigms, which sometimes makes people feel uncomfortable." [3]

The counter to critique #3 is that there are no examples of this. If the teacher is "challenging assumptions" that "make people uncomfortable," it is highly probable they have entered the realm of political, religious, or sexual beliefs that have views previously learned in the home. Certainly science and engineering lessons are not going to make people uncomfortable since it's hard to argue about things like gravity. If learning was to "give students what they need," and that view is counter to their personal belief, well, that's not really a school anymore; it's indoctrination. Other teachers chose the route of debunking, as in, "In order to protect students from emotion-focused propaganda, the debunkers 'fortify the minds of young people against emotion.' Yet, in so doing, they harden students' hearts and moral sensibility."[4] In other words, by the mere statement of this critique, the hidden motivations of institutional elitism are exposed to not just introduce and initiate the student in common knowledge, but to actively override pre-existing beliefs.

As has long been the indictment by homeschooling communities and private schools, propagandizing or debunking postures in public schools are some of the reasons that consumerism may grow with a vengeance, in a similar way to the growth of charters and private schools and the unschooling movement. It is not a wanted thing by most families to have children come home from school in a "critical of mama and papa" state of mind. Or families in poverty might feel as if they will never be able to get out of it. If the consumerization of learning brings down the overall cost and greatly heightens access, like the revolution of album disaggregation to single-song purchase with iTunes, then a real shift is on the horizon that will reckon institutionalized learning with the will of the people to determine what and how they engage education. Essentially, consumerization has the promise of bringing new freedom.

Consumerization of learning has only just begun to scale in ways that will make it as ubiquitous as other consumer arenas, but it is on its way. Certain mechanisms should be in place before it becomes fully realized.

The tactic of criticism and avoidance will not work and may delay the boon that potentially awaits the individual teacher who is currently fettered economically, stuck in a singular job paradigm without the great alternatives available in other industries. The delivery mechanism after all is the Internet, which heretofore has allowed groups like Anonymous to hack governments on a global scale and allowed for a no-government paradigm that yet provided a thriving underground economy.[5] (Go ahead and research Somalia, presently the only country on earth that has no government and has devolved into a barbarism, but because of the Internet and cell phones, has had a thriving third-world economy, similar in some ways to America's Wild West, an example of the sheer power of the Internet. Weird, but true.)

The fact that consumerization of learning is more than an alternative school, that it is in fact an entire alternative *non-system* "system," should be the new target of discussion by governments, schools, families, and individuals.

Time Machine

Let's get in a time machine to put all critiques into a perspective of change through time. A famous saying is that "The more things change, the more they stay the same." Context that is not merely the last decade or two, but longer, is important to have in order to see where this new thing, consumerized learning, may go. Let's get in our time machine and travel back in time for a perspective of where education systems came from and where they could be headed.

> "The Massachusetts Puritans, who were followers of Calvin, passed a law in 1642, just 22 years after the landing of the Mayflower, which dictated that parents were responsible for their children's education. The law asserted the state's right to ensure that every child was educated. It made education compulsory, but made no provision for schools or for teachers. The teachers were to be parents or private tutors. Every family was responsible for the religious and moral upbringing of their children under pain of a fine."
>
> *– Collins, Allan & Richard Halverson (2009),* Rethinking Education in the Age of Technology: The Digital Revolution in Schooling in America, *Teachers College Press, by Teachers College, Columbia University;*

1642

The education system in the U.S. was one of our great national inventions, gifted also to the world at large and founded on a premise that someone must be responsible for a child coming up in the world with enough literacy and morals to contribute. Laws demanding that parents be responsible date back to 1642 when a colonial law requiring that children were to be educated was enforced with a fine if leaders determined parents were not educating their children well. Later, families and laws required that one person be assigned to teach the children to read and write if there were at least fifty families in a community. With one hundred families, a grammar school was required.

1837

Nearly 200 years later, in 1837, with the instigation of Horace Mann, and with the start of the Industrial Revolution and a great influx of immigrants into cities, education became a means of controlling and normalizing the population. This effort was especially pronounced in inner cities after child labor laws were enforced and there was a great worry about what kids would do without guidance while parents worked in big factories. Tax-supported schools came into being, as well as a shift away from family responsibility for education.

1848

The "graded school" and classroom single-teacher leadership came into being with an initial ratio of 1:56 students. Parents were already disassociating themselves from the responsibility of educating, faithfully putting all their children in the hands of the state.

1860

Lack of teachers and structure a mere twenty years later meant that thousands of students had no seats – an initial inequity.

1900s

By the early 1900s, the education system nationally looked a lot like factory work with compartmentalization of students by age, teachers as knowledgeable resources, organized and mass-instituted main subjects, textbooks, face-forward seating, testing, and Carnegie Units. These were the "technologies" of the 19th century for education. By the 1940s, people were routinely graduating from high schools, setting up America for a generation of economic and technological advance unprecedented in history. Public schools have lasted as a remarkable institution, nearly impervious to change and with only a call for modernized bureaucratic administration from the 1920s-1930s.

2037

If we count 1837 as the real origination year of socialized education, then 2037 would be the next 200-year mark. Perhaps because of the potentialities of consumerization of learning, we could say that by that year we will have had a complete new ideological shift to a new system, coming full circle back to original ideologies, an "un-system" to mirror the same effect the Internet has had in flattening and atomizing other industries.

The "un-system" system is already beginning with the move to a complete definition of individualized learning – that which is personalized by the student for themselves. Already Howard County Public Schools in Maryland and Pasadena ISD in Texas, along with many others, are applying a structure of individualizing learning that is way more than mere tweaks to lessons for different learning styles. It's actual individual pathways.

The lead up to consumerization has been most thoroughly wrought by teachers themselves, who are responsible for over fifty percent of all digital learning objects currently in use on the market today.

[1] "Consumerization" definition, excerpted from https://en.wikipedia.org/wiki/Consumerization

[2] Ben Wolfgang, "Teachers Outnumbered in Schools by Administrators, Support Staff in Many States, Study Shows," *The Washington Times,* Thursday, February 28, 2013.

[3] Laura M Harrison & Laura Risler, "The Role Consumerism Plays in Student Learning." *Active Learning in Higher Education,* Vol. 16, 67–76, Ohio University, USA, 2015.

[4] Brett Vaden, "C.S. Lewis on Three Kinds of Education: Propagandizing, Debunking, and Initiating," *Classical Latin School Association*, June 24, 2016.

[5] "Anonymous (Internet Group)," *NY Times*, 2016, http://www.nytimes.com/topic/organization/anonymous-internet-group

Reference Material:

Thomas Sowell, "Classroom Should Be Place of Learning, Not Propagandizing," *The Baltimore Sun*, March 2006.

the Learning Counsel, *"Digital Curriculum Strategy Survey & Assessment Tool"* results, 2015.

Chapter 22
Ungating Potential and Rigor

To "ungate" in software is to allow a user to proceed to the next level or into a new section. In some software, gating is a way for teachers to lever up or hold back individual students so that they can surge forward if they are high achievers or remain with a group.

A great innovator (and bow-tie wearing fellow with a lot of flair) named Cleon Franklin, the Director of Virtual Learning at Shelby County Schools in Memphis, said a very interesting thing about what happens when you ungate students. When you let them learn forward outside of their age group, it is like moving up to a new game level inside video games, and some kids find that opportunity inspiring. New software allows students to get more than run-of-the-mill digitized teacher-created and whole lessons, so they can surge forward through to higher subjects. Students can leave algebra behind and finish calculus as 9th graders or sooner.

When Cleon saw the students in Memphis doing just that, he said he felt schools "had been holding kids back for 100 years." With the digital curriculum software transition, learning could get to dimensions well beyond just un-gating and into a whole new golden age of unleashing human potential.

In practice, teachers find some students are easier and that they enthusiastically intake lessons, projects, and the programs planned for them. Others seem to be unreceptive. Their minds are

Key Points

- The consumerization of learning will have market dynamics determining how to "ungate potential" both with what objects and with what is gained, on an instantaneous and international scale.
- The "gifted" minds would be allowed to accelerate, fueled on basics but allowed instant access to all other human knowledge without normalizing, where they could flourish and become the future leaders we so anxiously need.
- Those that need a high amount of careful remediation, also flourish because they are attended to, and can therefore attain more.

distracted or perhaps not capable of pushing thought through the bottleneck of speech and other forms of communication to connect well with other people and life. We can observe student types. But we may not have regularly observed a certain type of student mind, the one that can step well beyond the guardrails of commonality and throw off anything but the foundational information, basic conceptual language, and math, to soar into unexpected greatness. This kind of mind is often labeled "gifted" and allowed to accelerate, but within somewhat normalized arenas. Those students, fueled on basics but allowed *instant access to all other human knowledge without normalizing*, could flourish and become the future leaders we so anxiously need.

Imagine that. Now imagine that it is possible via custom software and virtual world learning environments.

Imagine as well that those minds that need a high amount of careful remediation, also flourish because they are attended to and can therefore attain more.

It's important to note that normalized gifted programs or lowest-common-denominator whole group teaching are usually not individualized or personalized learning the way that software could enable it. Teacher-differentiated learning is working to adapt a lesson so that certain learners can intake the same lesson as everyone else but at their own pace.

Intelligent learning engines inside immersive courseware will allow future teachers the ability to leverage the best in software development and systems. These future teachers will be able to program journeys for individuals, starting points and requirements, and masterfully inject social collaboration along the way. It will be more like travel planning for learning than teaching in the traditional sense.

Leveraging Tech without Gating

While idealized, this promises two eventualities:

1. Student minds shackled by our present system which typifies them and slots them into a normalized routine may gain a freedom heretofore unseen, networked through technology to unprecedented amounts of knowledge and community at the same time, and

2. A reinvigorated teaching profession with a new modality that allows any student to get gains based on their needs. This will no doubt help remove the great demoralization of teachers who get too few joys in their teaching by rarely seeing true accomplishment. Along the way, a need for more teachers with more specialties, directly associated with schools or acting as market free agents, will potentially change the whole industry.

These are exciting potentialities, and ones that are already provided for with some courseware, so why are we not already embracing it everywhere?

Rigor

Besides all the reasons already given in previous chapters, there is one more: the question of rigor.

Rigor is that fun word bandied about by educators that makes outsiders believe there is some secret sauce to how teaching has to be done, how instructional design works. There is a good reason for this: some publishers in the past have offered products that just don't do the job. They lacked "rigor," meaning they were not academically needful and were not intellectually or personally challenging for students.

Fear of lack of rigor is natural when the new learning modality looks and acts in many pieces of courseware like a game. This is called "gamification" and it does not mean that the learning is less rigorous, it is just different.

Here is where the past still holds us back from needful change.

Schools have been used to years and years of "learning trials" to validate a single textbook as worthy of the needful rigor of teaching and learning. There is a great hue and cry for things "that work" and "are proven." All new digital learning objects are expected to be validated the same way because of this past way of doing things.

This cry for trials proving rigor has prompted a response from industry in the form of multiple companies doing evaluations of products. The problem with some of these evaluations is that some of them are mere commercial labels placed for the benefit of earning income from the company being evaluated – directly or indirectly.

The federal Department of Education (DOE) has proffered grants for rapid-development learning trials to try to help with the great barrier of time-to-trial that has been the industry norm for years when adoption cycles were long and arduous inspections. Faster inspections while still doing a detailed rigor inspection is the aim.

Some of the large districts, places like Houston Independent School District (HISD), oversee their own evaluations. They not only have a team in place to evaluate digital curriculum, they even have a specialized team to evaluate whether a single app has the security clearances required to be downloaded into the HISD environment, and that evaluation is given in a 24-hour or less period by the dedicated team.

In actuality, the allowance for the market to determine on its own what works and what doesn't is already a function of our open free markets, albeit a a pretty unsystematic one. Confusions as to quality and actual rigor are added by the OER preferential language of the feds and the states. In the future, policies related to the characteristics of software by teachers and schools, now mostly road-mapped by the Learning Counsel's work and being extended by professionals in districts, added to verified user comments, will act as an instantaneous "trial" in the consumer domain. This is similar to the comments anyone can see on Amazon or other major ecommerce hubs about any product. In Knowstory, little light bulbs are used as the ratings symbol. Where favorable, that product rises in purchase and use. Where unfavorable, the product wanes and falls off the catalog. That is the free market mechanism. Since this has yet to be seen at a high national scale for learning objects, the reality is that the market still demands "trials."

The consumerization of learning will have market dynamics determining how to "ungate potential" both with what objects and with what is gained, on an instantaneous and international scale.

Chapter 23
Love, the Anti-Tech

It's easy to get lost in technology detail and forget core values, like surviving this digital revolution with our humanity intact. With that in mind, I'd like to take a brief, but important, detour.

The first year the Learning Counsel went on the road with our Digital Curriculum Strategy Discussions tour, we met the incredible Dr. Adam Fried, the Superintendent for the Harrington Park School District, and Takecia Saylor, the Director of School Innovation for the New Jersey Department of Education (at the time; later she landed at the federal Department of Education). We learned some interesting things about "teaching with love" and raw persistence in the face of adversity.

In this context, let's just say that love has meaning in education: it is the demonstration of genuine caring. You would know that if you were in the room that day as Adam and Takecia both spoke – you would have felt it.

Adam inspired us with a whole lesson about leading his staff and students with love, a warmth and genuineness we honestly had not encountered with such gusto anywhere else. It struck us that this was an anti-technology, an "analog," and we afterward spoke at length about it and what it meant. The same day, Takecia Saylor awed us with her tale of leaving the private sector to teach and landing in a primary classroom with a lot of failing students. By the end of her story of getting all of her students through despite all odds, more than one of us was tearful.

Key Points

- Love is still the greatest technology of all to free minds.
- To teach when surrounded by technology innovation, it is even more necessary to understand what life is doing in order to enhance it to survive amongst machines and even compete with machines.
- This tool, or anti-tech, love, is the differentiator that consumerized learning will not be built to deliver.

It struck us that on that day Adam and Takecia were unaware of conspiring to bring forth a significant lesson. *They* were doing something that had nothing to do with the tech itself and they were winning. It wasn't the digital curriculum or the devices at all, but they had introduced a sort of winning move. Many other places were failing as they adopted technology, and these people were cheerfully going forth and winning. They had something others did not.

Let's break this down.

To teach, it is necessary to understand life to a degree. To teach when surrounded by technology innovation, it is even *more* necessary to understand what life is doing in order to enhance *it* to survive amongst machines and even compete with machines. Even if we don't understand everything about our fellow humans, we can still admire them and love them. After all, humans have something we can call creative inception that "jumps the rails" of direct linear code of machines and works non-linearly to think.

Life *is* the antidote, the opposite of tech. It is *actually* alive, not pretending machines.

Love may be the greatest *ability* of life.

It is wise to remember this about life.

Life also seems to be the telling of a story, from birth to achieving something and then eventual decline and death. The journey of life has the same beginning, middle, and end of a good story. It's more than just showing up and observing, or mimicry and memorization. It's not a docile data intake. This business of living is a deeply involving, contributive, rigorous activity, and we need to talk about it because we are so *into* it. Yet there is an interior complexity to our individual minds that is bottlenecked in connecting exteriorly. We can talk or write, physically interact, or build a piece of art or our whole lives into a sort of art, all to achieve a high level of communication through to others. Still, we are without an ability to directly mind-meld with any other human coherently or completely at the high volume and speed of thought and with all the nuances paralleling the actual intricacy of a mind. Thus, when we are our most alive, we feel compelled to tell stories, even play act like little children, building stories and even creative illusions on top of the real story of what is happening to us every day. We also do this when we dream. This skill is called *creative inception.*

It is interesting to notice that the human mind is this most sophisticated thing, creative well above and beyond the actions of daily life. It is superior to any present-day machine in this respect, even if it had all the capabilities of fantastic algorithmic inference. Additionally, as any good literacy champion could attest to, a mind uses a good story to escape its present-time environment on merely the wings of thought with no other conveyance required. If it cannot, it is not a free mind and is to that degree "illiterate" on a whole other level beyond reading comprehension. I have friends who have argued that this is the precise reason any idea of a technology "singularity" moment of artificial intelligence takeover can never happen.

A really high degree of comprehension combines with creativity, which is different from person to person. A trapped mind would be a mind that thinks *only* like a machine – linearly without an ability to "jump the rails" with creative inception. A mind like that might be able to memorize and do straight functions like math, but would not be very interesting as a dinner companion. It might not be able to extend creatively beyond itself interiorly to *love*, which, as anyone who has ever loved can tell you, is an act of extension outside of oneself.

The biggest driver for most teachers is the saving or freeing of a mind. They usually did not sign up to be testers and compilers and researchers and discipliners, but to help others find the freedom of mind that they themselves have experienced. To show something that gives the mind new space, new meaning, and new dimension is perhaps more significantly rewarding than other fields, because it achieves a mind-expansion beyond one's own mind, a freedom. That's causing creative inception. That's love being shared and being ignited in others.

When most other fields are attempting to drive consumption of things and solutions to various problems, and are therefore selling minds a mere accessory, or worse, an inhibition that must be overcome to live (you have to buy this machine that is like everyone else's machine so you can hope to keep up), education stands apart as a field that provides an expansion and freedom when it is truly causing learning.

Yet the freeing of minds has been nearly the opposite of what most formal education has focused on. Lots of memorization and history that hasn't necessarily been massaged with extra-interesting aspects or a live-it-like-you-were-there experiential interactive software has been the norm.

Technology that is leveraged to allow the ingestion of the data students need to master, while obtaining that mastery by letting them participate in a real experience, has the promise to bring the mind-expanding freedom that is being sought. This is possible, provided teachers guide them along their path with love. This is what teachers do that tech can't do.

This tool, or anti-tech, *love,* is the differentiator that consumerized learning will not be built to deliver. This anti-tech, then, is one that is in the arsenal of institutions and the teachers employed in them already. This is *their* differentiator. They can add love to the new mechanism of consumerized learning to find a solid place in the Age of Experience.

Chapter 24

Becoming Software Mavens

What does it mean to have a good user interface and user experience (UI/UX) with learning software? That is, a good user interface and user experience with an educational institution? If you answer the question from the viewpoint of interaction between *people*, you are still in the 20th century. Most captains of industry today lead from a different viewpoint – from "behind the screen," so to speak, as in what you see on the screen, how you see it, and where it takes you.

This is not to say that there will be no *people* in education or the learning journey in the future, but real survival will depend on how the interposition of technology between those people helps them get to objectives they would not otherwise be able to attain.

For example, one teacher truly individualizing every lesson on every subject for every child in the arbitrary grouping of a "class" is unrealistic for the average human teacher. One student, were he or she be allowed to progress in just math through un-gated courseware (no barriers to moving up to next lesson, chapter, or related subject) may be in "9th grade" but already complete on calculus. Fifteen others may be just getting comfortable with basic math, while a handful of others are strung out in between algebra, geometry, and trigonometry. One of the groups might even have done all of these things but all mixed up and backwards according to our current usual pathways.

Key Points

- Educators must address user interface and user design to engage authentic experiential learning.
- When the technology is not the real technology of the subject combined with a highly crafted delivery mechanism and highly artistic articulation of the concepts, what you really have is a barely digitized same old means of teaching and learning.

Let's just be real – what single teacher can do that for every kid, every class, and every subject without the intervention of a lot of technology?

The ideal of such potential falls down in two places:

1. Inadequate technology system structure.(Too much "nesting" or files within folders within sections, within systems, within larger numbers of systems – all with their own passwords, etc.)

2. People unable to keep up. (Being organized, scheduled, following through.)

This is simple but oh-so-complex at the same time. When the technology is *not* the *real* technology of the subject combined with a highly crafted delivery mechanism and highly artistic articulation of the concepts, what you have is a barely digitized same old means of teaching and learning. It's the Pong of electronic games compared to the uber-digital Minecraft, Pokémon Go!, or virtual reality field trips. Let's call the real technology that has been built with much attention to user interface and user experience this: *immersive environment courseware*. It's the professionally coded-type software mentioned in the chapter on evaluating digital curriculum.

When the teachers, and administrators in education, as well as students, are exposed or relegated to *non*-immersive environment courseware, the mode has all the usual old flaws, even if it's a little fancier looking.

With regards to the technology being the *real* technology of a subject, what is meant is that the method of teaching that does or *does not* use technology for a subject is the real question. There are ways to teach things with technology that may be way better, and the nuances of how that would be done are not fully explored across every subject. Some things aren't good at using technology right now, like playing most of the extra-curricular sports, but even that could change. The right technology of a subject is one thing that remains to be determined finitely, by learning degrees and perhaps ages.

User interface is the art of communicating via the code and screen with good utility. Buttons have to be in the right place, the flow of the lesson must make sense, and it probably moves (in the English culture) from left to right. In advancement, screens flying in from the right or below are expected.

The interface should fit the topic and not be random and non-sequential. There is an entire ocean of discipline already in the code programming and design world for what works commercially, but the depths of what constitutes good user interface in *learning* may not be the same as those that drive consumers. This knowledge is in the domain of real educators and research scientists, and in these coming decades, the depths of significance to their knowledge will cross with developers and web designers such that a real UI science will evolve for learning. This is one of the things publisher associations have been protesting – the potential for a *lack of science* in digital teacher lesson building, since so many are not trained instructional designers or UI/UX experts. In other words, there is a potential rigor problem.

Jay Diskey, the executive director of the Association of American Publishers' (AAP) pre-K-12 division, told *Education Week* that the association does not oppose open educational resources, but it is wary of government officials promoting them in the marketplace in ways the group believes will hurt companies and leave consumers with fewer choices.[1] I feel the same way – free resources are of course important, but must be contextualized for their proper place within a greater schema that includes the efficiency of the education enterprise. New companies coming into the space like Amazon may be excellent for making this happen. Personally, I think the free and open resource world holds even more promise for *student* discovery learning if it could be enabled. Student discovery, curating knowledge resources as part of the learning itself in the same way that teachers do when they develop lessons or publishers do when they build a textbook is something that holds enormous potential for learning digitally.

According to Diskey in his article in *Education Week*, "Materials created as open resources might provide good academic content in isolation, but many districts need a broad range of wrap-around support for content, the kind that commercial companies devote significant resources to providing. It's about much more than just content, in most cases, what districts want are really innovative projects that involve data analytics, assessment features," and other components.

The association effectively argued that the federal Every Student Succeeds Act (ESSA) proposal flouts an executive order by President Obama that requires agencies to base their regulations on "the best available science," among other federal policies. Those arguments have hit home with many schools who *do* want more than free bits of open education resources that they must curate and develop into scope-and-sequenced whole courseware that is still less than commercial grade available elements.

Game and web designers have a working knowledge of how facile code can be and how elements are presented typically, and they have also mastered things like click through rate and view time. User interface is all about accomplishing user maneuverability.

User Experience is a little more ephemeral to describe. It is in the field of aesthetics. It comes down to the engagement factor and, hypothetically for education, can be broken down to measurable engagement factors, including completion rates. New educational software publishers are already into subjects like "eyeball tracking" for time on task, which bring the idea of educational attention directing and measuring. Yet user experience is just like it sounds – is the user having an *experience*, or are they plodding through a boring digital recorded lecture or surfing through links before writing up a paper?

When you consider that personalization is a major goal of educational institutions already, if the resource used is just a flat file for the ingestion of data, some Word document on screen, it misses the wonders of audio, motion video, and animation, as well as a host of interactive challenges.

The survival of schools, teachers, and learners, particularly in a form resembling a formalized partnership between an institution and individual learners such as is the present norm, will necessitate having leadership that thinks like a software company. It will find a plethora of ways to first win students and parents into the idealized online community that is the institution; then it will deliver a dynamic interrelationship between assigned teachers to individual students.

More than mere survival, this will constitute a new abundance in the relationship. It will hopefully be well beyond just an automation of grade books and student information into authentic experience – perhaps a virtual and physical world seamlessly interrelating.

The future school administrator will be or have on staff a new sort of software maven, creating a proprietary mix of code with great UI/UX and humanity. This may begin with surveying and taking inventory of what software is available and in use already. After that, details of how things are being used and what is covered in the inventory of existing learning objects will help administrators to know their coverage models.

From there, administrators and companies that support them must craft and create a valuable digital user interface and user experience for students, parents, and teachers as they journey towards knowledge and community. Discussions of user engagement will become common as learning is being consumerized, as well as other common areas that software companies and most industries worry about, like web traffic, page loading speeds, and more.

[1] Sean Cavanagh, "Open Education Resources Get Major Boost From ESSA," Jan 2016, http://www.edweek.org/ew/articles/2016/01/20/open-education-resources-get-major-boost-from.html

Chapter 25

Digital Development & Administration

As has been already mentioned, a lot of focus on the lower-value free learning objects that have little upkeep by their original developers could be a hindrance to the transition to digital. Anything that doesn't have a commercial reason behind it to keep it up, something that pays the developer back for all the investment of their time, is at risk. Additionally, really well-designed systems are the province of industry, since software building is not the core competency of schools.

There will be companies who will build good free learning objects because they *do* have a commercial interest in doing so. Others will do so because they are embedding some advertising or are doing some sort of commercial data collection that might be objectionable.

The thing is, if you can make money doing it, you will invest money in it. If you can't, then it should be funded in some way or else it becomes no one's program, an orphan. It is wise to be suspicious of things that are considered "free" if they have actual value and are kept up by professionals, at least while our economy runs on money and not just good will.

Educators should understand the software coding world, which breaks down to this simplicity:

Coding or development or programming, essentially the same things, are the work of putting an orderly progression to a communication the machine can understand. It's a *language* to

> **Key Points**
>
> • Software coding and the development cycle is not so alien to educators as you might suppose.
>
> • It pays to introduce teachers to all of the possibilities in development and animation, in machine-based learning, and in becoming time conscious for themselves in lesson building.

learn, but more importantly, it's just being able to think sequentially.

If you can put things in order, you can code.

If you can understand strategic planning, you can understand the development cycle. Development includes the same things you would have to have to do for lesson planning or curriculum mapping, really. This means it should be a highly familiar arena for educators.

Building an application starts with requirements or needs analysis. This is kind of like a pre-assessment but is called by developers a "system investigation" or "system analysis." These could have slightly nuanced separate meanings, but you get the gist.

Next you'd have the actual design, like the lesson *plan*. Next you'd do the actual build or coding, like delivering the instruct.

Next you'd do some testing and "QA" or Quality Assurance, which is a lot like formative assessments – tests or quizzes.

Finally, you'd end up in operation and maintenance. This is the part where the building of curriculum often falls down in the educational system, *not* because all of the above steps couldn't be done with lesson plans and loose objects that are custom coded into grand online gaming with intelligent learning engines and analytics behind them, but because of upkeep.

Any teacher worth their salt has always prided themselves on keeping up with the times and their subjects, but what happens when the speed of change is such that no one can keep up and maintain quality personal interactions with students? Or keep up with subject and instructs and custom digital lesson planning, while also building great hands-on projects?

What happens when they can't build software that competes with the really engaging consumer-grade apps, so that they are further disconnected from the reality of students?

Therein lies the reason for doing one or more of these solutions:

- Spend a lot of time finding and curating the quality paid professional resources.

- Use the outside paid professional industry to build great digital objects in whatever mix can be truly afforded.

- Give teachers the training to be developers and animators.

- Give teachers powerful authorware tools that fake their being developers and animators.

- Hire a bunch of developers and animators.

It pays to introduce teachers to the possibilities in development and animation, in machine-based learning, and in becoming conscious of the time they use in lesson building. There is no reason everything has to be super-duper awesome digital, but perhaps the more there is, the more time those things give back to the teacher to build *other* activities, like field trips and class discussion sessions. Those are the things that will deliver on the personalization promise, while also providing the valuable experience sought by the present generation.

Chapter 26
Teacher Metamorphosis

School administrators who do not want a wholesale insurrection as they move schools towards consumerized learning need to be as inclusive as possible with the ideas in this book.

Merely implying that teachers need to change is enough to get you hints of revolution. And it's not that they need to change – that would not be a proper way to say it. It's that the world is changing, and they need to develop the skills to be something more.

What's being asked by schools is a metamorphosis into a new being, with new super-powers, including being equipped with knowledge about consumerized learning and what it means *for* them. What do they get out of it? Ideally, they get the magical ability to provide truly individualized learning automatically *and* gain back tons of free time, including time to pay attention to all the learners for real.

The shift to teachers as digital lesson planners without true consumerized learning objects is taking a great toll. It *appears* to most teachers to be an unfettered free-for-all to use any app and create lessons at will from as many free open education resources (OER) as possible. In fact, it is a greater burden than most realize. As Michele Alvarez, a charter school teacher with twenty-five years of experience said in the Visalia Times Delta newspaper on February 6, 2015, "The teachers are exhausted. We're being overworked and the district is taking advantage of their definition of

Key Points

- Teachers need to know that real consumerized learning makes them a superhero with individualization capabilities for every student and gives a ton of their time back.
- Teachers get the magical ability to provide truly individualized learning automatically and gain back tons of free time, including time to pay attention to all the learners for real.
- Leaders have several ways to give hope to teachers to help them to transition.

> "The teachers are exhausted. We're being overworked and the district is taking advantage of their definition of what is a professional day since we're not hourly employees."
>
> *Michele Alvarez*
> *Teacher, Charter Alternative Academy, Visalia, CA*

what is a professional day since we're not hourly employees. We're only paid for 7 hours of work. They're assigning more work and mandating more work than can be completed. They're getting lots of work that we're mandated to do for free."

The article also cited Karl Kildow, the president of Visalia Unified Teachers Association, addressing the school board saying, "Teaching is a contracted profession which regularly extends beyond usual work hours. Grading, lesson plans, after school meetings and more are done on a teacher's own time typically. But with the adoption of new curriculum, textbooks, planning resources and more, the workload has been extended tremendously this year."

"There's a host of things an educator has to do," Kildow continued. "It's part of the gig. The issue for us is the district has continued to pile on things that take time outside of that seven hours. And particularly this year, that outside time has even doubled or tripled depending on the assignment they have. It's affecting personal life, it's affecting health.

"More regularly now than ever before (I) hear of scenarios where teachers have to choose between personal family functions and classroom prep time outside of classroom time, with work usually edging the other out."

"When we have people who must choose between their daughter's dance recital or getting ready for the next day, something's gone wrong," Kildow said. "Those are the stories I'm hearing now, people having to make those choices."[1]

To this point on how teachers' lives are changing, Elliot Soloway, a professor from the

Department of Computer Science and Engineering at the University of Michigan, wrote to the Learning Counsel in August 2016 to say "Apropos of our conversation there (at a recent conference), here is a quote we recently copied down quickly from a conversation with a 3rd grade teacher":

> *"In the absence of textbooks, individual teachers are forced to spend hours searching the internet for resources. The process is not only time consuming, but much of the material online has little to no editorial oversight. With no textbooks, every teacher becomes an improvisational curriculum designer, which they try to do on-the-fly while also teaching their classes every day. When this amount of effort is multiplied by all the teachers doing the same thing around the country, it is clear that the wheel is being reinvented nightly, to the detriment of both the students and the teachers."*

This is a tale of woe told nationwide as schools shift to digital curriculum. The Learning Counsel asked one superintendent in Boston to "do the math" of what it was really costing his district. He did, as a roomful of other senior educators coaxed him on. At the estimated twenty-five percent of teacher time spent searching around and custom building lessons out of free open education resources (OER), his cost across all teachers was in the tens of millions. It was easily enough to have paid for software development professionals to not just purchase, but to *build* custom sophisticated digital curriculum content with educational rigor.

Notable Fact:

"In our efforts to ensure a positive experience for our teachers and avoid resistance to adoption, we started our Learning Management System (LMS) implementation by introducing teachers to the most simple communication, collaboration, and assignment submission tasks in the LMS. In retrospect, it would have been a good idea to provide teachers with brief preview-demos of our digital library search and personalization features. Many of our teachers were unaware of these tools.

"In some cases, teachers were unaware of the more than 1½ million high-quality digital learning objects from more than 30 publishers, searchable by topics and learning standards. A number of teachers did not know until recently that they can link assessment questions to specific learning standards. Upon completion of a properly meta-tagged assessment, the library automatically produces a list of potential resources for re-teaching and re-learning. Such preview-demos would have provided teachers with a powerful incentive to learn more and move at a faster pace."

L. Beatriz Arnillas, MFA, SPHR
Director, IT - Education Technology

There are systems emerging to create greater efficiencies. Knowstory has been built expressly to create the story of a teacher's own inventory of digital learning objects, however they have been created. When a teacher associates to a school, they join a community forum of shared learning objects and inventory controls, while still retaining their own independent page and lists. Analysis of coverage models can be done, and more. Being a social forum, Knowstory allows users to see what others use in other schools, rate objects, and promote their own special mixes. It is built, in other words, to bring structure to the chaos and changing learning object universe for individual teachers and institutions.

Give Hope

The answer for administrators includes giving hope to teachers about their future. They need the relief of consumerized learning to lead towards differentiated learning for each and every student. In this future, teachers function as learning tour guides, chefs, designers, air traffic controllers, or orchestral leaders of digital courseware and objects. They do not have to be "all" as classroom leader, finding and building all their own digital curriculum. They can win at directing students' learning from the software.

Leaders can also give hope in these ways:

- Paid professional resources can be funded to ease their burden. Learning Management Systems and single sign-on solutions can help make sense of all of the learning objects.

- Have everybody use Knowstory to keep a dynamic inventory of everything and watch what is working nationally.

- Try to find the good courseware that is super awesome (consumerized) and giant collections sites with tons of learning things all seamlessly accessible.

- Admit that Open Education Resources (OER) is great but can be a burden when teachers have to be in charge of every little thing while riding the bucking bronco of changing technology.

- Time can be dedicated and paid to help get teachers through the transition.

- The transition to tech will be never ending and teachers' jobs will need to be remodeled to provide for the regular acclimation to tech use.

- Assist teams and even online professional support groups to be used.

- Support development of skills that give teachers the ability to freelance digitally as well as be creative so that they have long-term viability even working from home and even if they ever disassociate from the institution.

- Allow the mixing of digital learning objects into an artful and practical scope and sequence. This is itself the new "know-mixing," just like music playlists, and is a sellable commodity in the future, divorced from the content – the list in sequence and projects and tests around it. This is the secret sauce of custom learning for any subject, and when customized to individual learners, is the new teaching or mentoring online or in person with supervised screen learning.

- Shun awkward terminology that points just to generic pedagogy, like blended, virtual, flipped, or online in favor of celebrity for the individual teacher. Use words that describe new person-to-person realities, such as "Guide," "Mentor," "Mixer," "Pro," "Agent," and other titling conventions that make much ado about the new glamour of consumerized learning brought to you by (insert teacher name here).

- Teach teachers that they are part of a team– not alone. Individually they are important, but as a team and group, they are unstoppable in creating a great experience hub for students that competes with fully online consumerized learning.

- Let them know that teaching online, being a student's guide rather than source of all

> knowledge, is the new "thing" happening globally and that the future is wide and bright for those roles.

At a Learning Counsel discussion in San Diego, Kim Knight, a teacher and instructional coach from Beaumont Unified School District, told a story about how her school started a 1-1 initiative so that every student had a computer. Teachers were on their own to build out a software set of lessons. One day a central office administrator trotted by and mentioned that she could use a log in for a math system. She checked it out. She started to use it as supplemental for students, a sort of game for the high achievers or slower students. The more she got into viewing the program, the more she understood what it was actually doing. Soon she slid other materials aside and was using the courseware as the core resource for teaching math.

She delighted in telling this story because she saw significant gains for students and could tell the story *statistically* of their gains.

This is the truth of the transition to digital – help teachers to look and know what they are viewing and what the software can and should do to help them teach students.

It's the story of student gains because of something as mild-mannered as a willingness to try, to look, to play with software, and to just see.

[1] Stephanie Weldy, "VUSD teachers discontent with working conditions," *Visalia Times Delta Newspaper*, February 6, 2015, http://www.visaliatimesdelta.com/story/news/education/2015/02/06/vusd-visalia-teachers-discontent-working-conditions-black-shirts/23004093/

Reference Material:

Karsten Strauss, "10 Great Freelance and Part Time Jobs for 2016", *Forbes.com*, June 2016, http://www.forbes.com/sites/karstenstrauss/2016/06/16/10-great-freelance-and-part-time-jobs-for-2016/#5451ca483d1c

Adrianne Bibby, "5 Top Companies for Remote Teaching Jobs", *Flexjobs Website*, April 2014, https://www.flexjobs.com/blog/post/5-top-companies-remote-teaching-jobs/

Stephanie Coleman, "What are the benefits of teaching online?", *WorldWideLearn*, August 31, 2010, http://www.worldwidelearn.com/education-articles/benefits-of-teaching-online.htm

Chapter 27
Expo Arrival

Expo is short for exposition, meaning a show or exhibit. I like to think of it as Disneyland or a state fair. It's a place pretty much everyone *wants to go to*, rather than sit at home and do their learning on their mobile devices. It has attention on the future and inclusion, a future which may potentially be a world largely without work because of automation.

I think the real challenge for education is the creation of both a virtual and real "theatre of experience," an Expo Center of Learning. This is because the environment is as much *a knowledge* as the subjects and topics taught in schools. When it is a compelling environment filled with projects and activities, it has relevancy in a time when a physical location is increasingly optional for learning delivery, especially when figured against consumerized learning. The digital learning objects can be the "furniture" being moved around in a digital universe as individualized, chunked mixes of knowledge, and the physical spaces, real furniture, mirrors this dynamic mobility with teachers and students in various modes of learning, decoupled from the "classroom" structure in an Expo of learning.

With a vision of Expos, the school is itself marketable social knowledge. It is a stimulating arena that challenges students by being bright, beautiful, and able to mutate from warmly casual to rigorously professional in a flash. Certainly, the vision is *not* one of marching through drills of data and

Key Points

- To arrive at "Expo Education," where the experience of learning has been redesigned, there will also have been a complete redesign of any physical center.
- The environment is as much a knowledge as the subjects and topics. Remodeling for digital learning helps establish schools as Expo Centers of learning.
- A "world without work" may be a reality for education to prepare students for – new curriculum steps.

lectures before a bell rings and a student dashes to the next class. It is new in the respect that it is centered more on activity, not sit-and-get.

Arriving at a real Expo, one that has a seamless interplay between screen learning and meeting up with teachers and other students in a physical location or across multiple locations, even nomadically, *is* the way to co-opt consumerization and bend it to the benefit of schools. It is a way to play with time and form to deliver meaning flexibly.

The important thing is that teachers and administrators must understand the digital things and their increasing sophistication and character internal to software and devices. Once those are understood, they can be used to recast learning and scheduling. Next, the new flexible learning will necessitate a remodel of the form, the academic structure, and the enveloping physical environment to most thoroughly compete in the coming century. It probably looks more like an office, a theatre, amusement park, gym, football field, library, and lounge. The software is so sophisticated that the physical environment shifts to engage on par with what's going on in the screen.

Expo Centers for Learning are already here for both grade schools and colleges or universities dotted across the country, most usually small centers of innovation.

Being an Expo is a place that is not a place *necessarily*. It could be a no place and many places, moving between the local zoo to local farms, from museums to stadiums and places of business. Online, it is everywhere with anyone, globally. Local attendance from elsewhere is via video chat and virtual presence. It is more of a crafted experience, a schedule with a lot of options.

The Expo Center of Learning

Creating an Expo is designing a central hub for the experience of learning for individuals, groups, or a club that forms into a grade and needs a teacher or coach. It's the creation of a platform that has the flexibility to leverage consumerized learning and digital objects of all kinds, but it adds value on top of that with things that give it relevancy to learning consumers and entices them into some sort of membership. This might include project-based learning, music, arts, social functions, math workshops, and more. The deconstruction of mandatory grading framework and classes opens up a world of new creative possibilities.

This is not a comment on all the barriers that already exist to accomplishing this. It's a comment on how to survive as any sort of school because of imminent consumerized learning.

Schools becoming Expos is the way teachers and schools will compete in the future with consumerized learning. It will appear, in fact, that consumerized learning was never a real threat if schools start to act now to make major changes. Some of them are.

At Houston Independent School District this project is already underway. They are ripping down walls and upgrading networks in a grand remodeling effort to bring the entirety of their school community into Exposition Centers that are terrifically engaging and imbue the population of students and teachers with a sense of thrilling innovation, compelling them to achieve. They already have the largest system of digital curriculum in the nation. Other schools are also planning for this.

To accomplish real transformation quickly will require some legislation changes, a whole lot of evangelizing, some technical capabilities, and new commercial-grade standards for learning objects. Schools can ignore these for now and focus on what they *can* do, which I will cover here.

In the realm of strategy, starting to spread the idea of competing with consumerized learning from a craft view (i.e., how well a school is digitally self-actualized with tricked-out software) is an important starting point.

In really readying a school to arrive at Expo environments for learning, it is important to envision tactics, such as:

1. Marketing the "Mix." Custom "mixes" of digital curriculum will be the critical brand move. Branding will be super important for K12s just like it has been and will continue to be in colleges and universities. Schools are already getting wise to this. Dr. Sharon Johnson-Shirley, the superintendent at Lake Ridge New Tech Schools, attended the September 20, 2016 Digital Curriculum Tactics Discussion event in Indianapolis and proudly brought the district's list of digital curriculum learning objects. She represents only a handful of schools nationally that are that organized and even aware that having that list is actually a positive marketing function.

2. Skilled Management. There will be a new "golden age" of school financial management, strategy, and recruitment. Software enablement of this is arriving from new companies.

3. Remodeling. There will be new layouts of the physical environment.

4. Experiential Learning. This will go well beyond old-school lecture-style whole-group teaching.

5. A new curriculum for a world *without* work.

Let's briefly take these tactics one at a time.

Marketing the Mix

First, let's discuss general school marketing as a backdrop to the internal mix-mastering of digital curriculum and in-person activities.

New York City's mandated choice program is a microcosm of what the new demands for schools will be when public schools are not only competing with private schools and charter schools, but also state-led online charters and pure consumerized learning – not just locally, but internationally.

One really interesting study titled "School Brand Management: The Policies, Practices, and Perceptions of Branding and Marketing in New York City's Public High Schools" came out in 2014, written by authors DiMartino and Sara Butler Jessen and published by Sage Publishing. It stated,

> *"How and to whom schools market themselves, as well as the nature and type of information students and parents receive in negotiating the school choice process, can directly affect enrollment. The branding decisions a school makes – from the name, to the official theme, to decisions about gender enrollment – affect how parents and prospective students perceive the school and, in turn, who decides to enroll. At the same time, schools with a low marketing profile can*

> *be passed over by students, simply due to lack of familiarity; schools that make misleading claims or ineffectively convey their mission or purpose can also result in families making erroneous choices."*

While the rest of the study offers a lot of interesting points about school marketing that are new and interesting, the usual fare, such as holding open houses for prospective students and parents, is also mentioned.

An in-depth awareness of marketing, promotions, and public relations is going to be needed by school executives. This is the same sort of training that the private sector gives brand managers. This is a new field for schools to consider in K12, although it is already well-tread ground in higher education.

One of the fastest ways to get savvier as a K12 is to form a coalition with top recruiter and marketing experts at area colleges and universities. More than likely they have staff who are interested in area K12 students eventually arriving on their campuses and will team up to help.

Whole "technologies" of how to market and how to think about consumers shopping for learning or where to send their child will be emerging from expert firms including knowledgeable news hubs like the Learning Counsel. Tracking local interests and geographic voting behavior is already a part of some of the new software offered by analytics platform publishers like GuideK12.[1]

The real work of marketing, though, is going to be the digital learning brand. The student and parent user interface and user experience is going to be central. What the actual learning software is doing, though, is more important than the niceties.

If it stays teacher-centric when the consumer world well surpasses it in gamified, social, engaging, and rigorous individualized learning, schools will be left behind.

The fact of digital learning transforming the landscape must be thought of as the ability for students to autonomously gain learning. Schools could become an intrusion into that. Schools must market themselves as places of hands-on discovery, project learning, and culture. They must not rest on their laurels and take their populations of students and parents for granted, or even their teachers, who could leave in droves to work from home over the Internet. If schools do not adopt this alternate view, this seemingly alien new reality, they will eventually fail.

When schools create an appealing mix for their local area, they will be able to win back the local learning consumers – or never lose them in the first place. The number one mechanism to find out what your mix should be is to survey, and not just students and parents, but businesses as well. Having a view to where the local economy can go, what is happening with growth or potential in the greater region, is also important.

Skilled Management

The isolationism of the education community, considering complete authority and an immunity to its customer's wants, will end. Schools and districts will be forced to transform through economic circumstances that drive the middle class out and the lower classes to find the most expedient low-cost means of education.

To prepare for this, school leaders will need to seek new levels of school financial management with programs like Allovue[2] and major systems that help them predict and manage where they spend extremely well. Knowstory will help track the inventory story and also present a marketing page to show off a unique digital mix of learning objects.

Setting a "sellable" strategy that makes sense for students and parents may include some of these features:

- Creating themes, such as "Technology" or "Arts" or "Virtual Reality Academy."
- Using freelance adjuncts and mentors to fill in specialized areas via online distance teaching.
- Using services such as online homework help and special needs teachers for speech therapy and more.
- A seamless orchestration of virtual and in-person attendance would use the efficiencies of home study and parent groups. Online schools would dub a parent as the "learning coach" and help them understand all the parts of their new role.
- Create scheduling to reduce costs, perhaps closing buildings and not running buses for two or three days a week while remote learning happens with mobile computing devices.
- Promising specialty digital learning curation to create individualization and rigor so that parents don't have to do it all themselves, giving them back parental roles that are bearable.

- The potential to structure so that smaller groups are catered to well, which could remove a lot of the bullying issues as well as parental fears of school terrorism attacks.

- Financial transparency.

- Workable social times, especially for parents to be with students when they are not working.

- Promising fantastic learning activities that may include multiple ages in groups that work together.

- Hiring subject-matter-expertise teacher networks.

- Providing quiet spaces that are supervised so parents can drop off their kids, but only that.

- Providing a sense of belonging to a group and manners and etiquette for social achievement that is more difficult to deliver in purely screen learning.

- Sports, dance, and physical activities.

- Anything else that makes sense locally, including self-defense classes.

A real skill in the understanding and selection of digital content and curriculum, perhaps even in building it from the raw lesson plans that already exist, is going to be an increasingly interesting role in the consumerization of learning. School administrators will become part of the new reality even as they compete with it, as they already have been.

Remodeling

There is room for schools to create new physical environments once there are a lot of digital objects being used by students, with a lot of screen learning going on in school or in various locations including home.

Just like office buildings, with their cubicle farms and conference rooms no longer resembling manufacturing lines in the plants of old, so too will education change in its form.

Layout Options for the "Expo" Remodel

These definitions describe some of the settings as they vary from schools of old. Many are adaptable within existing schools and some can be part of actual structural remodels to provide new spaces set in new ways.

Single-setting whole group – a space with desks or seats all facing forward with the teacher as the central delivery point via lecture with some illustrative content points in analog or digital chunks. Usually, there would be a podium or teacher desk, a blackboard/regular or interactive whiteboard/projection, and a television for video clips. This setting does not lend itself to rearrangement, and desks may even be bolted down.

Single-setting whole group interactive with multiple delivery modes – same as the above except technology is taking center stage as the delivery mechanism. The teacher is directing attention mostly to outside sources (video, projection, courseware, apps), not predominately lecturing. Students may also be called on to use technology such as calculating on the fly or look ups. Technology may include all or some of the students on computing devices with dynamic interaction during whole group lessons. If computing, the teacher's device may lock-screen on all other devices and force attention to one source, and that one source may be on the teacher's tablet and/or projected to a large screen. This is typically what is known as "blended learning." Typically, there is one arrangement of desks or chairs in any configuration, like face-forward rows, rounds, a horseshoe, or a giant circle.

Single-setting stadium – same as single-setting whole group or interactive above, except totally stationary and set up with riser rows. Typically, the room is extra-large and requires super-sized screens and voice amplification for any lecture or digital source. This is the common configuration in universities and generally atypical for K-12.

Independent study desks – the single desk configuration is for independent study when students need to focus on their own projects, especially for taking tests.

Independent study cubicles – similar to a single desk configuration for independent study and useful for middle and high schools when full, individualized learning is in use. Similar to typical businesses of today, these can be high or low-walled or simple carrels taking up limited space. Career readiness and high school intervention are typical applications.

Meeting room – boardroom meeting spaces for small or large groups that are typically equipped with projection and non- or interactive whiteboards.

Divided setting, pairs – a section of one room that has pair-up desks or tables, ideally mobile with wheels that can be configured into working pair-ups.

Divided setting, teams – same as pairs except with a larger, separate configuration of desks or tables.

Divided setting, project based – a section of one room that has a project orientation with larger table space. This may be ideally suited for art/maker/robotics projects with specialized impact-resistant surfaces.

Divided setting, advisory – a particular type of one-on-one setting using teacher desk and student chair, desk or table; student-and-student desk or table in a sectioned off area; or half-moon table for multiple students working in a group while teacher leads or oversees that dialog or work. Flat screen monitors commonly included in configuration for group viewing.

Divided setting, multi-use soft seating spaces – set up for working while lounging, including items like beanbag chairs and plush carpets to lay around on while reading from books or tablets, couches or poufs and some side tables for having an informal chat about a project. These are common for elementary grades for "reading" periods.

Divided setting or separate room, lab – maker spaces with access to technology. Typically high tables with power and tops with specialized high impact surfaces and mess resiliency for science or art work. May be in-room with other settings or a stand-alone dedicated room for lab work. May be a robotics or virtual lab for tools from such companies as RobotLAB, LEGO, and the acclaimed Dash and Dot from Wonder Workshop.

Divided setting or separate room, studio – for video or sound editing, with specialized audio/visual equipment and potentially a theatrical space preset for video backgrounds/green screen.

Divided setting or separate room, arts – for music creation or arts work, with specialized equipment and table or desk settings and potentially an orchestral seating with risers.

Divided setting, intensive computing – this type of space used to be known as a computing lab, but is now a separate space typically with computers with high speed graphics cards for rapid rendering capability for graphic art, video, and more.

Divided setting, manipulatives – an area in a classroom set up for individuals to play with or use objects, such as blocks and toys, mini-whiteboards, interactive whiteboards, and robotics; a dedicated editing computer; a dedicated distance-learning computer with headset such as those used for speech therapy lessons online (for programs like PresenceLearning); and a set of manipulative objects that interact with the computers including shapes and science equipment that may be used also in Labs, such as Tiggly, OSMO, and other more sophisticated lab equipment that can connect to computers for analysis.

Divided setting, quiet space – a separate space that may be in-class and semi-walled off or an entire separate room for students to escape to or be assigned to. May contain work desk or lounge setting and be a subdued lighting space that is extra quiet.

Divided setting, communications space – a separate space that may be in-class as a video-conferencing table for external communications, or a phone-booth-like space for students and teachers to visit to make external calls in private that could contain a power outlet and desk and chair.

Divided setting, small- or large group social emotional circle – smaller, more subdued spaces containing a circle of chairs for group discussions.

In addition to the above list for the redesign of existing schools and classroom spaces, there are many other spaces within school grounds to be included in the complete

Key Questions in Forming an Expo Learning Center

- Can the walls move and shift to facilitate a lesson, video, or group activity?
- Does the furniture adjust for reading or slide for a demonstration?
- Can the students freely draw or write on walls or tables?
- Does the space lend itself to instructors developing assignments that include real-world situations and have projects that are collaborative by nature and hopefully even culturally relevant?

redesign of teaching and learning environments. Spaces to consider in this regard would include:

Niches within corridors and circulation spaces – these make for ideal spaces for students to engage with technology and each other where they can see and be seen in conjunction with other educational activities going on around them.

Commons, or areas within common spaces, including views to outside and nature – this could include window seats, lobbies, and any area that would allow students to simultaneously work and enjoy the benefits that viewing nature has on the student.

Lofts or balcony overlook spaces – allowing students to work in different size groups, while still being spatially and visually connected to their teachers and classmates.

Outside play space – play is essential and the outside spaces of education institutions are widely recognized to be vital in the transformation of teaching and learning. These spaces include synthetic grass and other soft surfaces, as well as writable art walls with non-toxic paint or other markers for creative expression.

A New Curriculum for a World Without Work

Modern-day concerns about robots and the automation of work have led many writers to consider the issues of politics – managing humans when there is little for most people to do. For educators, a new question arises about the needed curriculum for learning in a world without traditional work. When schools step into becoming Expo Centers of Learning, there is a potential to deliver to both potentialities: highly-skilled work preparedness as well as a new creative non-work. In doing so, schools could perhaps become permanent hubs of enlightenment and community rather than preparatory shops with a finite graduation point. Expo Centers of Learning may be the cure of no-work, where learning, creativity, and organizing one's human-ness become a new social imperative carried on indefinitely. The investment in automation at every level of industry should open up ever more attention to travel, to gardening, to literature, to games of all kinds, and to arts that can be exchanged for the enjoyment of others in the new experience-oriented economy.

A market correction that rewards actual human service over industry's heavy computing power investments and robots is already starting to occur due to the "weight" of automation. The rapid pace of change already overwhelms humans, inhibiting the rate at which industry can rake in revenue by pushing even more new gadgets and features in. This natural cap will reduce the valuation of more common technologies and drive industry to care for both sides of the equation, the product *and* the health and quantity of consumers. Industry will naturally turn towards experience-oriented brands, incredible-level technologies, space travel, increasingly great design, controlling media attention, and especially politics.

To understand why a world could survive without work and what it will mean for education, it's important to consider the human condition. Work boils down to the important concepts of purpose, giving valuable exchange of labor or goods for money, and the human feeling of being essential. Without that feeling of being needed or sufficient, humans rebel or succumb to depression, drugs, or various criminal activities. Given free "basic income," or anything else free without any exchange by the receiver, tells them they are without merit in and of themselves. They cannot contribute and are worthless to society. Part of the self-evidence of this is in children. Often two- and three-year-olds recognize they are completely dependent and seek to self-actualize and contribute by helping around the house. They will play with toy vacuums, toy kitchens, and toy tools and are happiest when they make you smile. It is their "pay." A curriculum that will enhance our humanity to deliver personal purpose and importance will be as important as traditional core subjects which can be delivered systematically with digital courseware.

Step 1. Return to Vocationalism

Curriculum that will address the creation of a work and non-work-ready population would need to help all students be comfortably capable of a variety of non-work contributions to society. Governments across the world already require non-work for basic welfare incomes. Artisan crafts and the resurrection of rare and expensive skills, like metal smiths of old, home repair and woodworking, sewing and gardening and cooking and aiding the sick or infirm all show great promise. Many of these were part of the great curriculums through the 1960s but through program attrition have been largely forgotten until new maker-spaces began in earnest only a few years ago. Maker-spaces will need to widen in scope beyond 3D printers and into these older skills that enhance the experience of life and art more directly. Society is being enabled to return to these pursuits because of technology.

Step 2. Teach Volunteerism

New social media sites for posting potential tours of duty with purpose already exist, like VolunteerMatch and Indeed. Reading to, visiting with, and walking with our aged population, as well as oversight of children while they are in the process of learning on-screen or socializing, are needed in all societies. Being testers of new software, marketing survey subjects, and users of social media could all be paid "volunteer" positions for major corporations in the future. Helping students approach the need to help in their immediate social circles with a serious attitude, including how to build local interest for mini enterprises that will show direct benefit to others, like leaf raking and box pick-up, is the entrepreneurship attitude that will be needed in all students in a world where less and less traditional work is available. A new dignity in service, pride in one's empathy, and ability to connect with people will cause schools to emphasize social-emotional learning as a skill more essential than ever.

Step 3. Bring on the Interpersonal Skills

Interpersonal skills of good manners, respectfulness, public speaking, reasoning, and eye contact in communication already make the difference in many careers. Education towards the values of world-class customer service and creating quality experiences has the potential to birth whole new human-intensive industries. Personal travel guides could come back, public relations guides, actual live telephone answering as a means of brand improvement, event planning, the inventing of stories for virtual reality programs, and perhaps infinitely more new ways to have humans create value because they are human.

Step 4. Tech Awareness

Education will also need curriculum that exposes students to the full breadth of existing technologies so that they can create *beyond* them. The youth mind is particularly capable of thinking at the "incredible-level" of science-fiction-like make believe that could help take technology into higher realms. Space exploration will require a "renaissance man" approach to education where all math, science, mechanical, and more will be needed in everyone, rather than specialties only. The design of things, system theory, and philosophy will also be needed for a well-rounded awareness to problem-solve on the fly.

Step 5. Reasoned World View

It is already self-evident that commercial and political philosophies are bending media attention in an increasingly volatile barrage aimed at controlling populations. Staged events are subsidized expressly to cause behaviors that favor one or another party or objective. Without a reasoned world view that looks at survival factors for the race, at history, and especially at social dynamics, people are manipulated and used. They are isolated as individuals by preference or trait, and then ruthlessly managed into acting on those single issues emotionally, overriding the inherent sense of humanity in nearly all of us. The ensuing disassociation from mankind, the degradation into mindless allegiances, can only be managed through the exposures to such curriculums as 1) journalism's prior tradition of verification and concise truths without opinion, with a breakdown in meaning behind each of those operative terms for genuine understanding and application, and 2) debate's discipline of defending both sides of a single proposition. Exercises in both can be fun activities for learners of all ages.

Local debates held in the evenings at Expo Learning Centers, where all citizens can engage and watch under strict rules of conduct for the combatants, could relieve tensions and elevate the democratic process into a game of wits and intellect.

[1] http://guidek12.com/

[2] http://allovue.com/

Reference Material:

"A World Without Work is Coming – It Could Be Utopia or It Could Be Hell," Ryan Avent, *The Guardian*, Monday 19 September 2016, https://www.theguardian.com/commentisfree/2016/sep/19/world-without-work-utopia-hell-human-labour-obsolete

"Would a Work-Free World Be So Bad?" Ilana E. Strauss Jun 28, 2016, *The Atlantic*, http://www.theatlantic.com/business/archive/2016/06/would-a-world-without-work-be-so-bad/488711/

"When Robots Take All the Work, What'll Be Left for Us to Do?" Marcus Wohlsen, Aug. 8, 2014, *Wired*, https://www.wired.com/2014/08/when-robots-take-all-the-work-whatll-be-left-for-us-to-do/

"Welcome to World Without Work, Ryan Avent, *The Guardian*, Sunday 9 October 2016, https://www.theguardian.com/commentisfree/2016/oct/09/technological-revolution-sparks-social-unrest

Chapter 28

New Roles

Taking advantage of the best of consumerized learning while building a new Expo Center for students with a virtual administration means new roles in addition to new policies and new structures.

What might some of the jobs in education be like in the future? Besides the fictional chapters later in the book, what follows are some probable job descriptions in the future education sector. The way schools will get there is how they are getting there right now – promoting teachers into new roles or repositioning existing administrative jobs. I have met plenty of these hard-working administrators whose titles behind their names list out numerous duties as if their bosses have added more and more jobs onto the same person. Since no one really knows what the future looks like for certain, a lot of creativity is already going into defining job responsibilities and titles for what *could* happen with the digital transition. What absolutely *needs* to happen is for reallocated staff to have a distinct posture to co-opt consumerized learning and to reposition their institutions as Expo Centers of Learning.

Here are some of the new potential titles and responsibilities:

Learning Travel Planner

This is a teacher with new superpowers who crafts an individualized learning path for any one individual learner based on various characteristics

Key Points

- New roles and way more jobs in the education field are probable in the future.
- What absolutely needs to happen is for reallocated staff to have a distinct posture to co-opt consumerized learning and to reposition their institutions as Expo Centers of Learning.
- Consumerized learning may force the hand of unions and schools to provide for the teaching profession to enjoy far more telework.
- The administrative challenge is to juggle posting a new organizational structure of learning leaders and shifting the scheduling of all personnel by discovering a reciprocal balance in more and more powerful software.

and interests. It may also include virtual travel planning for learning. Lots of teachers are already doing this, but calling them this new title makes it way cooler.

Mentlancer

This is an anagram made of two words, "freelance" and "mentor." It is someone who associates to institutions at will as a substitute teacher or manages individual learners with their own special mix of learning objects and online or in-person meet-ups. This is the new "untethered" teacher who is not always associated directly as staff of an institution but could be part-time or on-demand.

Social-Emotional Leader

This is a specialized administrative role that interacts on-demand for certain teaching functions for groups or for individuals, perhaps serving up the latest in anti-bullying lessons or online privacy lessons.

Experience Manager

This administrative position is the student's individual experience manager, sort of like a homeroom teacher combined with a counselor.

Activity Learning Specialist

This teacher is focused on the activity using up 60% of any student's time, curating all sorts of subject-based activities that provide a lot of group or individual things to do, physical hands-on, or experiments.

Project-Based Learning Specialist

This person develops activities and more and

relates the activity level and *relevancy* level of what is learned with greater curriculum maps for that learner or group/class and the greater business community to align all of those.

Data Analyst

The data analyst is looking at macro trends and helping all teachers and administrators use their masses of learning object data.

Business Analyst

This administrative position is looking beyond the school at local, national, and international trends that might be useful in what is happening in teaching and learning. Perhaps a business far away needs a lot of animators and some students in one group have a high number of artists that could be given extra units on animation to help them get work one day. The business analyst helps identify these trends for schools to act on.

Curriculum Developer

This would be an actual coder, someone doing more than just the mapping out of things, but actually building them or customizing them. There could be dozens of these on school staff.

Curriculum Animator

Another useful resource for curriculum teachers' use, an animator helps to build animation into what schools are using for digital objects or to teach it.

Learning Object Curator

This is a new skill for the librarians and media specialists of old, who mostly already are the most fabulous vetters of digital objects ever.

Digital Subject Specialist

The subject of how you teach math or any core topic today should be considerate of developments with digital objects and the greater tech field of delivery, including virtual worlds and more. The specialist in this area will craft the mixture of digital learning objects, discrete texts, and full courseware to deliver learning for various levels of comprehension.

Group Dynamics Expert

This administrative expert draws on experience with student interactions to pair up screen learners and help teachers in actual physical classroom environments to pair up the most helpful sub-groups. This is perhaps one of the most overlooked areas for schools – the sub-dynamics that impact learning because of the way they deliver education. New dynamics can be created by moving most of the ingestion of information in learning to the screen.

Some of these positions are already appearing on the landscape of school administration in the guise of added functions given to curriculum managers, counselors, teachers, or administrators of some sort for part or all the definition of their jobs.

It is important to remember that most teachers are cut off from the rewards of technology regarding mobility. Telework is rarely enabled for teaching for the obvious reason of required student attendance. Consumerized learning may force the hand of unions and schools to provide for the teaching profession to enjoy far more telework. With technology, there is no reason not to allow a lot more teachers to become experts and to teach or run learning communities from anywhere. Mobile experts online also give administrators options in crafting a curriculum that uses different employment contract structures. When individual teachers become specialists just like college professors, it could also mean bringing up the quality of all learning in grade schools.

With these new roles, we probably will see *more* teacher-level staff. We will also see a new sophistication to the organizing of teaching and learning via changed scheduling and teams of subject experts leveraged across multiple schools. Software systems that provide for better automated scheduling and curriculum administration will free up some of the needed budget for more teaching staff in new roles.

The administrative challenge is to juggle posting a new organizational structure of learning leaders and shifting the scheduling of all personnel by discovering a reciprocal balance in more and more powerful software – all in the direction of highly personalized learning delivered out of thrilling Expo Centers.

Chapter 29

Who Is on the Way?

The consumerization of learning is providing a different experience of learning already. Learning math or economics in a game with repetitive training, "failing forward," and feedback loops on exercises are different things than being in a classroom with a teacher and taking a test.

If it is purely and only screen learning, it can still accomplish a sort of "experience." That is why people go to movies. They discuss them afterward, and they've definitely had an experience.

Thinking that the only way to deliver an experience is in the real world is false now. Pokemon Go! has proven that software can also engage people in the real world. Virtual reality has great promise as well.

Teachers are usually great at project-based learning and activities.

The new trick is building experiences around digital courseware, letting the bulk of the information download and knowledge acquisition happen on screen so that they can particularly craft experiences *for that individual student*, similar students, or even letting that student "teach" older or younger learners. Perhaps one student is struggling with some subject and a trip to a pottery wheel has just enough hands-on activities that they can write a paper that shows they are no longer struggling. Perhaps the student is having trouble with physics concepts, and a group project with drones is just the thing, which also serves to help some of the other students who need some of the

Key Points

- A lack of purchase behavior by schools to intake and use more of the industry's digital courseware, and instead to favor teacher-led and teacher-created materials, is forcing the industry to circumvent selling to schools and go straight to the consumer.
- The new trick is building experiences around digital courseware, letting the bulk of the information download and knowledge acquisition happen on screen.
- Schools will ultimately provide a level of service that makes learning like having a family – an always available, always encouraging essential to life.

social aspects. "Stations" of teaching excellence, perhaps even spread across a city in different buildings, may be a model.

Schools creating these sorts of experiences, especially alongside parents, create more than just learning experiences – it's helping craft the life of the student.

Who's on Their Way?

There are a lot of school leaders who are having the realization that consumerization of learning is on the brink of arrival and that expositions of learning are necessary. There are schools all over the world doing interesting things, although it does not appear that there are many that are the real hybrid Expo Centers of consumerized learning idealized in this book. Those mentioned here are either schools or software companies selling to schools, with a few in that magic space of appealing straight to consumers. A few to mention include:

Mountain House High School

Ben Fobert, a school board member turned high school principal, is one of the most charismatic visionaries we have met on our travels. He stepped down into the principal position out of a serious interest in seeing real innovation occur with a brand new school that had been built by the Lammersville Unified School District.

In November 2016, he addressed the group attending the Digital Curriculum Tactics Discussion event held by the Learning Counsel in Palo Alto, California on the Stanford campus. He described his new high school building, but then made a serious turn off the usual discussion of school leaders being prideful about their buildings and talked about innovations in scheduling.

The new schedule of the school day instituted includes an hour in the middle of the day that breaks for teachers to have a short lunch and then meet on technology and student management. In the meantime, students have an hour of "Success" and lunch. It's their time to keep up digitally. In addition, Fobert has promised to allow homeschooling families to remain untethered via a digital enablement, while still using his school's sports programs and other in-person activities that will give digital learners access to the community.

Fobert is setting an example of the new Expo Center of Learning, as well as the example of a restructuring and rescheduling – a change in timing and staffing. This type of leadership is unprecedented and most definitely the "right stuff" of the future.

HMH

With their development of a comprehensive curriculum of learning objects, courseware and collections, HMH can boast they have a complete go-to-market coverage plan. More importantly, they have done something extra by building their "HMH Player" app. A first of its kind, they have taken on the really complex technical work of tying in a multitude of back end systems encompassing a vast array of knowledge pieces and various software interfaces into a front-end navigation that is built with the type of strong consumer interface one expects to have. HMH Player makes the access mobile and both online and offline for students.

K12, Inc.

This company, and others like it, is a are models that allow a fully online grade school service for students, across all subjects and topics. This model is available in nearly every state as either a state-linked charter service available across that entire state, or attached to a district or a private school.

K12, Inc. describes their service as "a high-quality, individualized education online," where "the classroom is in the home or on the road, wherever an Internet connection is available."

They describe the full-time students' days as a combination of these things which are overseen primarily by the "learning coach" and a member of the family in combination with the oversight of online teachers:

- Online lessons, interactive activities, and virtual classroom sessions in the online school.
- Independent activities not on the computer using the K12 provided materials, including textbooks and workbooks.
- Interaction with teachers and classmates online or by phone.
- Planned student activities and parent support as needed.
- Students are expected to complete schoolwork each day and attend virtual classroom sessions as scheduled by their teachers."

Students who have started in their program as kindergartners are already graduating in several states – and testing high on exit exams.

This alternative for parents is gaining ground, and there is some use of intelligent courseware and gamified learning objects. The company uses an advanced learning management system to log in students and present courses, many of which are lectures, assignments, and documents.

They also sell one-offs, or single courses online, and the student pathways are definitely individual, although still somewhat oriented to the typical grade and class structure.

Florida Virtual School Global

Florida Virtual School Global (FLVS) is an online school that is technically a district in Florida in service to other districts. It has developed a comprehensive virtual K-12 education solution for students all over Florida, and in the last few years extended those across the U.S. and the world. It is a non-profit, public entity competing with for-profit industry. Founded in 1997, it was the country's first state-wide Internet-based public high school. Today it services students in grades K-12 and provides a variety of custom solutions for schools and districts to meet student needs.

Florida residents take courses for free, while non-Florida residents take courses based on tuition rates.

Students in Florida have the right to choose Florida Virtual School as a complete educational option, not as a partial option. It is not fluidly set up for consumerization, but is more rigidly following the school model; it cannot grant diplomas and can offer access only if local school counselors deem it appropriate for a student. FLVS also cannot offer a real consumerized model and limits adult access to only a few courses. Florida state statutes limit and protect the existing delivery structure of their schools.

Visions in Education

One of many online charter schools, this one is hung off of the San Juan Unified School District in California. It allows students and parents to enroll locally and offers a full K-12 homeschool program. Parents and guardians take an active role in their childrens' education when they enroll a student. It provides all the materials, including renting laptops for academic instruction in the home. Credentialed teachers work with families to ensure curriculum meets California state sontent standards and that students are assessed periodically for achievement. Credentialed teachers help parents and students take advantage of a flexible instructional program, curriculum, enrichment services, and other resources to enhance their home schooling experience.

In this program, families commit to providing at least four to six hours of in-home instruction daily, and as they do so, Visions in Education[1] provides these things:

- A credentialed teacher, available Monday – Friday, 8:00 a.m. to 4:30 p.m.

- A flexible spending account (up to $1,800 for the school year) to use for a student's personalized learning plan. (The virtual charter school distributes the money directly to students for "enrichment activities and more.")

Whether the students are citizens or not is unclear, nor is it clear if this is a contracted spend or actually has supporting legislation for appropriations distributions, meaning if it has budget authority or not. This is a direct financial distribution in support of student educational goals by the (probably) authorized local district itself. The money can be used by parents with more than 1,000 vendors throughout the nine-county service area the school covers, and even beyond that geography for outside services, such as athletics, tutoring, enrichment, and digital curriculum to Visions homeschool families.

- Online ordering systems to ensure quick easy curriculum purchase (full e-commerce). 24/7 access to systems to manage student budgets and curriculum orders, enroll in classes/events, and participate with the online community.

- A wide variety of courses to choose from in their home school high school catalog.

- Access to community college courses with approval from a Visions counselor.

- Vocational apprenticeships through the California Apprenticeship Program.

- Field trips, picnics, and other activities with other homeschool students and families.

- Technical education and regional occupation programs (ROP).

- Support services including academic and career planning.

Amongst all of these, the "physical" environment is missing except for certain classes, which may have taken space at local strip malls or other inexpensive retail or business space to offer hands-on classes in science if desired. Other home experiments use manipulatable items that are shipped to students' homes.

Ithaca City School District, New York

At this school, there is a focused effort to create student "thinkers" as a strategy. Dr. Luvelle Brown is the superintendent and was named one of the nation's most "tech savvy" school superintendents in 2014.

To create thinkers, he has focused on the environment more than the consumerized learning objects, but his tactics are setting the stage for a total assimilation of consumerized learning.

"As we talked about how to do this, how to promote skills like collaboration, problem-solving, creating, and analyzing, it required us to change the spaces," said Brown in an interview in July 2016. "We have many spaces now with writeable walls, writeable desktops, and flexible seating options. Kids are not sitting in rows in desks and chairs anymore, they're sitting in flexible seats, seats that move, tables that transition."

He talked about how, in Ithaca schools, you'll see students creating on walls; they're working in digital spaces, using digital tools and mobile devices. "The color, the look, the feel can be shocking at times," said Brown. "For the teachers who were very successful in the school district many years ago to come back and see it now, they wonder 'Wow, that's not the place where I taught. It looks very different now,' and the conversation has been about how to be comfortable with it looking so different."

Dr. Brown has talked with architects about the design of schools and discussed the common trends that are now the expected: day lighting, how the sound is being handled with baffling systems, the look, the feel, and color, all which promote learning. But beyond the architecture, they also surveyed their students and teachers to find out what they felt the spaces should look like without spending a lot of money.

They've used the latest furniture and Idea Paint, but it's not only new materials. "We even repurposed old furniture," said Brown. "The kids will make their own chair or desk in a shop. And we've bought hundreds of yoga balls for classrooms. It's more about the pedagogy – how we want to shift the teaching/learning process, and then it's the tools, i.e., the mobile device or the table or chair which support that. And we've had that conversation again and again with architects and they've been helpful in designing these spaces with all this taken into consideration."

Wisconsin's Connects Learning Center

For Stacey Adamczyk, the lead teacher at Wisconsin's Connects Learning Center (CLC), a four-district consortium alternative high school for youth at risk, "Creating the right learning spaces for (our) students to thrive in has been an integral element to our students' success." The school started with students sitting at desks, but with no assigned seating.

Through trial and error, CLC's learning spaces evolved to become less like traditional classrooms and more like a "home away from home," according to Adamczyk. "Much like college, our learning spaces are filled with comfy couches, chairs, and lounge furniture for student use, as well as areas conducive to collaboration." These shared spaces create a sense of community and give CLC's students "the feeling that they are not alone, that they belong."

Using cloud-based curriculum from Odysseyware, CLC couples its non-traditional spaces with a non-traditional daily schedule. "We operate two three-hour sessions per day," said Adamczyk, "with 80% of student time being spent working individually online. Thanks to the flexibility of Odysseyware, our teachers are able to create and customize online courses and content based on students' individual needs."

Odysseyware is one of the companies on the market with a wide array of course options, although not all of them are full digital courseware, but are content that has been chunked into knowledge objects that can be mixed into various lessons to make courses. Full animations, gamification, and the intelligent learning engine are not autonomous, but teacher-led. Odysseyware is one of many companies offering solutions that are not yet consumerized, but are being sold to schools because they still require a teacher leader.

The Connects Learning Center courses all focus on applied knowledge, creative problem-solving, and decision-making. The synergy of software and space "allows our students to find their ideal spot for learning, and to learn at their own pace," Adamczyk said. This school is on its way while still somewhat attached to the teacher-student model and non-fully-immersive digital courseware.

Companies to Watch

ST Math by Mind Research Institute offers visual math learning, using no words in many of the digital gaming-like lessons to teach mathematical concepts in an entirely innovative method.

Myon, a Capstone Digital company, is a personalized literacy environment that incorporates a large collection of digitally-enhanced digital reading content with an envelope of the state-of-the art learning platform. It incorporates the Lexile® Framework, a reading level determinant, and cutting-edge literacy tools with analytics.

DreamBox, a K-8 math games product that adapts to the learner's level of knowledge and supports teacher decision interjections.

GoLeaps from The Life Excelerator, Inc., a K-12 full-subject coverage digital curriculum model that includes special attention to social-emotional learning.

Fishtree, an adaptive learning platform that curates, aligns, and personalizes online courses.

TenMarks, an Amazon Company, offering adaptive curriculum math for all levels.

Awesome Stories, a unique platform started by a concerned citizen offering a story-board format for teacher- and student-created digital lessons.

HMH, with its Read180 and Math180 programs and hundreds of other offerings, is one of the "major" publishers doing a good job of whipping into digital mode.

eDynamic Learning, born out of a keen interest in student work preparedness, offers a lot of career and elective courses online.

Gale Cengage Learning, one of the better "discovery learning" research-type sites for students that includes their own created materials along with titles from 120+ notable publishers, thousands of newspapers and journals, and more than 175 million pages of primary sources.

Achieve3000® provides the only patented, cloud-based solutions that deliver daily differentiated instruction for nonfiction reading and writing that's precisely tailored to each student's Lexile® reading level.

Adaptive Curriculum offers deep concept-aligned and standards-aligned middle and high school curriculum that is true immersive digital courseware.

Imagine Learning is an innovative language and literacy software program for English Language Learners, struggling readers, early childhood education, and special education students.

Triumph Learning provides research-based print and digital solutions for instruction, intervention, and test success, including an all-inclusive program that adds depth, understanding, and practice for all of the Common Core standards and skills.

Apex Learning provides digital curriculum designed to actively engage students in learning, combining embedded supports and scaffolds to meet diverse student needs, actionable data to inform instruction, success management, and virtual schooling for partial or whole operations and online tutorials.

Follett, with their Lightbox educational platform, Digital Bundles, and special emphasis on maker spaces that include the arts, Follett's offerings are coming along to transform the purely paper focus they once had.

Waggle provides individualized math practice and "productive struggle" for students.

Ogment is a learning platform that allows students and teachers to clip relevant, real-world content with the "Web Clipper" which are not just links but actual videos, articles, images, and websites.

BrightBytes is a learning platform that effectively transforms complex research and an increasing number of disparate data sets into simple, actionable roadmaps that educators and administrators can understand.

i-Ready by Curriculum Associates offers an adaptive assessment and instruction for math and reading in grades K-8.

Istation, a pre-K-12 digital curriculum is an assessment and intervention and English Language Learner program for reading and writing.

Knewton, an adaptive learning platform that customizes educational content based on student needs.

itslearning, an intuitive learning management system that allows districts to personalize learning by putting curriculum resources, instructional strategies, objective-based lesson plans and assessments, into one central location.

LearnBop, offering an automated online math tutoring and analytics tool for 5th-9th grade students.

MyLab, which has leading collections of online homework, tutorial, and assessment products designed for higher-ed students.

Think Through Math, an adaptive math program providing adaptive instruction, motivation, and live support.

Final Note

There could have been fifty or more examples of schools in this book showing which ones are on their way in addition to what has been seen already. There could be thousands of companies listed who are offering for-sale digital objects, courses, courseware, and whole online schools.

It's important to note that the schools cited are on their way, and like *most* schools, haven't seen fully consumerized learning – yet.

Only a few thousand companies are offering it in the U.S., but many are busily building quality learning objects. A lack of purchase behavior by schools to intake and use more of the industry's digital courseware, and instead to favor teacher-led and teacher-created materials, is forcing the industry to circumvent selling to schools and go straight to the consumer.

The educational focus on *locating* learning into a geography is the opposite of consumerized learning, which is gaining ground internationally for all the same reasons that catering to consumers online benefits companies and governments. The focus on individualizations, on the highest technical sophistication that can be rendered using not just technical software aspects, but also research into human learning via the screen, is creating a growing tide of digital learning objects and courseware.

All of this has implications for the greater economy. A great gain will be had after learning that personalization is *real.* Exactly how to do this is with software that does the bulk of the heavy lifting to adapt around a learner.

I have been criticized for not giving a more exact step-by-step guide, but I must concede to the facts of place-specific needs. No overly authoritarian plan has been working anywhere universally, despite the billions put behind some lovely schemes. The facts of utility for the consumer are also not all in – what do *they* want? How do we change operations and regulations to enable them directly and not keep trying to protect structure? That is really the question today already driving the consumerization of learning. It will be what drives teachers and schools whether they like it or not, a three-hundred-sixty degree turn from century-long aggressive prescriptiveness and central control. It does not mean public education will not survive, but it must change, or it will increasingly become only the last resort, the least desirable option, and by nature, something that is not in equity with other options. It will miss its chance to build a fantastic expansion of our economy through knowledge.

Now is the time to create an economy that buys learning or, by public contract, earns learning by arrival, instead of mindless escape games; to build an industry where students can grow up using digital learning, and where schools will provide a level of service that makes learning like having a family – an always available, always encouraging essential to life. It is for this reason that I am building Knowstory, so far without any outside influencer or investment forcing it into the common mold of working only for institutions or only for consumers. It will be both. The freedom of learning in the Age of Experience should be one that is a foundational right for all – with any mix of guidance.

Reference Material:
Link to Florida State statutes: http://info.fldoe.org/docushare/dsweb/Get/Document-5250/dps-2009-007.pdf

Chapter 30
Paying For It

What is a myth? Well, there are two primary definitions of "myth," according to the Oxford Dictionary. One is "a traditional story, especially one concerning the early history of a people or explaining some natural or social phenomenon, and typically involving supernatural beings or events."[1] This definition of myth is like a folk tale, fairy tale, or legend. While it might feel like in schools that one is in some ancient legend, another definition of myth is "a widely held but false belief or idea."[2] That is the appropriate definition here.

What is the most widely held but false belief or idea in education? The "there is no money" myth.

It really is one of the most interesting phenomena, that a market with a trillion and a half dollars rolling through annually has this ever-persistent rhetoric that there is no money. This is always contextual to how budget is allocated, with complaints that the different sources all have different strings attached, which does have some truth. Education is always the largest portion of state budgets, and many times the same is true for local county/community budgets. During the recession, the federal stimulus monies evened out the great dip-that-really-wasn't. In tracking the stimulus funds, one of the anomalies was the fact that there was a lag of years in some areas for spending their allocations.

During the recession, you could walk through a good 2,000 square feet of interesting foam-core boards with fantastic pictures of brand new

Key Points

- Schools have a lot of money they could redirect but actually do need a lot more funding for the tech transition. By becoming their own "net centers," and even selling learning objects, they could earn some or all of what they need.
- Beyond the vision of always-on digital learning, where consumer choice and utility create ever-better works of digital aesthetics, is a time when the global micro-learning market may be larger than the music or movie industry. Children will learn while playing. Adults will play while learning.

$30-$350 million dollar new buildings going up all over the U.S. at the annual National School Boards Association (NSBA) events. Big school construction is still such an enormous industry that there are whole magazines dedicated to it. Meanwhile, the ever-growing charter schools that are delivering on a shoestring budget take space in emptied commercial buildings or old malls, and they still manage to create interesting "expo" learning type centers. Rhode Island and a few other states late in the recession had placed temporary moratoriums on new public school construction, while other states like Georgia questioned spending on a single school construction project "$147,893,989 for about 1,650 students."[3] Do the math. By anyone's estimation that is beyond exorbitant.

Many districts are not, in fact, transitioning to digital but simply rearranging budgets. And many of the schools that are innovating often find they are under-budgeted intentionally because of another pervading myth that virtual is way cheaper.

There is a culture of "place-as-important" for many districts and school leaders. There is a pride in the big beautiful buildings that younger generations may have gladly traded for less class-time and more mobile learning. This is perhaps restricting some of the creative thinking – thinking that is obviously going on with charters and private schools. It's true – far too many superintendents have said that they will keep buying textbooks while trying to make the transition to digital curriculum. This means the budget didn't move, so of course there is "no money." Those same Superintendents are probably forwarding the idea that there is no money to the troops while spending $25 million a year on textbooks, perhaps a new building or two, and another chunk on tablet computers. The troops, or teachers in this case, have also been well indoctrinated all their lives in the idea that there is no money. Upon hearing yet again that there is no money for the curriculum to run on the devices they were just given with no accompanying training, the "no money" campaign continues.

Interestingly, there are stories of districts who, sometimes by no fault of their own but some sort of procurement over-encumbrance complicity by their state, have warehouses full of unused textbooks worth thousands, if not millions, of dollars. Stories abound, but to mention a few places that made the news in just the last few years with their purportedly wasteful spending:

- West Contra Costa Unified School District, CA in 2014
- Clark County School District, NV in 2012
- Washington, D.C. in 2007
- Irving Independent School District, TX in 2012
- Detroit, MI in 2008
- San Francisco Unified School District, CA in 2011

What's interesting about these is that almost universally the articles mention reasons such as "out of date" or "the teacher didn't use that workbook" or "new edition replaced those that we never opened." At $10-$150 per book or more, those poorly planned allocations that went unused are representative of an enormous potential upside to education *and* the digital publishing community.

Honestly, with poor administration software to support inventory controls, it is no wonder a lot of this has gone on in the past. This is another reason for the inventory mechanism inside Knowstory – to help schools avoid these sorts of news-making issues that shame schools.

If somehow schools can consider the potential vast efficiencies when they are not warehousing books or throwing away books no one uses, and redirect those budgets into purchases or training for teachers, there is plenty of money to create well-marketed Expo Centers of Learning. You will probably never hear administrators say that, though. That would be very poor form for any executive officer in any industry – bragging about savings and giving people ideas that they could spend more on something else.

Education as an industry needs an explosion of more people, energy, enthusiasm and change than ever before. This does not *necessarily* mean more money, but it does mean change and a campaign pulling in community involvement from every quarter – parents, associations, and other community groups.

Every district has their horror stories of waste because of poor planning, which, while not palatable to the tax-paying public, is understandable given the incredible change being pushed by various accountability requirements onto schools. What's irritating is that the direction of demand on the budgets for capital outlays on buildings or books, in addition to the waste, is not necessarily the correct one for the future.

There needs to be a way to pay for the transition to a posture that puts schools in a power position with consumerized learning so that they survive.

This will not be just a budget shift and reallocation of normal funds to new things. Unbelievable as it may seem, there is a need for self-sustainability financially with some grade-school level services *and* vastly *more money* allocated to a dramatic education transition.

Retooling costs money. Other countries like Singapore are doing it, and the U.S. should be no exception. I've mentioned earlier that the cost to make a fast transition could be at in the neighborhood of $150 billion, a number that hinges on both the size of the market and the estimated costs of a lot of new technology across 97,000 schools and 50.4 million students. That is roughly $2,000 additional per student for a one-time purchase of devices, networks, and a lot of software, plus another $50 billion for developing staff, continuity, and up to five years of refreshing technology until the efficiency of the system re-shapes itself back to existing budget levels. This must not be administered federally but in block grants to states with technology and planning required. Consider that what is going to be most useful is to set up a sort of commission in every state that temporarily runs the alternative super-structure of administration, incubating and aiding schools and industry to develop their action plans. If I were writing the legislation, I would set it so the commission expires in five years.

I envision this could be like a New Deal for teachers and schools that provides a similar program to the Relief, Reform, and Recovery [4] program of Roosevelt's presidency, giving students the learning needed to rebuild our future.

Relief is needed – actual money, to drive schools to a new architecture of delivery through digital learning objects and full coverage models of digital learning plus remodeled physical environments. Then we must reform a lot of the laws and encumbrances, plus train personnel in efficiency and marketing and all things digital. Additionally, like the road-building and communications network investments of old, our country needs a new recovery program that gives grants to the publishing industry to redevelop itself to be a world-class superpower of millions *more* digital learning objects that rival any game or app out there, plus a clear path to market them internationally as one of our largest exports. Other countries are already in this global race.

As mentioned earlier, there is a near infinity of value in the experience economy for learning. The attractive ways it could become experiential are limited only by our imaginations. People will *pay for experience* in the new economy – it's how you market to them to cause it that matters.

It is already commonly agreed that learning accompanied by the impact of real experience is better than any rote memorization or placid receipt.

When service levels of digital learning are extraordinary, and schools figure out how to use their "net center" of information for their *own* gain, they may actually also become more self-sustaining financially. They do not have to give away all the power of their information commercially, but they could potentially use some of it without harm to attract business, to help business locally, and more.

Schools and teachers may even start selling a lot of their own digitally created learning objects to defray costs.

Beyond the vision of always-on digital learning, where consumer choice and utility create ever-better works of digital aesthetics, is a time when the global micro-learning market may be larger than the music or movie industry. Children will learn while playing. Adults will play while learning.

Beyond this corner we are turning may be a change to a time when the global collaborative knowledge generation and crowd-sourced vetting refine human knowledge and hone it to perfection.

Beyond the digital learning transition is a real balance of humanity with technology, because we level the playing field for all.

It's possible.

[1] Oxford Dictionary, https://en.oxforddictionaries.com/definition/myth

[2] Oxford Dictionary, https://en.oxforddictionaries.com/definition/myth

[3] http://www.wsbtv.com/news/local/new-north-atlanta-high-set-be-states-most-expensiv/242202570

[4] https://dp.la/exhibitions/exhibits/show/new-deal/relief-programs

Book 3

Fictional Future

Chapter 31

Future You in Pre-Kindergarten

Welcome to Book 3, where you have now left future musings and practical advices and entered the realm of fiction.

The following chapters are hypothetical – just a fun look at where the tide of cultural change and technology can take education. We start where it starts for the youngest of us, and you get to pretend it's *you.*

Future You, in Pre-Kindergarten

You got to pick out your own outfit today – your first day of POD, which mom said was "Parents Over Development" or something. You picked pants and a shirt that could not have clashed more, but it doesn't matter to you because that shirt and that pair of pants are each, individually, your favorites of *all known shirts* and *all known pants* that are yours. Bright green and bright orange, especially with a ducky on the front of the shirt, are the best.

At four years old, you have a limited wardrobe anyway because you are growing so fast. Mom said this is your big day and you get to pick out your favorites. She goes with what you chose and you are off, down the street to the Maxwells' house. Mr. Maxwell is the Leader for today, your first day of POD.

Mom says this is not going to be like daycare, that you will have to "learn," and to you that means, more or less, "behave," because "learn" has very little meaning to you just now. You've pretty much been doing that already anyway, haven't you? You did get "learned" about not stealing cookies and not putting dirty clothes under the bed or picking your nose. You aren't a *baby*, so now you can go to POD.

You have met Mr. Maxwell before, because last year Mrs. Maxwell had you in her daycare. You know exactly where you are going – the big and brightly-colored basement of the tan-colored house! It's where the "big kids" got to go before, when you only got to go to the converted garage with the other babies when you were in daycare. Tomorrow you will get to go to Ms. Simpson's basement, because Mr. Maxwell is only Mondays and takes turns. Every day is a different house, because all the parents take turns in the neighborhood POD. Daddy said, "This is just savin' the govment money," and Mommy said, "It's better anyway."

Friday you will get to stay home and go to your own basement, where some of your new toys with letters and numbers on them already live.

One of the POD parents is not a parent at all but a grandparent, Mr. Obahinti. He doesn't even have any kids in POD, but he can do at least one day a week and volunteered.

You arrive and get to meet some kids you met last year in daycare and a couple of new ones. There are ten of you in your "POD." Mom says you are in POD 556. Mom knows that the full name is POD 556-CA-USA and has its own Skype address, website, and registration with the state and the federal government. It is part of a "Garden" made up of many PODs in your city. Gardens themselves are part of "Branches," which also have "Schools," a pretty old-fashioned term for collections of "Rooms" around the city for older kids to meet and do projects, like science labs and robotics, and "Places" for activities, like sports and big gatherings.

You hop and skip up to the big white door of the tan-colored house and don't wait for Mom to knock-knock-knock. "Hello? I'm ready to come in!" you say. No one answers and the door doesn't open. A camera mounted high on the wall near the door swivels and then lights up the doorway. Mr. Maxwell's voice comes from a speaker by the camera says, "Oh, is that you? Coming for POD? Well, welcome!" Then there is a "bzzzzzt" from the door, and it pops open. Mr. Thompson is just coming up the stairs to the door and takes your hand. You are off to POD.

"Bye Mom!"

The future of design learning spaces, game spaces, simulation spaces, and the immersion-VR (Virtual Reality)-type spaces for PODs is already here. They incorporate elements including motion-tracking and kinesthetic learning and foster exploratory work and dreamtime.

Grateful thanks to GameDesk and their supporters for okay to reprint photographs from their Playmaker pilot school.

Down the stairs, the first thing you see is that the room has a large table-screen and two other kids are already using it, playing a game that has huge letters with legs on them running all around the table. If a hand catches a letter on the table, the letter shouts "I'm a B" or whatever letter it is.

There is also a large touchscreen on the back wall with a lot of squishy kid chairs all around it.

Some of the kids are also in a corner playing with big blocks, each of which have tiny screens on them that currently have numbers or quantities of little things in a picture. Kids are trying to find the right block to click into the corresponding other block that has that number of things on it so they can build a tower of blocks. Another kid is tugging on Mr. Maxwell's shirt.

"Missseerrr Maxwell? Can I listen to Maria now?" says Renee, a 4-year-old PODder.

"Yes, you go ahead; we will wait for a few other kids to get here before we do a group project with the Air," he says. Renee goes over to lay on a squishy chair with one of the larger blocks, into which she wirelessly links pink 3D glasses with built-in headphones and starts her Spanish lesson. "Hello teacher?" she says.

A teacher soon pops onto her small screen and greets her. A scene for the Spanish lesson also comes up on the big screen, and Renee watches her small screen to pay attention to the teacher while occasionally glancing up to the larger screen as it depicts three-dimensional environments that show her things that go with the words she is learning in Spanish. Renee talks back to the teacher and becomes agitated in her chair. She jumps up and goes to the big screen and touches a vase on it, "This one?" she says out loud to the block, which currently shows her online teacher on it. Her teacher must be telling her "no," because she goes to a window in the scene and touches it and says, "This one?" Again she must be being told "no," because she is now hopping up and down, fairly agitated.

Mr. Maxwell comes over and touches her shoulder and the large block Renee is holding at the same time. He pops on his own headset and links in with the online artificial-intelligence teacher. "Oh," he says, "I've got it." He smiles at Renee and says, "You missed a word before, go back to Part 2 like it says and start from there." He pushes some buttons on the block, and Renee grimaces. "I didn't want to go back, I wanted to keep guessing," she says. "It's okay, Renee," Mr. Maxwell says, "I know you would have gotten it sooner or later, but let's just make *sure* you do so that you can be *great*, okay?" Renee says, "Okay," and pokes the block to start her teacher back up at Part 2 of her lesson.

You are excited to start in POD. After everyone gets there that day, Mr. Maxwell stops everyone in their individual play activities and gathers them around the big screen. He speaks and makes several arm gestures which logs him into a program. He chooses some music with words and, much like current-day karaoke, all the kids sing along with an alphabet song. More songs follow, and then a short video of a bird with the sound of the birds singing, and then everyone gets to put on their special glasses at once.

Mr. Maxwell puts on the Air game, a program which projects lights from the floorboards and corners of the ceiling and allows all the kids to "draw" in the air using their fingers in the light, tapping the right lens of their glasses to change colors. They can save what they individually drew so that others can see their light drawings on the big screen later. Mommy had told you about this. She said, "It's so you can learn the right ways to move so that later you can tell machines with your arms and fingers and face what to do, not just talk to it."

Mr. Maxwell says to all ten of the PODders, "Let's now draw a bird and after we draw it, we hit 'save' and sing how we think the bird we created is singing and then save again. Okay? Does everyone get that?"

Jax, a three-and-a-half-year-old says, "No," and sits down grimly. The other kids are going on drawing in the air. Mr. Maxwell takes Jax aside and tries to explain, only to find that Jax doesn't want to draw at all but to do more with the blocks. He is allowed to bring one block to play on but has to stay with the group so that he can learn about birds. All the other PODders are dancing about, drawing whole environments and birds and then singing the way they imagine birds sing. It is a full half hour of movement and some running and some crashing into others and a small bit of crying over being accidentally bumped. Mr. Maxwell handles each incident well. At one point Jax decides to join in with his special glasses and Air draw.

"Are we ready to share what we did?" Mr. Maxwell finally asks the PODders. "Yes, I am," you say. You really had liked that red-breasted bird and you drew a forest and red bird the way you had seen it, but of course you used a lot of green and orange as well, because it goes with your outfit that day. You had to be shown a couple of times how to tap-and-save, but you had no problem creating with your arms and even your feed and head in the air. You erased a lot, but you also created about 20 different completed pictures. You want to share the last one, so Mr. Maxwell shows your set of saved ones. You walk over to the big screen and touch the last one, and it "rolls" to show not only the final picture, but the creation of it and then the final picture again and the sound. You are a good singer! You sound just like a bird, you think.

The other kids give their various murmurings of approval and Renee runs over and hugs you and you both tumble to the ground and laugh. Then you get to look at the other kids' birds while you laugh and skip in place and sometimes fall down on purpose.

Then it is time for lunch. The whole POD goes upstairs to the kitchen and gets to have lunch together and even help a little bit with the daycare kids who are there as well.

In the afternoon there is nap time with special music lullabies that sing numbers and "say Please and Thank You and you will be so Pleased and Thankful and…"

You get to go to recess at the corner park, you and the whole POD, all of you wearing your "Alert" wristbands that light-up if you get too far away from the POD or Mr. Maxwell. It is important "security," according to Mom, to always wear the Alert. Some kids have a different kind of Alert *inside* them in a little pill under their skin and not on the outside, because their parents wanted to be extra careful.

Chapter 32

Future You in Primary & Middle

"Don't forget you have to meet with your Story Guide later today," Mom says.

You know you are going to meet with one of your all-time favorites from the online "Garden," the Story Guide who helps you write your own Story of what you know. Your Story Guide might have been what used to be called a "teacher" combined loosely with a counselor and curriculum director. Her job is to know what you are capable of, where you are in mastering everything required of you, and what your interests are, so you can keep being challenged and keep learning. She even helps with discovering what you could be interested in learning that you didn't even think of being interested in before, even with the help of all the advanced directories and marketing coming at you from online learning media and apps.

"Okay, my W says 2 p.m., and it already told me a long time ago," you say. Your "W" is your wristband, which talks to you and helps keep you on track for your Story Guide learning day and pretty much your whole social life, reminding you in advance of things you should probably prepare for and even people you should probably call since you have named them "friend" but haven't talked to them for a while. It also answers incoming communication in your voice and in the ways you would normally answer using artificial intelligence. It will only prompt you for definite decisions or creativity in answering. If it's just a reminder to be at Timko's birthday party, for example, your W answers for you and puts it on your calendar since it knows you will want to be there. It tells you of these minor decisions at some lull in the day in case you want to change any of them. If it is a commercial call, like someone selling something, those get automated replies unless W knows you are in need of new shoes or a new headset.

You've been studying plant life and biology a whole lot because the regular common standard lesson piqued your interest. After you mastered the requirement, you chose the "Arrow Up" and got a whole list of other things you could study beyond the simple concept of from-seed-to-mature-plant-to-death-and-recycle idea. You are now totally into seeds and the whole idea of genesis. You are even asking Mom where babies come from. Seeds? You have searched for lessons on any plants that "get fat" before they have babies. It seems one similarity in the plant world is the pea-pod.

At 2 p.m. you discuss this with your Story Guide.

"I see you've mastered Primary 206 and gone beyond, well done!" says your Story Guide, Jessie, over live video interface. She says, "Have you considered this conception of life from any other perspective, like maybe how it works mathematically?"

"I haven't picked any math-side discoveries (lessons), no," you say, "but I am wondering more about seeds and biology and what about *people* and *babies.* I asked my mom… and she said it is not time for me to know all that yet but that women do *not* swallow watermelon seeds no matter what my friend said."

"No, no they don't," says Story Guide, Jessie.

"Well, what am I supposed to do to find out? It seems like there are links that I can't go to…" you say, very frustrated for an eight-year-old.

"First, let's talk about why you want to know about seeds, because I can see that's the first thing you wanted to link on to get more information," says Jessie.

"I picked seeds because it's the start, and I want to know what starts things – just putting them in the ground and watering and sun – I found that stuff out – but still…" you say, unable to put into words exactly what you are suspicious is missing from the biological equation.

"Oh, I see, that's very good that you have found out more of what goes into plant growth. I am going to give you some extra credits in your Story account for that, and then I will tell you that what you are searching for is what many people try to figure out and have through all of time. You are trying to figure out the spark of life, what makes that happen. There are many philosophical references for this, and I will send you the links at your reading level, but this is also something that you should talk to your mother about, because it comes also into the field of religion. I am sending her a reminder on her W to talk to you about this," says Jessie. "Now, let's talk about math Standard 475, because I have a new game that uses ocean adventure that can help. Aren't you and your family going to the ocean this summer on vacation? This could be helpful for math and also identifying the fish you will see. How about that?" Jessie puts up a window showing the game live for you to see.

"Yes, that sounds good," you say, seeing on screen a glimpse of the game Jessie is talking about and getting really interested in all the fish floating by, numbers flashing on their gills.

"Good," Jessie says. "I am recommending you use it in 3D for now, and you could earn extra credit later if you come back and do a report after vacation on the ocean."

Future You, in Middle

None of the kids in your original POD, except for Renee, are in the same Standards class as you are anymore. All the others are working in different parts of the Standards, either above or below, or are on Tangents. A Tangent means they are off on some sort of travel-study or work-study or life-study.

One student you knew from Primary who was in the same set of lab classes with you, is now helping in a convalescent home for a six-month Tangent, because his grandmother is there and very ill. She may not live too much longer. He reads to her every day and helps her finish her Story. She wanted to write up what she learned from doing one of her own Tangents, star-gazing on a ship at sea a few years ago. Tangents are, after all, learning that you can do any time in life. Her voice shakes and so do her fingers, so any machine artificial intelligence is not able to help her keep up a Story. He is helping. His Tangent is getting him extra credits towards his plan to be in medicine later, and he gets a lot of credits for Compassion. It is a requirement of one of the High Standards anyway, but he is doing it in Middle because his Story Guide says it aligns with the time in his life and his grandmother and he can do it.

Your parents and your new Story Guide for Middle tell you that you are doing very well, and could actually slow down and enjoy being 12 for a while if you like. You decide to plan a Tangent and reach out to ask about this with your Story Guide. You got a male Story Guide this time, because your dad wanted you to have a male influence at this time in your life rather than female.

"Hi Matthew, I want to plan a Tangent rather than just hang. I want to learn something and not just play around like you and Dad said I could be doing right now since I'm ahead. I'm thinking something in art. I want to explore color and how color is affected by things like culture, and maybe how it relates to math. Does it? Is there a sort of scale to color like we learned about the rainbow? What else is there to know?" you say.

"Well, this is exciting for you. A Tangent is well-timed for you. I took a note on art, culture, math, rainbows, and interrelations. I'll be glad to create a special Tangent for you." Matthew the Story Guide says.

"Great, and let me know if there is anyone else in our Garden or Branch, or even anywhere, that would like to Tangent with me. I'd like to maybe do my Tangent *with* someone else," you say.

"Mmm, that's really a good idea, and if you do want to really get cultural implications, it's a perfect thing to do with students from other cultures, even possibly more than one. I will create a lesson plan and shop it internationally," Matthew says.

"Okay, let's do that," you say.

A week later, you have attracted the attention of a Chinese student, a South American student, and a European student. All students speak English, but you also use online artificial intelligence interpreters between you as needed during the Tangent.

Your Story Guide builds an original lesson plan that is later modified by a Chinese Story Guide and also one from Switzerland who is working with the European student. The finished Tangent is projected to take the four students at least four months to complete.

The first set of discussions are around videos all four students make up of a selection of twenty-five colors chosen jointly. All four students have to video each of the colors or make something of each color, and write about that color and share.

Projects involve reference works around color and math and discussions.

Pottery becomes a major historical journey, and present time pottery examples are sought in each country. Each student finds local potters who can give lessons on the art of pottery, and all lessons are videoed and shared. Each student has several lessons and creates pottery that they ship to one of the other students.

The Chinese student sees a relationship between the color vibrancy based on a mathematical principle having to do with how high the heat was in the furnace, an idea that was surfaced by the European student who had watched a video on early Egyptian pottery methods to make brilliant turquoises and glazes.

All four write papers on how all the ideas tie together and win a whole Tangent Badge for their efforts. Much to their delight, the work culturally allows them to cross off High Standards that they hadn't even gotten to yet.

Chapter 33

Future You in High School

You've graduated to being your own Story Guide for all the Standards. You are given enough lear-credits to hire a Mentlancer (Freelance Mentor) for a handful of subjects you want to go deep in.

Your first day of your next Story – technically you are a "9th grader" in historic terms – you are excited to log in to your new courseware and calendar. First, you tweak your avatar to show you've now got glasses and prefer to wear blue. You march into the virtual campus you are a part of and are greeted by a new character, the administrator for your new POD. He says he will start introducing you as soon as the others join.

Two Chinese students, one from Kenya, three from Canada, one from Venezuela, and six other Americans, all from different states, all join in. You discuss calendars and advantages and disadvantages for certain work based on the work times for the far easterners, who are fourteen hours ahead. Based on the work the POD is set to do, most of the interactions will not be live. The administrator helps set six convergence dates that all POD members will have to attend live, regardless of time zone.

Once assignments are handed out, you turn next into a virtual room that pulls up your history and shows you a dashboard of skills you need to work on and all of the subjects you will cover this year. It provides you with certain advices based on your skills for how much time you should allocate and what you should concentrate on with each subject. Reminders are set for certain advices on these, while you kill off others as annoying and just not your style. You don't care about being a great speller since you are on an engineering track, and you'd rather not have so much repetition in that area.

You set yourself up with an adequate amount of time for each lesson and make sure your calendar syncs up with the others in the POD. You do some of the research you need to do and explore some of the resources and virtual environment for the subject. After your first hour, you are distracted by your pet bird and realize you never fed it this morning.

As you head off to the kitchen, a video call comes in on your wrist phone. It's your mom, reminding you to get your exercise in and feed your bird.

"Yeah, yeah Mom," you say, "I was just going to the kitchen to get some feed for Billibird, and Sanjay's dad is going for a run at 3 p.m. with both of us. Besides that, I have baseball team play two days this week."

While you're feeding your bird, you check your wrist phone for your fitness goals and ask your computer how you're doing physically. You're told you need to stretch more and to sit up straighter. Without asking for it, you're also reminded by your computer that a lot of extra activity will help with your moods and concentration. You're young and full of hormones, so being really active is important. Just the thought of hormones makes you think of that special someone you have your eye on, and the computer giggles at you and flashes a pop-up of your heart rate. It thinks it knows what you were thinking.

Later in the week, you join a few students, most of them near your age, from other PODs at a live lab on campus at a local school. You decide to spend the whole day on campus that day, hoping to see that special someone you think is so cute. Your one lab class goes quickly, and you spend the rest of the day doing your regular work in a canopied chair with a power outlet so you can stay plugged in. At one point a seminar is held in a larger room for half an hour that features several local companies giving short talks about what they do in hope of interesting some of the students to sign up for their learning paths in order to later join one of those employers.

On another day, with your learning work all done, you decide do some online socializing. You already have enough social-admiration points stored up, but you really like doing some of the social activities and games, so you log on for an hour. While you are playing, a pop-up query from your computer buddy tells you about a new math topic developing on another social site that you might want to go check out. You do, and quickly realize it's a new nano-math conversation about adaptive algorithms that really interests you, but one of the students is off on a political tangent. You realize you want to say some nasty things to them, but you might get kicked off the forum, so you watch and wait. A little while later you are able to join in with your views, and you've learned a lot more about what's happening in some of the foreign countries. You decide to pay to be a member of this group and use some of your online coins (a new "bit-coin") to purchase a brief reservation.

Your POD does a lot of extra-curricular work going out and seeing local work environments and sharing them with each other via live streaming. You also interview work-from-home folks and watch a lot of video interviews about all kinds of different work being done – everything from auto mechanics to store clerks to molecular biologists to sand farming and more. You did a lot of exploring. You also took a lot of "work dating" sort of tests as to your proclivities and what you would be good at or interested in.

Months later, your POD learning journey is almost complete. You were gratified that you also were able to contribute by way of the new things you learned from online socializing about nanomath. The POD ended up experimenting with some nanobots in a live lab in Argentina via their rent-a-lab online program that could prove fruitful for the future of paint. The experiment proved that there are some promising ideas behind specifically adaptable bacteria and enzymes mixed with paint that could be genetically "programmed" in complement with nanobots to allow for paint to "grow" and then "die" after it finishes its painting job. Essentially, your POD proved the likelihood that paint could be programmed to put itself on the wall once placed in a glob onto a surface. The paint, if the right bacteria and enzymes were mixed in with nanobots that would "warm" and then "cool" them at the right times and locations, would grow to cover an area that is warm and then die when cool. The idea and initial experiments got your POD's paper a National Science Foundation Award.

The rest of your work in other subjects was not as thrilling, and that's okay with you, because you've decided to pursue your engineering ideas further as you go into college and life. You already have a student and professional circle of admirers and can network to take your next step.

Chapter 34
Future You in College & Life

You spend some time in college, although really what you do is pursue lines of interest with a professional institution you choose that can custom-fit you with subjects to study across a vast network of professionals worldwide. For example, your SmartPaint idea gets some thorough grounding in the history of making pigments. You study with a Mentlancer in Cairo who knows all about the original Egyptian pigments that created colors that weathered the centuries in clay. You study the art of fabric dyeing with some Chinese and Indian people. You study enzymatic action with a Mentlancer who has a background in cheese making in Sweden. You visit paint manufacturers in the U.S. on short field trips. You fly to Japan to study nanobot manufacturing.

At twenty-one, your grandmother passes away, and while spending a week hanging around all your relatives again during the funeral period, you discover you have an ancestral branch of the family in Ireland. You research some of the colors and symbolism of the culture and discover you have a deep affinity for it, especially since hearing your great-great aunt talking about the ancestral home and explaining some of the weird quirks of language your family seems to have. More family stories help to give meaning to your wanderlust and fascination with paint – it turns out you had a relative who was a professional painter of some great renown!

While still studying to attain a custom-certificate, something somewhat equivalent to a degree, you decide to start making money. Your parents are deeply interested in your moving on, after all, getting your own place.

You contract with a think tank doing research in nano-tech and solicit a grant from a big paint manufacturer. This work pays you enough to live very comfortably and put away money for your first company, which you hope will actually *make* your SmartPaint.

This Future You keeps in touch with all your old primary, middle, and high school POD-mates so that you can also hear about what they were doing and learn and grow with them. One of your best friends in Middle has gone on to do something with a new sort of Styrofoam that could actually clean up the oceans, mostly because she just loved the ocean and all sea creatures and would talk about it endlessly all through Middle POD. Through social networking, and partly by failing in some of the science end, she ends up working to help save the whales by tagging some of the last few of a certain species and selling wealthy people the right to "name" each whale tagged and studied. She also helps market the whale-saving effort through social media and awareness campaigns, using her gift of gab and promotional skills. She has found her perfect "fit."

In fact, through social networking, virtual worlds, and live major conferences, most everyone in your social circles has one way or another found their fit.

Future You, in Life

Conceptions of working *for* someone, rather than working *with* someone, have mostly left society. The way education and learning is done now, with a highly customized and personalized journey, has given most everyone, including you, a sense of being a free agent. You have a perception about yourself that you are highly mentally and physically mobile. You use sites and networks to fit in, and if things are not working quite the way you like, you have no hesitation about reaching out to learn something new or hire a lifestyle design coach. In matters of love, you can easily use a multitude of dating sites and found one that suited you perfectly that catered to, of all things, star-gazer singles.

You "lifehack" by moving to new countries, but you keep essentially everything else the same, including taking your mate and children, maybe your whole family. You join things and do work that is meaningful or meaningless, depending on what else you are doing. Perhaps you are out of shape, so you drop the intellectual work, sell that company, and get a line-manager job with some manufacturer or food producer that doesn't require mental innovation but does give you a workout every day.

The journey, the experience of life, maximizing the enjoyment or meaningfulness or meaninglessness is the ultimate lifehack for you. Money is a far lesser goal when you feel you are fully capable of providing value in some way and surviving. You might actually choose to experience the difficulties of no-money or no-place. You're interested in the interactions, the discoveries, the histories of things and places. Commonplace or large experiences, dark or bright, happy or sad, your brand of You is your unique story of each of those moments strung together.

Through freedom of learning and personalization, enhanced by dramatically increased networking between individuals, and sharing vast individually gained knowledge between them, Future You has a lifetime experience that is solely your own.

Chapter 35
Future Administration

"Well, if you ask me, the most *lost* freedom we have today is the freedom to be *nothing*," said Wells with some emphasis, his pale face a picture of disgust.

Taja thought about this for a while and answered without bothering to turn around from the wall-sized touch screen she was dragging digital icons around on. "Well, that is interesting. What you are saying is that from the day we are born, we are busy *becoming* something. We can't just lay around and saunter through life being unimportant… nothings. How… unfortunate," she said rather dryly, as if she had already considered all that his comment meant and was able to summarily dismiss it with hers. She brushed a long tangle of her black curls off her shoulder, her face a picture of placidity and concentration on the wall of digital work once again.

"Yes, well, even so, a lot of people do anyway. Be nothings, I mean, pretty much," Wells said, biting into a donut and scrunching up his nose.

The donut was already pretty stale. He laid the rest of it back down on the conference table and brushed off the crumbs so he could again start typing on the keyboard section of the table. He had lost focus and stood up to stretch.

Taja continued her dragging and dropping on the screen while Wells stared out the window of their twenty-story building. The door to the planning room was ajar, with a large number of cubicles just outside the glass wall of the room facing the interior of the building.

"Yes, but that's what *we're* here to fix," said Dr. Abrams, walking in through the open door. "Not letting people end up being nothings, I mean. Well, unless they *want* to be."

"Oh, welcome, Dr. Abrams," said Taja, turning for the first time. "We've been getting a lot done for Bundle 275 today."

"Great, tell me about it," said Dr. Abrams.

"Well," said Taja, "since this group has been self-selected by our student management system due to mutual characteristics in math and interest in spatial dynamics, we think that we should plan a project to tie them into Tylton Corporation's research on teleportation, for one thing."

"That sounds promising. I assume that was your contribution, Wells, since you're from the business research division for the state," said Dr. Abrams.

"Yes, since one of the students did a project explaining time motion studies, I thought it would be a good fit," said Wells.

"Bundle 275 has three Outsiders, which we need you to approve for us to send invites. One in Europe, one in Minnesota and one in Africa, just for the project work," said Taja.

"Okay let's save that for last. Show me the Bundle," said Dr. Abrams.

"Alright, I'll go first since my work is already up here," Taja said, turning back to the full-wall screen. "Here is the list of students in the group. As you can see we have five hundred forty in Bundle 275 from across the state. And here are the new Bundle Leaders we want to assign. Fifteen of them we are keeping for continuity's sake, since these are only tenth graders."

"Give me a chance to scan the characteristics

and achievements of the students. Can you pull up the Bundle's aggregated achievement window?" said Dr. Abrams. He spent the next ten minutes scanning lots of pie charts, scores, and lists of characteristics.

Wells left for a personal break, saying he would be back soon. Taja stood silently by, scanning all of the information again herself. At one point, the screen on another wall lit up with some trend analysis bullet points coming in from the federal Department of Education on the collapse of one of China's preeminent clothing factories, the sixth to fall in three weeks. Parts of Africa had better statistical outcomes, and jobs were moving there for the clothing industry. Other people on that floor wandered in to view the data on the bigger screen, making side comments to each other while ignoring Taja and Dr. Abrams, and then wandered back out. Wells came back in.

Wells came back in. "Almost done, Dr. Abrams?" he asked.

"Yes, I think I see what's happening here," Dr. Abrams said. "My concern is that besides the core subjects, we need probably another forty-five hours of work for this Bundle of students. Their combined IQ scores are quite high, and we need them active, pushed further than this. Taja, I know you're the Mixer, but some of these students are up to four years younger than the rest, and twenty percent are up to three years older. This is going to be tricky, but have you talked to the Vetters to see what's new that might fit?"

"As a matter of fact, I am awaiting their report. Dora, a Vetter who works from home up north, was an English Mentlancer for years and is our assigned Vetter for language for this Bundle. She is the first to get me these learning objects to consider, but I need ten other Vetters to send in their recommendations. They're due by the end of today," said Taja. She tapped a button on screen and up came the learning object recommendations from Dora.

"Ah, I like this first one," said Dr. Abrams. "I am going to commend her. This courseware promises to take this Bundle on a courseware journey through historical language mutation, right up the alley of kids already interested in space and time change. Let's pick that one and assign it to a Leader to manage on this Bundle."

"Excellent," said Taja. "But if we do pick this, I am going to recommend an independent Mentlancer who knows this courseware, since none of the Leaders we already have will have time to learn this fairly new courseware before we schedule it into the Bundle. And, my apologies, Dr. Abrams, but I just remembered we only have Wells for another fifteen minutes. He's due on a conference call with a different district who needs his expertise."

Dr. Abrams leaned back in his chair, a quizzical look coming over his face. He looked up at the ceililng, considering. "Wells, I did want to ask you for your input on Bundle 147, which is a mixed bundle all of the same age eight-year-olds, but structured to be uniquely close geographically in a sort of supporting mechanism of physical closeness. They spend much more time physically together. Most are from split families or wards of the state – that's why. They meet three times a week in a local center for physical activity. We're getting decent work on the core subjects, but scores are low for the social-emotional caring by

366

this Bundle, which is probably to be expected. What's new that we can add to physical activities that will make the core subjects come alive *emotionally*? We think it's important to add mental activity to the physical a whole lot more."

"Interesting...I assume the local center has all the usual climbing walls, science labs devices, and games," said Wells.

Dr. Abrams nodded yes.

"Okay, then why don't you have the facilities department dedicate one of the rooms at the local center with the new 360-degree projection for a virtual room that will require them to play superhero roles and save others? Some of the new games from Animatrix Corporation give whole-virtual scenarios where the group or individual using the room is flying through the air and spotting emergencies and having to save people. Their courseware either interacts with touch walls and floors, or you can invest in student pullover suits that wirelessly connect into sensors you install with the projection. Depending on the city, I think Animatrix may be opening time-rental virtual rooms there. You could just have the district buy that time and plan it into the curriculum map for the Bundle," said Wells.

"Excellent idea, and we can do that with this Bundle, because it's pretty much all in that geo. Lots of planning and scheduling work has to be done when the Bundle is geographically dispersed," said Dr. Abrams.

"Well, not quite as much as it used to be. The new Learning Management System has a new algorithm for Bundle scheduling that draws on the calendars of every local learning center, *and* we can plug in outside services like Animatrix. I think they're building the interface now," said Wells.

"That is news," said Dr. Abrams. "But we must still actually look with human eyes, have a care to exactly what is happening. Thank you, Wells. I believe we are done."

Wells left the room, and Taja pulled up another screen. "Just a quick detour, Dr. Abrams, please, I want to show you Timmy Chancery, who is not in any Bundle but lives in this state. He has already achieved Stage Five in six of the Core subjects. He is thirteen, and we are going to need an early release signed for him to move into the labor force if his parents approve."

Dr. Abrams started to peruse the study history of Timmy, looking at each of the achievements and manipulating the data from where he sat so that both he and Taja could do more of a deep dive.

"Interesting case. He is smart and has achieved decently in all subjects, moving fast through them, but not achieving really high scores. He's not apparently very ambitious. What has his Request been?" said Dr. Abrams.

"We don't have that yet since he's not quite done, but an interview with one of his Leaders last year was recorded. Let me show it to you," said Taja. "His Home-Hour Leader does talk about how well-adjusted he is emotionally, though, and has a great friendship with the mother via live online chat."

Taja pulled up a video of an interview of Timmy. In it Timmy was explaining that his family was planning to travel and see all the continents in the next few years, even though he wasn't sure he really wanted to do that. He had a younger brother, Zac, who was going to have to join an international Bundle soon so that the family could go. Timmy wanted to be finished with all of his Core subjects and graduated from district before the start of travel. It was his parents' plan for them to all travel until the two boys were of an age to really work and have independent lives. Timmy said he wanted to be able to work in foreign countries, just in case, but he only saw himself doing restaurant service or helping in retail shops for now. He didn't want to decide what to do until he was older. He wasn't planning to be anyone super important.

"Well, I think we should get his First-Hour Leader to calendar his Request for Release. Let the Leader make the call, but I approve. There are more and more of these non-Bundled students it seems, and I'm afraid our Segment in the district is overburdened with them. We have enough to do just doing all the curriculum mapping in our Segment for over a hundred Bundles, but now there are some thousand kids un-Bundled who we have to deal with," said Dr. Abrams. He also made some motions to check off his approval for Timmy right there so that the only person left to do so would be the Leader.

"Yes, but I think it will be okay. The algorithms are going much deeper now, and the un-Bundled are really not a worry. It's easy to mirror individuals with similar or statistically significant traits out of the regular Bundles anywhere in the nation for curriculum maps that match the un-Bundled students into the same sort of map," said Taja. "What *I* want to know is how much influence the curriculum lobbyists are having on the state. I hear that there is a call for Core consolidation, and two of the states are trying to push Washington into being the only ones with Bundles for the Mars agricultural teams. Politics!"

With a chuckle, Dr. Abrams said, "Well, I can't stay to gossip. We need to finish Bundle 275 today. I will do more analysis on my own in my office. The superintendent is plugging in a new distance service for some of the cognitively impaired students in one of the bundles, and I have to double check on the integration and something the development team wanted to ask me."

Tara smiled at him and turned to close the work she had on the wall-screen, saving it and sending it to her own mobile device for work on her commute. She could get another hour of work in with her autonomous driving car, which was a neighborhood rental she only used for the one day a week she was at the district office.

Dr. Abrams ambled down the hallway, stopping to chat with two other district employees.

This district and the others in the state managed more than twelve million students, not to mention the other one million students the state adopted from disadvantaged countries without learning planning systems, with Leaders to help students achieve their own personal maximum achievements across core subjects and interests.

In some instances, students could make requests and somewhat opt-out of learning to just work, but the majority went through all the Core to an equivalency of graduation in the olden days, with lots of extra-curricular interests along the way, until they or their families felt they were ready to work. Then they kept alive the attachment to the district, or in some places colleges. So the act of "graduation" was really a "release" that lessened their obligation and numbers of hours of learning, but as an individual they could still get more learning at any time. As adults, they would associate at will with any administration, all of who were constantly refining the digital knowledge objects and projects they developed. Some competition between the various administrations kept it all interesting, and some of the private administrations were particularly innovative with how they "branded" the experience of being educated with their particular mix of learning objects, projects, and leaders (a.k.a. teachers).

Many of the former teachers, now known as "Leaders," hold super-stardom status in their subjects, and are often affiliated with multiple institutions and handle thousands of students, aided by algorithms, great courseware, and continuous student feedback and student choice.

Teaching and learning has changed so that some teachers have quality project leadership roles for groups of students, others run whole Bundles of learners from a curriculum crafting viewpoint, and yet others watch over all of the dynamics to ensure both individuals and large classes are winning and learning.

Ultimately, the entire industry of learning becomes a service mechanism that that doubles both the number of working jobs and the economy as a whole, while also enjoying dramatic increases in outcomes for learners.

About the Author

LeiLani Cauthen, CEO & Publisher of the Learning Counsel

LeiLani is well versed in the digital learning object universe, software development, the adoption process, school curriculum, and technology coverage models, and she is helping define this century's real change in teaching and learning. She is an author and media personality with twenty years of research, news media publishing, and market leadership in the high tech, education, and government industries.

Nearly every week, she is on the road meeting school superintendents and their staffs, telling them about the Learning Counsel's national research and helping spread change. She traveled to 87 cities between February 2014 and December 2016. The discussions she started so energized the nation that hundreds of thousands of educators are now avid followers of her work.

The Consumerization of Learning, the book you hold in your hand (or read on your tablet), is a deep dive into the disruption at hand for the way leaders lead education digitally. It highlights consumerization as the act of making something desirable and consumable by the individual. Educators like to think of this as the personalization of learning on computing screens using the capabilities of the software that make it intuitive and highly adaptive just for that learner. If schools fully discover and adapt to consumerization's ingenuity, it has the power to give teachers back time spent custom building every digital resource themselves, time that can now be turned to attention on students, to create more hands-on learning activities, and to guide students in the fullness of a digital learning experience.

Consumerized learning is also an alternate delivery mechanism that has the potential to disintermediate on cost, immediacy, and effectiveness. It's time for schools to know and co-opt this trend. This book is meant to be a discussion about how schools are finding a new relevancy at the natural end-point of digital transition: maximized live experience and quality digital learning, also known as "expo" education.

LeiLani's hope is that this book provides you with practical advice, such as a digital software model architecture and definitions of things like screen learning versus other trending terms. At the end of the book, she does something rarely seen as a way to view her suppositions and theories concerning the future of education – she provides a fictional story about the future to illustrate where things can go for students, teachers, and schools.

LeiLani continues to travel throughout the country, leading discussions and keynoting on the transition of education to digital curriculum. You can find out more and follow her work and the work of the Learning Counsel at learningcounsel.com.

CPSIA information can be obtained
at www.ICGtesting.com
Printed in the USA
LVHW051447130120
643227LV00003B/123/P